SWEELINCK'S KEYBOARD MUSIC

PUBLICATIONS OF
THE SIR THOMAS BROWNE INSTITUTE
LEIDEN

General editor: A. G. H. BACHRACH, *D. Phil. (Oxon.)*,

*Professor of English Literature in the
University of Leiden*

GENERAL SERIES NO. 4

Jan Pietersz. Sweelinck. Anonymous painting, 1606.

SWEELINCK'S
KEYBOARD MUSIC

A STUDY OF ENGLISH ELEMENTS IN
SEVENTEENTH-CENTURY DUTCH COMPOSITION

ALAN CURTIS

PUBLISHED FOR THE SIR THOMAS BROWNE INSTITUTE

LEIDEN: AT THE UNIVERSITY PRESS

LONDON: OXFORD UNIVERSITY PRESS

1969

Distributed outside the Netherlands by the
Oxford University Press, Ely House, London W. 1

GLASGOW NEW YORK TORONTO MELBOURNE WELLINGTON
BOMBAY CALCUTTA MADRAS KARACHI LAHORE DACCA
CAPE TOWN SALISBURY NAIROBI IBADAN ACCRA
KUALA LUMPUR HONG KONG

Printed in the Netherlands

PREFACE

THE following pages deal with the musical relations between England and the Netherlands during the 'Golden Age' of Dutch culture. Although all Dutch keyboard music surviving from c. 1570 to c. 1670 is treated, the emphasis falls naturally on the works of Jan Pieterszoon Sweelinck (1562–1621), who was by far the greatest Dutch composer of the era. Nearly every writer concerned with his music has cited the English influence evident in his keyboard works. A stylistic analysis of these English elements, however, has not previously been undertaken, nor have they been placed in the context of a widespread vogue for English music in the Netherlands. Before stylistic comparisons could be made, it was found necessary to establish a canon of Sweelinck's keyboard works. Problems of authentication and of sources, therefore, occupy a considerable place in the argument.

The neutral designation 'keyboard music' is employed in the title as an intentionally inclusive term, calling attention to the lack of rigid distinction in Sweelinck's day between compositions for the manuals of an organ and those playable on a harpsichord or even a clavichord. The use of the word 'Dutch' brings up another terminological problem. The rather arbitrarily evolved modern-day border lines between the Netherlands and Belgium often unduly influence historians to project this separation too far into the past. A distinctly Dutch cultural milieu developed only gradually during Sweelinck's period and thereafter. For that reason, 'the Netherlands' here denotes the entire area now roughly covered by the two modern states, while 'United Provinces' and 'Dutch' are used to describe the seven provinces of the North; 'Spanish Netherlands' denotes the ten provinces of the Catholic South; and 'Holland' refers only to the province (in modern times divided into North and South Holland) in which are located such towns as Amsterdam, The Hague, Haarlem, and Leiden. Keyboard composers of the Spanish

Netherlands, such as Pieter Cornet, have not been included unless, as is the case with Peter Philips and John Bull, they have a direct bearing on the subject. In general, quotations in French or German have not been translated unless they are problematical; all citations in Dutch have been rendered in English by the author.

With gratitude I acknowledge the painstaking care with which Professor Dragan Plamenac of the University of Illinois guided this study through its first stage. For subsequent assistance and encouragement, I wish to thank the staff of the Music Library and my colleagues at the University of California, Professors David Boyden, Daniel Heartz, Lawrence Moe, Stephen Orgel, Colin Slim, and particularly Joseph Kerman whose untiring efforts to convert long stretches of my unwieldy prose into readable English began at Berkeley and continued even during his recent year at All Souls, Oxford. Countless valuable suggestions of theirs have been silently incorporated into the text. The kind help I have received from libraries, archives, and individuals in Amsterdam and elsewhere throughout the Netherlands will long be remembered with gratitude. I should particularly like to record the kind and friendly assistance of the staff of the Public Music Library, Amsterdam, whose Librarian, Professor Frits Noske of Leiden University, has helped this study at various stages, both directly and indirectly, through his excellent work in related fields.

It was Professor Noske who first suggested that I submit this book to the Sir Thomas Browne Institute; I should like to express my gratitude to the Director, Professor A. G. H. Bachrach, for accepting it for the General Series of Anglo-Dutch studies brought out by this institution; and to its staff for aid in collecting historical information, for preparing the manuscript for the press, and for translating Appendix I. For his excellent study of the now-vanished organs in Sweelinck's Oude Kerk, I am most grateful to Mr. Cor Edskes of Groningen. Mr. Anner Bijlsma kindly gave his help and hospitality in the final stages. I wish also to thank Mr. Gustav Leonhardt of Amsterdam, to whom I owe the topic of this book. Over the years his stimulating friendship has been a source of constant encouragement. Finally, it is to my wife that the book is dedicated, for without her endless patience and assistance the project would long since have been abandoned.

Amsterdam/Berkeley, 1968

CONTENTS

ILLUSTRATIONS

ABBREVIATIONS

A. 1–16*   The Chorale Variations edited by Alfons Anne-
           garn in the 1968 edition of Sweelinck's *Instrumen-
           tal Music* (Fascicle II). Asterisks signify *dubiosa*.

Bachrach   Bachrach, A. G. H., *Sir Constantine Huygens and
           Britain: 1596–1687*, I (London/Leiden, 1962).

BM   British Museum, London.

Breig *Sch*   Breig, Werner, *Die Orgelwerke von Heinrich Scheide-
              mann, Beihefte zum Archiv für Musikwissenschaft*
              (Wiesbaden, 1967).

Breig *Sw*   Breig, Werner, 'Der Umfang des choralgebun-
             denen Orgelwerkes von Jan Pieterszoon Swee-
             linck', *Archiv für Musikwissenschaft*, XVII (1960),
             pp. 258–76.

Cohn   Cohn, Albert, *Shakespeare in Germany*, (London,
           1865).

Dutch HM   Curtis, Alan, 'Dutch Harpsichord Makers',
           TVNM, XIX–1, 2 (1961–61), pp. 44–66.

D.D.T.   *Denkmäler Deutscher Tonkunst.*

D.T.B.   *Denkmäler der Tonkunst in Bayern.*

D.T.Ö.   *Denkmäler der Tonkunst in Österreich.*

Grove   *Grove's Dictionary*, 5th edition.

K.N.   Lüneburg, Ratsbücherei, series of MSS.

L. 1–40*   The Fantasies and Toccatas edited by Gustav
           Leonhardt in the 1968 edition of Sweelinck's
           Instrumental Music (Fascicle I). Asterisks signify
           dubiosa.

Leningrad MS.   Library of the Academy of Sciences, Leningrad,
                MS. QN 204.

Ly A 1, B 2,   Deutsche Staatsbibliothek, Berlin (Eastern Zone),
etc.   Lübbenauer Orgeltabulaturen, Lynar A 1, B 2,
                 etc.

MB   *Musica Britannica.*

MGG   *Die Musik in Geschichte und Gegenwart.*

MMB   *Monumenta Musicae Belgicae.*

MMN III	*Dutch Keyboard Music of the 16th and 17th Centuries,* ed. A. Curtis, *Monumenta Musica Neerlandica,* III (Amsterdam, 1961).
N. 1–13*	The Secular Variations edited by Frits Noske in the 1968 edition of Sweelinck's *Instrumental Music* (Fascicle III). Asterisks signify *dubiosa.*
Reinken	Curtis, Alan, 'Jan Reinken and a Dutch Source for Sweelinck's Keyboard Works', *TVNM,* XX–1, 2 (1964–65), pp. 45–56.
Riewald	Riewald, J. C., 'New Light on the English Actors in the Netherlands, *c.* 1590–*c.* 1660', *English Studies,* XLI (1960).
RISM	*Répertoire Internationale des Sources Musicales.*
S. 1–73	Sweelinck's *Werken voor Orgel en Clavecimbel,* ed. M. Seiffert (Amsterdam, 1943).
Speuy	Curtis, Alan, 'Henderick Speuy and the Earliest Printed Dutch Keyboard Music', *TVNM,* XIX–3, 4 (1962–63), pp. 143–62.
Tor G 1, 5, 6, 7 and F 8	Turin, National Library, Giordano vols. 1, 5, 6, 7, and Foà vol. 8.
(T)VNM	*(Tijdschrift van) de Vereniging voor* [*Noord-*]*Nederlandse Muziekgeschiedenis* [*Tijdschrift voor Muziekwetenschap*].
vdSM	van den Sigtenhorst Meyer, B., *Jan P. Sweelinck en zijn Instrumentale Muziek,* 2nd ed. (The Hague, 1946).
WM	Vienna, Musikarchiv des Minoritenkonvents, Kodex XIV, 714 (*olim* MS. 8).
Ze 1 and *Ze* 2	Clausthal-Zellerfeld, Bergakademie Clausthal Technische Hochschule Bibliothek (ex Calvörsche Bibliothek) MSS. *Ze* 1 and *Ze* 2.

INTRODUCTION

THE ORPHEUS OF AMSTERDAM

SWEELINCK's lifetime spanned a period of awesome change. When the boy from Deventer followed his organist-father to Amsterdam in the 1560s, he was brought to a Catholic city of essentially medieval appearance, a city of roughly 30,000 inhabitants, built around the dam at the mouth of the River Amstel from which the name was derived. Small wooden houses lined the narrow streets around the St. Nicolaas Kerk where Sweelinck's father played—a large Gothic church in the centre of the old town, boasting some thirty altars adorned with several famous paintings and a silver statue of the patron, St. Nicholas. Already Amsterdam was an important harbour, but the true heart of the Netherlands was Antwerp, which had recently surpassed even Venice as the focus of European commerce. Spain, under whose rule both Antwerp and Amsterdam fell, was at the height of its power; and particularly after 1580, when Philip II inherited the Portuguese empire, the open seas of the entire world belonged to Spain. In 1566, when Sweelinck was only four, a storm of iconoclasm had swept up to Amsterdam from Antwerp, launching a period of great religious turmoil and political revolt. Two years later we find the Sweelinck family living in a house on the Lange Niezel, which had been vacated by a Protestant forced to leave the city. The fugitives returned triumphant in 1578, and from then on the fate of Amsterdam was entrusted to the Protestant rebels and their leader Prince William of Orange, dubbed the Silent. After the hideous Huguenot massacre of St. Bartholomew's Day 1572, aid from France was out of the question and Dutch hopes lay with their Protestant sister-nation across the Channel. Shortly following the assassination of William the Silent, Queen Elizabeth complied with requests for support and in

1585 sent 6,000 troops to the Netherlands under Robert Dudley, Earl of Leicester.[1] With the destruction and dispersal of the great *Armada Católica* three years later, the Spanish 'Crusade' in the North had essentially been lost. However, Spanish troops had subdued Antwerp and the ten southern provinces, and floods of refugees began to move north. Thus began the decline of Antwerp as a port—the mouth of the Scheldt being held by the enemy—and thus began the growth of Amsterdam as a commercial and cultural nucleus of worldwide importance. Thus grew also that irreparable split between Northern and Southern Netherlands, so strongly evident today in the difference between the Dutch and the Belgian nations, and, within the Belgian nation, between the Flemish and the Walloons. Originally, the division had merely been due to the hazards of war—the outcome being hardly less arbitrary than the present separation between East and West Germany.

When Sweelinck died in 1621, the Twelve Years Truce had just come to an end. During this respite the warring of theologians (centering around the Arminian controversy) had replaced the clashing of arms. Although there were fears of a renewed Habsburg onslaught and hostilities continued until the Peace Treaty of Münster (1648), what amounted to a stalemate had already been reached. For the seven Northern provinces the Spanish yoke had been thrown off forever. The West India Company had just been founded, on the model of the already successful East India Company, and the rise of both helped to hasten the economic decline of Spain. Amsterdam now had a population exceeding 100,000. The famous half-moon of concentric canals—a brilliant stroke of city-planning which remains a wonder still today—had already been undertaken to accommodate the prodigious

[1] Upon entering Amsterdam, the Earl was welcomed with a Latin address by Jan Verhee, a friend of Sweelinck and co-executor of his mother's will after his father died in 1573. See J. Wagenaar, *Amsterdam in zijne opkomst* . . . (Amsterdam, 1765) I, p. 400; cf. also R. C. Strong and J. A. van Dorsten, *Leicester's Triumph* (Leiden/London, 1964), pp. 65–67.

expansion. As early as 1609 the local government was forceful
and foresighted enough to project, and begin to execute, an
area increase of 300 per cent. An early ordinance had forbidden the construction of wooden houses. Following the
lead of the city architect, Hendrick de Keyser, a contemporary of Sweelinck and a superb sculptor as well as designer,
the tree-lined canals, both old and new, were graced with
spacious houses of brick and stone in the late-Renaissance
'strapwork' style of which De Keyser was an outstanding
master. The Oude Kerk (formerly St. Nicolaas) had been
'cleaned' by iconoclasts of most of its decoration, with the
notable exception of the two organs on which Sweelinck,
employed by the municipality and not directly by the Church,
played recitals. The Calvinists had not only altered the old
churches, but were building new ones as well, towering over
the new South, North, and West extensions. Again they were
the work of De Keyser, who was also commissioned to convert
the collapsing and outmoded Gothic fortifications into decorative towers, several of them later supplied with carillons,
visible (and audible) from nearly every corner of the city.
Instead of the river, it was now the estuary, 'het Y', which
Amsterdam faced, and from which it sent ships to all parts of
the world. From the Arctic to Australia, Dutch vessels brought
untold wealth and knowledge back to Amsterdam, leaving
behind new settlements on such outlandish islands as Java or
Manhattan. With its bustling world trade, its immigrants of
every faith from all over Europe, with its wealthy merchants
collecting art treasures of every sort, Amsterdam must have
felt to a citizen such as Sweelinck like the very navel of the
universe.

In an age when Dutchmen gazed through telescopes at the
rings of Saturn, peered into microscopes to discover protozoa,
and sailed outward to the most remote, uncharted corners of
the globe, it may seem strange that the greatest of Dutch
composers was content to perfect an art established by others,
and showed so little interest in exploring the musical universe.
There is no evidence that Sweelinck ever travelled any further

than Antwerp. [1] There can be little doubt, however, that he kept abreast of new developments in Italy and particularly in England. The English composer Peter Philips was among those who came to visit him in Amsterdam as early as 1593; and, as we shall see, Sweelinck's works reveal his profound knowledge of English music. But while he remained in Amsterdam, receptive to anything musical which came his way, he also sent out a steady flow of disciples to all parts of Germany, Poland, and Sweden. Heinrich Scheidemann, Samuel Scheidt and his brother Gottfried, Jacob Praetorius, Melchior Schildt, Paul Siefert, Andreas Düben, Peter Hasse, and David Aebel may be mentioned as among the most prominent of the German-speaking pupils who flocked to Amsterdam between 1606 and 1621 and who took home with them not only a practising knowledge of Sweelinck's art but also a generous sampling of the master's works. Without these foreign students, and the copies their own pupils and descendants made, we should have little or no keyboard music by Sweelinck today. In his own country, every single Sweelinck autograph has been lost, together with all the numerous copies of his music which colleagues, friends, and Dutch pupils would have made, and nearly all the keyboard music composed by any other Dutchman of the Golden Age as well. In fact, had we been dependent on sources in the Netherlands only, we might never have heard of Sweelinck.

It is hardly surprising, then, that so very little is known of his life. We cannot even be sure of his religious convictions. It seems certain he was raised a Roman Catholic, and it is likely that he later became a Protestant, since we know that three of his children were baptized in the Reformed Oude

---

[1] In 1604 he bought a harpsichord there for the city of Amsterdam. For the possibility of a study-trip to Venice, see p. 85. Sweelinck occasionally did some travelling within the United Provinces, where his advice as an organ expert was often asked: Haarlem, 1594; Deventer, 1595; Deventer and Middelburg, 1603; Nijmegen, 1605; Harderwijk, 1608; Rotterdam, 1610; Dordrecht, 1614; Deventer and Rhenen, 1616. 'Den organist van Amsterdam' also came to Nijmegen in 1585, but it is doubtful whether the authorities were already asking advice of the 23-year-old Sweelinck.

Kerk. Composing a polyphonic setting of the Genevan psalter was Sweelinck's lifelong project and these psalms were, of course, published by and for Calvinists. One volume bears a dedication to eight 'Philomuses', prominent Calvinist merchants who had 'often sung this music' in their homes, presumably under Sweelinck's leadership. Among the eight was Philip Calandrini, whose brother Jean was the father of Jean Louis, Sweelinck's 'tressingulier amy', [1] and the sponsor of weekly chamber music sessions under Sweelinck's direction—sessions important enough to be reverently mentioned in his autobiography by Constantijn Huygens, who apparently came over from The Hague to play 'sub Joanne Sweelingio, viro incomparabili'. [2] Both the Calandrinis, who were well-connected bankers, and their circle of friends were staunch Calvinists. Yet near the end of his life, Sweelinck's *Cantiones sacrae* (1619) appeared in Antwerp with a dedication to his young Catholic pupil and friend, Dr. Cornelis Gijsbertsz. Plemp, and contained such texts as 'Regina Coeli' which could hardly have been intended to be sung at Protestant gatherings. Sweelinck's brother, the painter Gerrit Pietersz., [3] seems to have remained a Catholic; and a daughter, Elsgen, after her father's death but with consent of her mother, married a Catholic lawyer in 1635. Dirck, Sweelinck's son and musical successor, [4] was severely reprimanded by the Oude Kerk authorities in 1645 because he had played a kind of old-fashioned Christmas celebration ('kindeken wiegen') and 'invited many papists'. Such religious ambiguity was, after all, typical of the period when a militant Calvinist minority only gradually suppressed the outward traces of ancient Catholic traditions.

---

[1] Cf. vdSM, 62, where the author fails to distinguish between Jean Calandrini and his son, and is also mistaken in regarding Calandrini and Willem van den Heuvel (Bartolotti) as the same person.
[2] Bachrach, p. 58, n. 1.   [3] See Appendix IV.
[4] At his death, Sweelinck's position as organist was first offered to his blind Catholic pupil, Pieter Alewijnsz. de Vois, who merely used the offer to improve his own position at The Hague. Only after his refusal was the offer made to Dirck Sweelinck. See M. A. Vente, 'Sweelinckiana', *TVNM*, XIX—3,4 (1962–63), p. 186.

One such tradition which was never entirely erased was
the use of the organ in the service. According to orthodox
Calvinist belief, musical instruments had no place in the
church. In the new edifices, such as De Keyser's Zuiderkerk,
finished in 1611, no provision was made for an organ; and,
indeed, none existed there until 1823. In the older churches,
however, where fine and expensive instruments had already
been installed, the city government took possession of these
organs at the time of the Alteration, and continued thereafter
to hire 'municipal organists'. We know that Sweelinck had
such a position by 1580, and continued in the same job until
his death. Of his exact duties, however, we know nothing,
for no contract is preserved. His starting salary of 100 guilders
was doubled in 1586, and raised again to 300 in 1590, at
which time he was also offered, as a kind of wedding-present,
the option of an additional 100 guilders or free rent. He seems
to have chosen the latter and to have moved with his bride,
Claesgen Dircxdochter Puyner from Medemblik, into the
spacious three-storey house in the Koestraat with which the
city provided him until his death. The house must have been
attractive indeed, for his family continued to live there after
his death, eventually buying it from the city and selling it
only in 1661 to the well-known marine painter Jan van de
Capelle.

After a raise to 360 guilders in 1607, Sweelinck's official
salary remained constant to his death. It was not remarkably
high for the period, but this may signify a restriction of his
tasks rather than a lack of appreciation of his talents. Included
in the duties of many organists of the period was the playing
of the carillon and the frequent provision of dinner music for
municipal banquets. Cornelis Helmbreker, for instance, was
hired at Hoorn in 1612 and given a very elaborate set of
charges. [1] For his yearly salary of 350 guilders he had to play
the carillon and other instruments (harpsichords?) for the
banquets of the Burgomasters, Regents, and Judges, and for

---

[1] For the Dutch text, see *Bouwstenen* (1965), pp. 130 ff.

the entries of Princes or Lords. He had to play the organ
every sermon-day, both morning and afternoon, before and
after the sermon, [1] and for an additional hour at dusk. Then
he also was expected to play the carillon for an hour twice
every Sunday (7–8 a.m. and 12–1 p.m.), on Saturdays
(10–11 a.m.), on Tuesdays and Thursdays for at least half
an hour around eleven, on Fridays from June to November
because of the Cheese Market, etc. Since the harpsichord-
maker Artus Gheerdinck was hired as organ-tuner and *carilloneur* of the Oude Kerk, [2] we may assume that Sweelinck,
unlike many of his contemporaries, was never burdened with
such time-consuming physical labours. He seems to have been
paid extra for playing at banquets [3] and probably did so only
on special occasions. His principal income may have been from
teaching: we know that he received the equivalent of 200 guilders for giving a year's instruction to the young Brandenburg
organist Augustus Brücken in 1613. We can arrive at an
estimate of Sweelinck's financial well-being if we note that
this same student was allowed only 186 guilders for all his
other expenses that year, [4] and if we realize that Sweelinck
must have had at least ten—and could have had twenty—such
pupils every year.

Although the arrival of German pupils is documented only
from 1606 onward, there might well have been some who
came earlier, for Sweelinck's fame was international already
by the last decade of the sixteenth century. For instance,
when Count Philip Ludwig II of Hanau-Münzenberg visited
Amsterdam in 1594, he made notes of the most important
sights. For this German visitor they included seeing a live
elephant in the Hall of the Archer's Guild, visiting the Artillery

---

[1] 'Voor en na de predicatie', a phrase which recurs again and again in
these contracts as a kind of euphemism for including organ music—
forbidden by Calvin—as an adjunct to the service. The contract might
even specify that the organist should play variations on the psalms about
to be sung by the congregation—but even so, such a psalm prelude
was technically a municipal recital which just 'happened' to be tempo-
rally adjacent to the church service.
[2] See p. 144, n. 3.   [3] vdSM, 46.   [4] vdSM, 68.

House, and hearing the city's organist. [1] Some dozen years later another distinguished visitor, although he had no time for elephants, did not fail to hear Sweelinck. With but three and a half days in which to visit Amsterdam in 1608, the Venetian Ambassador Giorgio Giustinian was shown only the highlights. One of the Burgomasters and five other Magistrates of the city arranged a climax for his last evening, beginning with a trip to the 'Chiesa maggiore' to hear the organist, 'who is a great, excellent man, and has a good stipend from the city, which will never let it be with-drawn' (implying that it was a life pension). Later that evening they had an extended banquet, with many 'good healths' as was the custom of the country, and with music by the above-mentioned organist. [2] Perhaps Sweelinck was induced to play for the banquet by his friend J. Calandrini, whom the Ambassador had visited the day before.

Unfortunately, such ear-witness reports of Sweelinck and his music are all too rare. His praises are sung by the great poets of his day—Vondel and P. C. Hooft, for example—and by Carel van Mander, [3] the Vasari of the North, who calls him the 'Orpheus of Amsterdam'. Such praise is all highly impersonal, as is the lengthy and rather heavily mythological *Lyck-Klacht* published on his death by N. Voocht. [4] Apart from Huygens's reference, only Baudartius, a music-loving minister from Kampen, gives us one small glimpse of Sweelinck as a human being:

This Apollo had the manner of most musicians; that is to say, one cannot easily induce the best musicians to sing or play, but when one has brought them to do so they can hardly bring themselves to stop . . . . I remember when I was once with some good friends visiting Jan Pietersz. Sweelinck, who was my good

---

[1] For the German text, see K. A. Citroen, 'Een Olifant in de Doelen', *Amstelodamum*, LIV (1967), p. 13.
[2] For the full Italian text, which has been overlooked or misread by Sweelinck's biographers, see *Relazioni Veneziane*, ed. P. J. Blok, *Rijks Geschiedkundige Publicatiën*, VII (1909) p. 16.   [3] See Appendix IV.
[4] Reprinted for the first time as Appendix V.

friend and was among other good friends, in the month of May, and he being inclined to play on his harpsichord, continued to do so until about midnight, playing among other things the tune 'Den lustelicken Mey is nu in zijnen tijdt', which, if memory serves, he played with as many as 25 variations, now this way, now that. As we stood up and were about to take our leave, he bade us yet hear this piece, then that piece, not being able to stop, in such sweet humour was he, giving pleasure to his friends, as well as to himself. [1]

It may still give pleasure to recall Sweelinck at his harpsichord in the Koestraat. Today, however, his house has vanished—as completely as have his manuscripts—torn down only 70 years ago. The lot is vacant, there is no plaque, and the Koestraat has fallen into a state of perpetual filth, with the garbage of its miserable inhabitants piled high in the street. One is reminded of the four-part 'Vanitas vanitatum' canon which Sweelinck once wrote in an Album Amicorum at Harderwijk—and which can no longer be traced.

[1] For the Dutch text, see vdSM, 60.

I

ENGLISH MUSICIANS IN
THE NETHERLANDS AROUND 1600

An extensive repertory of English music is preserved in Dutch sources from the early seventeenth century. As Thurston Dart has pointed out, [1] its presence reflects a contemporary influx of English musicians into the United Provinces, and, in turn, the great influence these musicians had on many aspects of Dutch musical life. A contributing cause for the vogue of English secular music and a principal source for its dissemination over Northern Europe was the association of such music with popular English plays and jigs acted by various travelling companies. The activities of these comedians on the Continent have often been examined by literary historians. [2] As they have shown, music was a highly important aspect of such dramatic productions, and indeed many actors were players of instruments as well as of roles. Although most of them were merely performers, a few are known to have been composers as well. On the whole, these were minor figures (such as Richard Machin, two of whose lute pieces are preserved) but occasionally such prominent and prolific composers as William Corkine [3] or Robert Jones [4] may have joined the travelling companies.

[1] T. Dart, 'English Music and Musicians in 17th-Century Holland', *Kongress-Bericht. Internationale Gesellschaft für Musikwissenschaft. Utrecht 1952* (Amsterdam, 1953), pp. 139–45.
[2] Riewald, the most complete survey to date, summarizes most of the findings of previous writers.
[3] See ibid., p. 90, for a quotation of the pass for George Vincent 'to goe over to the Prince of Poland' in 1617 and take with him the musicians, 'Richard Jones, Wm. Corkin, Donatus O'Chaine, Thomas White, Wm. Jackson, Tho. Sutton, Valentine Flood and John Wayd'. The latter cannot be identical with the actor known from later sources (he would have been 10 in 1617); 'Richard Jones' probably was the well-known actor-musician (see below, p. 17 f.). This would seem, thus, to have been

Particularly in the earliest references, English comedians on the Continent are often referred to not as actors but as dancers, musicians, tumblers, etc. Since the troupes seldom, if ever, mastered foreign tongues (only the part of the Fool was more or less regularly taken by a local native), [1] it was only natural that music, dancing, and mimed scenes should be the most immediately appealing and widely popular. The famous Shakespearian comedian and dancer of jigs, William Kemp, [2] was known in Denmark primarily as an instrumentalist, and his companions Thomas Pope and George Bryan (later in the Chamberlain's company) were termed 'instrumentister och springere'. Kemp was in the Earl of Leicester's company, following him to the Netherlands in 1585–86. Sir Philip Sidney, in an oft-quoted letter to Sir Francis Walsingham, says 'I wrote to yow a letter by William my Lord of Lesters jesting plaier'. Probably Kemp was involved in the 1586 Utrecht banquet on St. George's Day (23 April, o.s.) when there was 'dancing, vaulting, and tumbling, with the forces of Hercules, which gave great delight to the strangers, for they had not seen it before'. [3] Also in the Earl's

a travelling group of highly skilled actors and musicians. Corkine was a famous figure in 1617, having published two books of airs in 1610 and 1612 (cf. the article 'Corkine' in *MGG* by Wolfgang Boetticher). Four excerpts from both books were edited by T. Dart and W. Coates, *Jacobean Consort Music* (*MB* IX, 1955, p. 201). Valentine Flood is also known to have held various positions on the Continent: he was serving the Elector of Brandenburg in 1627 and is found in Danzig in 1634–37 (Grove entry, 'English Musicians Abroad').

[4] See below, p. 16.

[1] See A. G. H. Bachrach, 'Jan Starter, Engeland en Nederland in de XVIIe Eeuw', *Levende Talen* (1957), p. 68.

[2] Several lute pieces, mostly jig tunes, are ascribed to him, but it seems more likely they were named after him than that he composed them. See for instance 'Kemp's Jig' (Cambridge, Univ. Lib., MS. Dd. II, 11, f. 99v).

[3] For a full discussion of the players and musicians in 1585/6, see Strong and Van Dorsten, *op. cit.*, App. I 'The Players'. 'The Forces of Hercules' was not a play but more likely an allegorical elaboration of acrobatic stunts, capped with the forming of a human pyramid. As suggested by Dart, *op. cit.*, p. 142, this may have been accompanied by the music of 'Le forze d'Ercole' (BM MSS. Royal Appendix 59–62).

company was a certain John Johnson. Although not listed among the 'Musicioners', he may nevertheless have been the well-known lute-composer, particularly in view of his probable connexion with Geoffrey Whitney's emblem-book prepared at Leiden with the aim of honouring the Earl.[1] Those who are listed as 'Musicioners' include 'Thomas Cole, Wm. Baniton, James Wharton, Wm. Edgley, Wm. Black, Jo. the Harper, and Walter the boye'. In addition, four trumpeters and two drummers,[2] all English, are named.

English companies when playing at Stuttgart in 1603 were described as 'four excellent musicians with ten other assistants'[3] and at Nürnberg in 1612 and 1613 were expressly mentioned as providing their audiences with 'lieblicher musica'.[4] A troupe visiting Münster in 1599 was described as having brought with them 'vielle verschieden instrumente, dar sie uf speleten, als luten, zittern, fiolen, pipen, und dergelichen....'.[5] Many more such instances could be cited, particularly with reference to Germany.[6] Yet only a small number of references to the musical activities of English comedians while in the United Provinces has survived. One of the few relevant documents preserved indicates that early in January of 1605, a company of 'Engelsche Commedianten ende musicyns' arrived in Leiden with a letter of recommendation from the Elector of Brandenburg and a letter of consent from 'His Excellency of Nassau'. The town authorities granted them permission

[1] See also Philip Brett, '*Musicae Modernae Laus:* Geoffrey Whitney's tribute to the lute and its players', *The Lute Society Journal,* VII (1965) pp. 40–44.
[2] The trumpeters were 'Benedick Browne, Jo. Jewkes, Rowl. Strange the L. Norths man', and 'Griffin Martin'. Some forty years later, another English trumpeter, Robert Fyson, settled at Utrecht, and was praised as superior to his Dutch colleagues (see *Bouwstenen,* 1965, p. 244 and cf. also pp. 236–38, 303). The drummers were 'John Keynsey' and 'Jo. Vodett' (Strong and Van Dorsten, p. 85).
[3] Cohn, lxxvii.
[4] From contemporary notes by the Nürnberg patrician Stark, as printed in K. Trautmann, 'Englische Komödianten in Nürnberg', *Archiv für Literaturgeschichte,* XIV (1886), pp. 126–28.   [5] Cohn, cxxxv.
[6] P. L. Mueller, *The Influences and Activities of English Musicians on the Continent* (typewritten Ph. D. thesis, Indiana University, 1954), *passim.*

to play and to exercise and exhibit their arts in the usual place, namely, in the great court in front of the library, . . . for the succeeding period of fourteen days, provided, for this gracious permission, they give a sum of 12 guilders, of 40 groats each, to the poor of this city. [1]

This troupe of 'comedians and musicians' was undoubtedly headed by John Spencer, and the same group appeared at The Hague (and most certainly elsewhere in Holland) in the following years. [2] Spencer was probably an accomplished musician himself, for he signs as 'Englishman, Chamber Musician and Comedian', [3] and at the baptism of his daughters in 1603, before he had left England, he is described as 'a musician', not as an actor. [4] In 1611 Spencer's troupe numbered nineteen actors and sixteen musicians. A year later they gave a spectacular production of 'The Turkish Triumphcomedy' at Königsberg, involving elaborate scenery, costumes, masks, swords, etc. On this occasion David Rose, the court painter, turned in for his services alone a bill for 117 marks, 42 shillings. Fourteen instrumentalists 'assisted in the comedy of Constantinople'. [5] In 1613 the company offered in Nürnberg

beautiful comedies and tragedies of Philole and Mariane, also of Celide and Sedea, also of the Destruction of the Cities of Troy and Constantinople, of the Turk, and other such Histories, besides graceful dances, lovely music, and other entertainments. [6]

Similar travelling companies may have appeared in some of the larger Dutch towns, but references are usually to English 'speelluijden', a term with the same ambiguity as 'players'. Such a troupe appeared in Nijmegen in 1602; and there were 'Engelsche speelluyden', too, to accompany Johan van Oldenbarnevelt and his companions on their journey from Vianen

---

[1] For the Dutch text, preserved in the Leiden Gemeente archief, see Cohn, lxxviii.   [2] *Ibid.*
[3] J. Bolte, *Das Danziger Theater* (Hamburg, 1895), p. 41.
[4] E. Nungezer, *A Dictionary of Actors* (New Haven, Conn., 1929), p. 338.
[5] Cohn, lxxxv f.
[6] For the German text, see Cohn, p. lxxxvii.

to The Hague in March 1616. In Amsterdam a company
under John Kemp appeared around 1600, and there were
others regularly in the succeeding years. [1] In the fourth scene
of Act III of Brederode's comedy *Het Moortje* of 1615, a
young man recounts a conversation which took place the day
before on Amsterdam's main square. There one Licht-hart
(Light-heart) is reported as having said:

'We've stood here long enough; good men what counsel, whereto
shall we be off? Come let's to the Hall and watch the wits play.'
But Grab-a-beer, he said, 'Such scoffing I can't bear. I'd sooner
be in the pub beside an excellent Moll. I don't care to be so long
with the Rhetoricians: because these folk always play the fool
with everyone, and like the ape, they can't cover their hindmost;
they recite their lesson so sedate and stiff, you'd think their
bodies stuffed with stave-wood! Were it the English, or other
foreigners, whom one hears sing and so lustily sees dance, that
they reel and turn as a top: they speak it from their wit [*geest*], these
[*meaning the Rhetoricians*] learn it from a roll.' [2]

From this passage we can imagine how entertaining and popular were the singing and dancing of these comedians—enough
to attract 'Packe-bier' away from the 'kroech' and his 'excel-
lente Trijn', i.e. from the tavern and the wenches. The same
character later sums up the difference between the English
players and the native Rhetoricians as: 'The foreigners,
they're frivolous, these [*Dutchmen*] counsel for the good'.

As to the question of what specific music the English actors
and comedians employed, we must be satisfied mainly with
speculative answers. Dart has suggested that the published
consort books give us a vivid picture of Elizabethan theatre
music. Since the tunes (of which they contain certain settings)
are popular also in Dutch sources, there is every reason to
believe the players brought such music with them to the
Continent. We can also be sure that the popular English
tunes, frequent in the Dutch songbooks and amateur instru-

[1] Riewald, p. 72.
[2] For the Dutch text, which is in verse, see *Werken van G. A. Bredero*,
ed. J. A. N. Knuttel (Amsterdam, 1924), II, p. 153.

mental publications[1] of the time, were sung, played, and danced in the various English plays and jigs, as well as the imitative Dutch *kluchten* or farces;[2] the actual settings, however, cannot be reconstructed. The famous 'Thysius Lute Book',[3] compiled *c.* 1590–1620 and preserved still in the handsome Bibliotheca Thysiana (1655) on the Rapenburg at Leiden, does supply us with some small works which—however badly corrupted and musically insignificant—may interest us at least for their having specific connexions with two English comedians.

One of the most prominent of English players on the continent was Richard Machin. Although he is not recorded as having visited the Netherlands, the presence of two pieces by him in the 'Thysius Lute Book' would suggest his having at least passed through the country, meeting some local

---

[1] Dart, *op. cit.*, mentions some of these. His list could be greatly augmented, but that would hardly serve our purposes here. Suffice it to say that the *Nederlands Volkslied Archief* of Amsterdam, headed by Miss M. Veldhuyzen, has undertaken the enormous task of indexing the tunes from all the early Dutch and Frisian songbooks (see Scheurleer's list in his *Nederlandsche Liedboeken*, The Hague, 1912) and other popular prints (mostly from the press of Paulus Matthysz. in the Stoofsteeg, Amsterdam).

[2] Such tunes as 'D'Engelsche Fa la la', 'Sir Eduart nouwels delight', and 'Engelsche Fortuyn' (see the discussion of Sweelinck's and Byrd's 'Fortune my foe' variations, p. 122) are mentioned in the only preserved Dutch editions of early *kluchten* (cf. J. Bolte, *Die Singspiele der englischen Komödianten und ihrer Nachfolger in Deutschland, Holland, und Skandinavien*, Hamburg/Leipzig, 1893, pp. 27–31). There are also frequent allusions to the comic character of 'Pekelharing' who, although the technique of pickling herring was a Dutch invention (there is a painting of the character by Frans Hals of *c.* 1629), was made famous by the English comedian Robert Reynolds in the play of 'Simple Simpkin', translated and renamed as 'Pekelharing in de Kist'. Reynolds was described as 'resident' in both Utrecht and The Hague in 1629, and his young associate, John Edwards, 23 years old, was given a pass that year to go to 'Rotterdam to remaine there'. See Riewald, 'Some Later Elizabethan and Early Stuart Actors and Musicians', *English Studies*, XL (1959) pp. 33–41.

[3] See J. P. N. Land, *Het luitboek van Thysius* (Amsterdam, 1889) who gave only the 'tunes'—often largely fabricated by him in cases where the tablature (or the setting) seemed to him ambiguous or not very tuneful. A forthcoming study of Dutch lute music by F. Noske will shed new light on this manuscript, including many corrections of Land.

musicians. [1] The two works copied in this collection, which comprise the only known music of Machin, certainly have not provided posterity with much evidence for esteeming his musical talents. One of them is, moreover, merely a corruption of another man's pavan: Machin's 'Pavyn de Lyght' has a just barely recognizable resemblance (clearest at the beginnings of each of the three strains) to the well-known 'Pavana Delight' ascribed variously to Edward and to John Johnson. [2] Nevertheless, a resolution by the Strasbourg city council, dated 11 May 1605, described 'Richardus Mechinus von London' as heading a group of sixteen, with a repertory of 24 comedies, tragedies, and pastorals, and said that 'sie ein solche Musicam haben, dergleichen nit baldt zu finden'. [3] Whether or not the council referred to music supplied or at least directed by Machin himself is unclear. P. L. Mueller thinks that Machin may perhaps have compiled and even copied the manuscript collection of instrumental ensemble suites at Kassel. [4]

Two pavans ascribed to 'Robyn Jhones' are also included in the 'Thysius Lute Book'. Although the nickname of 'Robin' need not always imply Robert, it does in this case seem likely. A Robert Jones appeared in Robert Brown's company at Frankfurt in September 1602. [5] Moreover, there are in these pavans harmonic audacities (such as major mediants) and unusual dissonances similar to those of the lute

---

[1] Dart, *op. cit.*, p. 143, and in his article 'English Musicians Abroad' in Grove mentions only the 'Pavyn de Lyght'; but later in the book (f. 391) is an untitled piece also attributed to 'Rich machyn.'
[2] See above, p. 12, concerning John Johnson, and cf. William Byrd's keyboard setting of 'Pavana Delight' in the *Fitzwilliam Virginal Book*, II, p. 436; and *An Anthology of English Lute Music*, ed. Lumsden (London, 1954), p. 21.
[3] Printed in H. Hartleb, *Deutschlands erster Theaterbau* (Leipzig, 1936), p. 50.
[4] Landesbibliothek, Mus. 4.° 72 (1601–03). See Mueller, *op. cit.*, p. 19, and G. Oberst, *Englische Orchestersuiten um* 1600 (Wolfenbüttel/Berlin, 1929), pp. 70–76.
[5] E. Herz, *Englische Schauspieler und englisches Schauspiel zur Zeit Shakespeares in Deutschland* (Leipzig, 1903).

I. Open air musical party. Drawing by Gerrit Pietersz. Sweelinck, 1593.

Figure 1. St. Cecilia. Etching by Gerrit Pietersz. Sweelinck, 1593.

accompaniments in Robert Jones's published songbooks. The latter often gave pause to the editor, Fellowes, [1] who found them so unusual he felt they must be either misprints or evidences of inexperience with the lute. The crudities in the 'Robyn Jhones' pavans are due to neither inexperience nor mistakes. They cannot stand alone as solo pieces; but they most likely were not meant to do so. Probably they are lute parts to consort pieces, and, like those of Morley and Rosseter, may well have been used in theatrical productions on the Continent. Along with his fellow lutenist-songwriter Philip Rosseter, Jones is known to have had connexions with the theatre. On 4 January 1610 the two composers, among others, were provided with a patent for a school of children in London to be designated the 'Children of the Revels to the Queene within Whitefryars'. Early in 1615 they were patentees for the project of erecting a playhouse for the Children ('Porter's Hall') on the site of a house occupied by Jones near Puddle Wharf in Blackfriars. When nearly completed, civic authorities forced them to pull it down and surrender the patent. [2] The possibility of his having toured the Continent does not conflict with the previously known facts about Jones's life.

The connexion of Robert Jones with the company of Robert Brown suggests a further link with the Continent and another possible addition to Jones's biography: he is likely to have been a relative (perhaps a son) of Richard Jones. When Lord Admiral Howard wrote a passport for his 'Joueurs et serviteurs' Robert Brown, John Bradstreet, Thomas Sackville, and Richard Jones on 10 February 1591, he announced their intention to tour Zeeland, Holland, and Friesland, and meanwhile 'd'exercer leurs qualitez en faict de musique, agilitez et joeuz de commedies, tragedies et histoires, pour s'entretenir et fournir à leurs despenses en leur dict

---

[1] *The English School of Lutenist Song Writers*, Ser. II: IV–VI and XIV–XV (London, 1925–27).
[2] J. Q. Adams, *Shakespearean Playhouses* (Boston, 1917), p. 343; and Grove, entry 'Jones, Robert (II)'.

voyage'. [1] It should be noted that the first of the 'qualitez' mentioned was that of playing music. Robert Brown had already been in Leiden in October 1590, perhaps with other of the players cited in the passport. In any case, this troupe carried out its intention and visited the Netherlands in 1592. Only one of their appearances is documented: that at Arnhem, where they performed with a license from Prince Maurice of Orange.[2] In August of that year the company had given, at the Frankfurt autumn fair, *Gammer Gurton's Needle* and some of Marlowe's plays. [3]

Brown and Richard Jones had already been associated at least by 1582, when they were members of the Earl of Worcester's troupe, and again in 1589, at which time Jones transferred his share in a stock of theatrical goods, including musical instruments, to another actor-musician of later fame, Edward Alleyn. Returned to England in 1594, Jones was singer for the Court performances by the Lord Admiral's company, and in 1597 he joined the Earl of Pembroke's men. [4] After extensive activity on the stage (including the role of Priam in *Troilus and Cressida*) he returned to the continent in 1610, but was back in England, ready to leave for service to the 'Prince of Poland', in 1617, and is found by 1622 as a musician in the service of Philip Julius, Duke of Wolgast. [5] On 30 August 1623 he asked permission, together with his colleagues Johan Kostressen and Robert 'Dulandt' (John Dowland's son), to leave Wolgast and return to England. [6] The following year, however, he wrote to the Duke that he had failed to find profitable employment in England, and asked to be taken again under his patronage. Whether the

---

[1] The original document in the Rijksarchief at The Hague has been lost. It was first printed in L. P. C. van den Bergh, *'s-Gravenhaagsche Bijzonderheden* (The Hague, 1857), I, pp. 41–42. The version in Cohn, pp. xxxviii f., is inaccurate.
[2] J. A. Worp, *Geschiedenis van het Drama* (Amsterdam, 1904), I, p. 312.
[3] Herz., *op. cit.*, p. 10.   [4] Riewald, p. 67.   [5] Ibid., p. 90.
[6] C. F. Meyer, 'Englische Komödianten am Hofe des Herzogs Philipp Julius von Pommern-Wolgast', *Shakespeare Jahrbuch*, XXXVIII (1902), pp. 209–10.

Duke honoured Jones's request is not known. We find a Richard Jones receiving payment for 'the Greenemen and fier works' in the Lord Mayor's Show of 1626, and being indicted for forging a license at Worcester in 1630. [1] Again, a Richard Jones was recorded as a puppet-showman at Coventry on 12 January 1638. [2] It seems most unlikely, however, that these later references would refer to the same man who was active in 1582. There was also a Francis Jones, 'Joueur d'instrumens anglois', in Lille in 1606; [3] but positive identification of this family of actor-musicians is hardly possible since their surname is so common.

A visit by the composer Robert Jones to the United Provinces must also remain a hypothesis; but we know in any event that his works were widely disseminated throughout the Netherlands. His song 'Farewell, deere love' [4] was particularly famous and is found in many of the Dutch songbooks, sometimes under its Dutch title 'Wanneer ick slaep'. Jacques Vredeman, music-master of the city of Leeuwarden, made a four-part arrangement of the air; [5] it was thus known in the far North even before the English-born Jan Starter included the tune in his *Friesche Lusthof* (1621). [6] Its popularity continued, and Cornelis de Leeuw's music to the *Christelycke Plichtrymen* (1648) included a fine three-part setting to the text 'Van de achterklap'. [7] The tune was also used in the numerous editions of Camphuysen's *Stichtelycke Rymen*, including that of 1652, to which Joseph Butler (a musician from Greenwich

---

[1] Riewald, 'Some Later Elizabethan Musicians'.
[2] J. T. Murray, *English Dramatic Companies, 1558–1642* (London, 1910), II, p. 253.   [3] Riewald, p. 75.
[4] Mod. ed. by Fellowes, *English School of Lutenist Song Writers* (London, 1925), no. 12, p. 24. A version of the text (but beginning 'Farewell dear heart') was sung by Sir Toby Belch and the Clown in Shakespeare's *Twelfth Night* (II, iii), perhaps to Jones's music.
[5] Printed in a 1608 Amsterdam edition of the *Livre septieme* (in continuation of the famous series begun by Phalèse).
[6] For more about Starter, see A. G. H. Bachrach, *op. cit.*, and 'Starter en Engeland', *It Beaken* (Assen, 1953), pp. 195–99. See also H. Brouwer, *Jan Jansz. Starter* (Assen, 1940).
[7] On p. 228; mod. ed. in *TVNM* VII (1903), pp. 210 f.

Cantus oft Tenor.

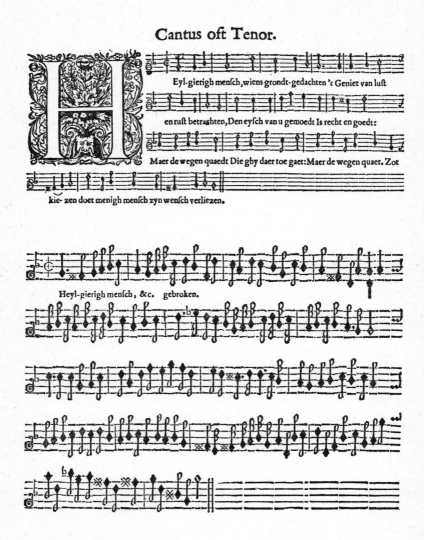

Figure 2. Cantus and Bassus of 'Heyl-gierigh Menchs' ('Farewell dear Love') in Dirck Camphuysen, *Stichtelyke Rymen*, ed. Joseph Butler, 1652.

BASSUS.

Eyl-gierigh menfch, wiens grondt-gedachten 't Geniet van luft

en ruft betrachten, Den eyfch van u gemoedt Is recht en goedt :

Maer de wegen quaedt Die ghy daer toe gaet: Maer de wegen quaet. Zot

kie-zen doet menigh menfch zyn wenfch verliezen.

Heyl-gierigh menfch, &c. gebroken.

who had come over as a young man and married in Holland) [1]
added optional divisions for violin and gamba (see Figure 2).
Butler may not even have realized when composing his old-
fashioned variations on a half-century-old piece (to suit the
taste of Dutch dilettantes) that the tune was originally the
work of a fellow Englishman.

Jones's friendship and business ties with Philip Rosseter
have already been mentioned. This brings us to another type
of English musician in the Netherlands: those instrumentalists
and composers who were not connected with the theatre but
nevertheless crossed the Channel and stayed. The Rosseter
family may have emigrated because of their religion (they
seem to have been Puritans who allied with the Dutch Reformed Church). Whatever the reason, the descendants of
Philip Rosseter found ready and varied musical employment
in the United Provinces—as performers, teachers, and instrument makers. It is interesting to note that the lutenist
Dudley Rosseter married the widow of Richard Bradford,
an English comedian on the Continent. [2]

Among the friends of Dudley Rosseter (Philip's son) were
the English emigrant organ and harpsichord maker, William
Deakens (Deacons), [3] and Edward Hancock, one of the English musicians who formed a band in Amsterdam under the
prominent lutenist-composer Nicolas Vallet, whose lutebooks
consequently include English music. (We may similarly
account for the prominence of English pieces in the publications of Joachim van den Hove, who was an associate of the
highly praised, and highly paid, John Jordan, English in-

---

[1] For further information on Butler and his music, see *MMN* III, xviii.
He married Josina (Janneken) le Febure (le Fêvre) in 1646, at Wijk aan
Zee, and died (in Amsterdam?) sometime before 1674. His brother (?)
John, who had married Josanna Lefebbure (le Fêvre) at Bloemendaal in
1642, probably had left England earlier, and may well be the player
'Jan Butler' who rented theatrical costumes from Isaac van Bochoven
(Boekhoven) at The Hague in October 1639 (cf. Riewald, p. 85).

[2] This and other details of the activities of a dozen different Rosseters
may be found in 'Rosseters in Holland', *The Galpin Society Journal*, XI
(1958), pp. 63–69.   [3] Dutch HM, 48.

strumentalist resident at Leiden already by 1608.)[1] In 1626 Vallet's band drew up the following contract, which reveals something of the social and economic conditions of English musicians in the United Provinces:

On this 12th of November, anno 1626, after mature deliberations, have agreed and consented Mr. Nicolas Valet, Mr. Richard Swift, Mr. Eduard Hancock, and Mr. Robbert Tindel, all musicians and citizens of this city of Amsterdam. And that in the addition here following, to wit, that the aforementioned contracting parties for the period of six continuous and succeeding years beginning today shall be in company and with each other during the specified period play together at all occurring weddings, banquets and other occasions according to the following conditions and stipulations.

1.—That everything earned be split evenly among each, except that Vallet receive in addition 10 stuivers (half a guilder) per night from each of the others for making arrangements. But if one of the other 3 engages for a wedding, banquet, aubade or other playing [*gespel*] he too collects 10 stuivers from the other two.
2.—Anyone who plays with other musicians (at weddings, banquets, etc.) will be fined 10 Flemish pounds, to be divided by his colleagues.
3.—To which end it is expressly wished, that all four go out together to play or all four stay at home.
4.—If necessary that only three be hired, then the fourth who stays at home earns a half salary from the other three.
5.—When three go out, the one who has arranged the booking plays and the other three throw dice and the one with the lowest will stay at home, on the conditions noted above in § 4.
6.—If two, then the three throw or else agree among themselves that the one who goes pays nothing to those who stay at home.
7.—If one is sick the other three pay him 10 stuivers each, and for every night they are engaged a guilder, so that every sick person gets a guilder every night there is an engagement: Be it understood that such payment will not continue longer than three months.
8.—In case of sickness, the healthy members may play with other musicians, but otherwise not.

[1] See Grove, 'English Musicians Abroad'. Jordan earned 12 guilders per performance in 1610 (Leiden, Gemeente archief, Burgem. maaltijd, 11 Jan., 8 and 9 May, August; information supplied by J. A. van Dorsten), and 36 guilders in 1617 (Riewald, 80 f.).

9.—If anyone is out of town he loses all claim to profits, even if he has left town with consent of the others. Solemnly accepted, etc. etc. etc. If any should wish to depart before the end of the period, they must pay their colleagues the sum of 40 Carolus guilders and further, as amends, must pay for the benefit of the poor of the English community [*gemeente*] the sum of 30 guilders, without any contradiction.

Further, the aforementioned Nicholas Valet and Eduart Hancock will establish a dance school, which shall be held at the house of the aforementioned Valet. They have agreed that the tuition money [*leergelt*] from the scholars shall be divided in the following manner, two-thirds to Valet and the other one-third to Hancock. They both shall be required to appear at the school to teach the scholars twice daily, namely, mornings from 10:30 until 11:30 and afternoons from 4:00 until 7:00 in the evening. And whosoever is late or misses the hour shall pay a *schelling* for morning and for afternoon, and if he misses the entire afternoon, two *schellingen*. The above fines are to go one-half to the benefit of the poor, and the other half for the company in general. All four must meet and play every Sunday in the summer for four hours and in the winter for three hours after noon at the aforementioned dance school. The gratuities given by those who come and exercise Sundays at the dance school, shall go one-third to Valet and one-third of the remaining two-thirds each to Swift, Hancock, and Tindel, but if one is absent, the others get 12 stuivers each, in addition. And all this for the period of six years. [1]

Hancock seems to have settled permanently in Amsterdam. We find another Edward, perhaps his son, in 1658, at the age of forty-three years, living in the 'Tower of Louvain' near the *Beurs*. [2] At this time he testified in favour of the *stadsmusiciens* against 'Mr. Matthijs, musicien' (Paulus Matthysz, the famous music printer?), living in the Romeinsarmsteeg, who late at night at the witnesses' house had called them 'thieves and rascals and uttered other injuries, blasphemies, and cursing'. Some years later, we find another relative, Richard,

[1] This and other relevant documents are given in the original Dutch in *TVNM* X (1919), pp. 148 ff.
[2] The noble stock-exchange, built by the great architect Hendrick de Keyser on the Dam in the centre of the town. It was destroyed in the early nineteenth century.

running a kind of musical tavern, also near the *Beurs*, under the rather elaborately painted sign of Parnassus, Pallas, Apollo, and the nine muses. There were several rooms with harpsichords, clavichords, zinks, lutes, and gambas. Concerts were given between four and ten p.m., and wine, beer, pastries, and oysters were served. [1]

Hancock's fellow English associate, Richard Swift, had joined Vallet still earlier in 1621. His contract was less complicated but otherwise similar to the later one, especially in its mention of 'weddings, banquets, and aubades'. One wonders if Vallet and his men with their broken consorts may have replaced the great Sweelinck with his *clavecimbel* as the most sought-after musical entertainment for a festive banquet. The date of their contract (11 December 1621—less than two months after Sweelinck's death) suggests this. A translation of the document follows: [2]

On this 11th of December 1621 Mr. Nicholaes Valet, lutenist, acknowledges to have taken into his service and board Ritsert Swift, Englishman, who hereby contracts to serve the aforementioned Nicholaes Valet in the exercising and playing of instruments for the period of the two succeeding years beginning today, for which the aforementioned Ritsert Swift shall obtain and enjoy free board and lodging, with in addition half as much as another player ['*speelman*', *implying an ordinary Dutch player, as opposed to this more expensive Englishman*] shall earn, whether at weddings, banquets, or aubades [*obaden*]. Furthermore, the aforementioned Ritsert Swift shall have and enjoy for himself as much tuition money [*leergelt*] as he shall be able to earn from any disciples he may instruct, provided that he neglect not the time necessary for the service of the aforementioned Valet, as hereby promised, but actively perform [his duties] in all diligence.

'Joost Thomas, musicijn woonende binnen deser stede', probably another English musician (Joseph Thomas) living in Amsterdam, is mentioned as having played with Vallet for a wedding at Leiden in 1614. Two years later, probably as a

---

[1] See D. F. Scheurleer, *Het Muziekleven van Amsterdam in de 17e Eeuw* (The Hague, 1904). [2] See p. 24, n. 1.

result of his professional contacts with English musicians, Vallet contracted to teach for the period of six years the ten-year-old son of David Gibson, named Jeremias, to 'play upon the lute and other instruments'. Above his signature, in a stroke of charming bravura, he added this impromptu canon:

Figure 3. 'Canon ex tempore' by Nicholas Vallet.

The list of English 'players', musicians, and minor composers in the United Provinces could be extended much further, particularly if we included the years after Sweelinck's death. The main point, however—that English music was widely known, appreciated, and heard 'first hand' in the Nether-lands—has been made: this is all that need concern us in approaching Sweelinck's keyboard music. Of more direct importance perhaps is the connexion between Sweelinck and the great English recusant keyboard artists who crossed the Channel to live in exile for the rest of their lives, in particular Peter Philips (1560 or 1561–1628) and John Bull (1562 or 1563–1628).

The possibility of personal contact between Sweelinck and Bull has been stressed by nearly every writer on the period.

Their statements range from the modest assertion that Bull 'was associated with Sweelinck'[1] to such a casual remark as that 'over in the Netherlands, Bull fell in with the great Sweelinck, Peter Philipps' colleague'.[2] There is not the slightest documentary evidence that Sweelinck and Bull ever met, though for several reasons it seems likely that they might have. First of all, remarkable similarities in their keyboard styles suggest mutual influence and imply that they had ready access to each other's works. Moreover, Sweelinck may have added a new ending to one of Bull's fantasies,[3] while Bull is known to have written a fantasy on a 'Fuga' by Sweelinck, probably as a *tombeau* upon his death. The presence of a canon inscribed 'Doctor Bull fecit'[4] as an example in Sweelinck's treatise on composition has often been cited, but this is less significant than the foregoing facts. His rules for composition are preserved only in a highly altered German translation dating from a half-century after his death. The canon, if it is indeed by Bull, could just as well have been inserted by Reinken, or some other copyist.

There are very few occasions when Sweelinck and Bull could have met. The earliest, and most likely, is during Bull's first trip to the Continent in 1601. By the time of Sweelinck's only documented journey outside the United Provinces—in 1604, at which time he bought in Antwerp a harpsichord for the city of Amsterdam—Bull was back in England and remained there until 1613. The following year Sweelinck went as far south as Dordrecht, and at the end of 1617, or early in 1618, Bull journeyed as far north as 's-Hertogenbosch.[5] In both cases they were paid to travel as consulting experts in order to inspect new organs in, respectively, Protestant Dordrecht and Catholic (until 1629) 's-Hertogenbosch. It seems unlikely that they met on these occasions, and both travelled even less in later years. Perhaps after a single meet-

---

[1] D. Grout, *A History of Western Music* (New York, 1960), p. 261.
[2] E. Cole in *Proceedings of the Royal Musical Assoc.*, LXXIX (1952–53), p. 58.   [3] See below, p. 62 f.   [4] Sweelinck, *Werken*, X (1901), p. 84.
[5] M. Vente, *Die Brabanter Orgel* (Amsterdam, 1958), p. 180.

ing in 1601 they corresponded or kept in contact through pupils or mutual friends.

Until recently, even less evidence could be adduced for assuming personal connexions between Sweelinck and Philips. It is now certain, however, that they met at least once: in 1593, when Philips went 'into Holland onely to sie and heare an excellent man of his faculties in Amsterdam'. [1] There can be no question as to whom, in Amsterdam in 1593, Peter Philips would have so described. Other newly discovered documentary material reveals interesting facts about Philips's life both before and after 1593 [2]—especially his subsequent arrest on returning from Amsterdam to Antwerp. Richard Verstegan gives a fascinating account in a letter to Father Persons, dated 13 January 1594, which incidentally reveals that Philips could speak Dutch:

Peter Phillipes the musitian, that was prisoner in Holland, is delivered and arryved here now at Christmas. He told me how one Roger Walton, somtyme page unto the Earle of Northumber-land that was slaine in the Towre, beeing at Midlebourg caused him to be apprehended, and accused him of many notable trea-sons before the Counsell at the Hage, whether they were bothe sent: all his accusations beeing such markable fixions of his owne hed, as they were soone discerned by the Counsell, who by the testimony of certaine Italian marchants (that to have his company and musick perswaded him to that jorney) were fully satisfied that he came not thether to passe into England to kill the Queene as the other affirmed. And he proved Phillipes intension thereto in this sorte, *videlicet:* that beeing some yeares past in Paris when the Baricades were made, there was an image made of the Queen of England and set uppon a great heape of fagots, and the King and all sorts of Religious men, coming in procession with burning wax candells, did give fyre to those fagots, and so did the Lord

---

[1] A. G. Petti, 'New Light on Peter Philips', *Monthly Musical Record,* LXXXVII (1957), p. 60.
[2] In addition to the article cited above, see also, by the same author, 'Peter Philips, Composer and Organist, 1561–1628', *Recusant History,* IV (1957), pp. 48–60, and *The Letters and Despatches of Richard Verstegan c. 1550-1640* (London, 1959), esp. pp. 204 ff, from which the quotation has been taken.

Paget, Sir Charles Arundell and all the English, amonge whome this Peeter Phillipes was one. At this Phillipes replyed that there was never any such thing don, and that the King at the making of the Baricades fled oute of Paris, and therefore went not in procession in Paris, and that such a publyke acte must nedes have many wittnesses besydes Walton. At this answere the Counsell began to looke at one another, and Walton in a great chaf said in English unto Phillipes: 'O Papist, Papist, yf I had the in England I would make shorte woorck with the.' 'Why,' quoth the other, 'what would you do?' 'Marry,' quothe Walton, 'I would aske the yf the Queene were supreame head of the Churche or not. And what wouldes thow answere to that?' 'I would,' quoth Phillipes, 'say she were not.' 'Then would I hange the,' quothe Walton. Hereunpon, Phillipes asked of the Counsell yf they did understand what Walton had said. They said no, but willed him to tell them. Then did he tell it them in Dutche, whereunto their President for the tyme (for they change often) replyed, *that he knew well enoughe what the justice of England was, but it should not be so theare.* Then did one Gilpen, who now is ambassador with the States in Bodley's place (for that Bodley is in England expecting Walsingam's place) aske Phillippes yf he had not bene at confession with the Jesuytes. He answered ye. 'Then,' said Gilpen, 'you were enjoyned to kill the Quenne, for whomsoever cometh to confession to them they do so enjoyne.' But notwithstanding Phillipes answered them well to every thing, and the litle proof they had against him, they detayned him untill letters came from England to certify bothe of him and of Walton; of whome the Earl of Essex wrote that of Phillipes they never understood other then that he had followed his soorte of musyck, and for Walton that he was a poore fellow and had nothing els to live by but by such meanes. And by other letters it was signified that Walton did in England make an occupation of accusing men, and that he had broughte 5 or 6 to the gallowes, as he would have don Phillipes yf he had had him there and the assistance of Topclif—which is not lyke he could have wanted.

Phillipes was in the end discharged, as is said, and Walton is yet in prison, and hathe bene racked aboute the cyphers that he had with Mr. Paget. And it seemeth that, notwithstanding the Counsell of Holland are ill enoughe themselves, yet they do abhorre such wounderfull monsters as our country in thease dayes dothe yeild.

The reason for Philips's stopping at Middelburg might well have been to visit the Grouwels family of harpsichord and virginal makers. [1] He would have known them when they were in Antwerp (and when Philips was maintaining himself 'by teachinge of children on ye virginals, being very cunning thereon'). By 1593 they had settled at Middelburg, for in that year Johannes became a citizen and Lodewijck bought a house. While there, Philips would have played some of their splendid new instruments, similar to the one now owned by The Metropolitan Museum of Art, New York. [2] He may, in fact, have encountered an unusual type of virginal in which the customary short octave had been furnished with split keys for the low F-sharp and G-sharp. The front halves would sound D and E (as normal for a short octave) while the back halves produced the accidentals F and G-sharp (as in a normal octave). This is, at least, the kind of instrument for which Philips wrote his pavan and galliard named 'Dolorosa'. [3]

One manuscript source [4] for this pavan and galliard pair lists them in its index as 'composta in prigione'. Former writers have assumed this was a mistake, resulting from confusion with the Tregian family imprisoned in the Tower of London. [5] Now we must reconsider that the scribe was after all correct, and that Philips's dolorous, chromatic pavan and galliard were composed in the *Gevangenpoort* (now a museum) at The Hague, between 27 September and 1 November. The date 1593, which Tregian ascribed to the pair in the *Fitzwilliam Virginal Book*, confirms this. That Philips while in

---

[1] Dutch HM, 50 f. Philips fell sick while at Middelburg, and a letter from George Gilpin to Lord Burghley (*Cal. S.P.*, Holland, vol. 47, f. 62) says he was detained there three weeks, 'conversant with such as delighted in musicq'.

[2] Illustrated in *MMN* III, xlv; Grout, *A History of Western Music*, p. 260; Hirt, *Meisterwerke des Klavierbaus*, p. 207; and Winternitz, *Keyboard Instruments*, pp. 16 f., including a detail of the rose.

[3] This is evident from the presence of both the low G-sharp and of chords playable only with a short octave.

[4] The former Berlin MS. 40316.

[5] This opinion probably arose primarily because the pavan of Philips's pair appears in the *Fitzwilliam Virginal Book* (I, p. 321) with the title 'Pavana Doloroso. Treg'.

prison should have been inspired to write for a very special type of virginal is curious. For him to be supplied with such an instrument during his confinement would have been an act of incredible largesse even for the nobler prisons of the time. A more plausible hypothesis is that he wrote the work as a very personal lament, while in prison, with the memory of a particular Grouwels virginal still fresh in his mind. None of his later works requires such an instrument.

After this painful experience in Holland it is doubtful whether Philips ever returned. He could have come to meet Sweelinck during the latter's Antwerp visit in 1604, although he had moved from Antwerp to Brussels in 1597. That they remained good friends seems likely, not only because of close musical relationships but also because of Baudartius' statement, written after Sweelinck's death but while Philips was still living, that Sweelinck was 'renowned as the most valorous and ingenious Organist of this age', which praise 'the artistic organist and musician Peter Philips, organist in Brussels, and all others gladly give, honouring him as a Phoebus or Apollo'. [1] It is also significant that Philips's pavan and galliard composed in the Hague prison are found in both the Gustaf Düben tablature and the (East) Berlin manuscript *Ly* A 1, the repertories of which seem to have direct descendancy from Sweelinck's school. This may indicate that he sent the work to Sweelinck, probably after his safe arrival in Antwerp.

Philips was not the only English recusant to hold a post as organist in Brussels. Nicholas Morgan, Countertenor and Gentleman of the Chapel Royal in 1567, after spending some time in France and at the Jesuit College in St. Omer, became organist to the convent of Augustinian nuns from 1612 until his death, at a most advanced age, on 3 August 1640. A still more important composer, Richard Deering, after visiting Italy in 1612, had become organist of the convent of English

---

[1] For the Dutch text, see *Memoryen ofte Cort Verhael der Gedenckweerdichste Gheschedenissen van Nederland* (Arnhem, 1624) II, Bk. 12, p. 163; cf. also pp. 8 f., above.

nuns at Brussels by 1617. 'Canzonette à 3 voci di Richardo Duringo, inglese' were published at Antwerp, [1] but have not been preserved. Joan Albert Ban of Haarlem wrote in 1642 of 'the excellent Richard Diringh my special friend', [2] which probably means that Deering visited Holland. He was still in Brussels in 1620, but returned to England in 1625 as organist to Queen Henrietta. Both these men came to the Lowlands too late to have influenced Sweelinck, and probably too late even to have met him. In any case, no music of theirs for keyboard instruments is extant.

A considerable quantity of keyboard music does survive, however, with an attribution to a certain William Brown, who may also have been a recusant organist. Nothing is known of his life, and his music has remained unpublished except for a single 'Phantasie' from a Liège manuscript. [3] Already in 1884 he was mentioned by Ritter, who suggested he might be identified with one 'Brouno', organist at the Utrecht St. Nikolaas-kerk in 1563. [4] Archival research at Utrecht [5] fails to shed any light on the matter, but the style of Brown's extant works indicates he was a later composer and would not have been active in 1563. [6] Since his music is found only in sources connected with the Spanish Netherlands (the Liège MS. 888, the former Berlin MS 40316, and Oxford Christ Church MS. 89), it seems likely that he was yet another of the recusant composers employed as an organist, perhaps at a convent. Further research in Belgian archives may reveal biographical

---

[1] *Musique et Musiciens au XVIIe siècle. Correspondance et oeuvre musicales de Constantin Huygens*, ed. W. J. A. Jonckbloet and J. P. N. Land (Leiden, 1882), p. cxcvii.

[2] Ibid., p. cxxix. Ban also met the Englishman D. Robert, who had written a treatise on song in 1642. See ibid., p. xlvi. This may have been the same 'Robert' who was Singing Master of the Chapel of the Duke of York, later James II, in 1677. See Nagel, *Beilage zu den Monatshefte für Musikgeschichte*, I (1894/95), p. 62.

[3] University Library, MS. 888. Mod. ed. of entire MS. by A. Guilmant in *Archives des maîtres de l'orgue*, X (Mainz, 1914), now extremely rare.

[4] A. G. Ritter, *Zur Geschichte des Orgelspiels*, I (Leipzig, 1884), p. 6.

[5] Kindly carried out for the author by Dr. M. A. Vente of Utrecht.

[6] See p. 118.

material, and perhaps also explain his curious alias of 'Jeanneton' (in the Berlin MS.). [1]

No list of Sweelinck's possible contacts with English music would be complete without mention of Sir Constantine Huygens (1596–1687), writer, statesman, artist, musician, virtuoso. As has been mentioned above, we know from his Latin autobiography that he played the viol at one of the weekly Amsterdam chamber music evenings in the home of Jean Calandrini on the 'Deventer Houtmarkt' (the part of the Nieuwezijds Voorburgwal now known as the 'postage-stamp market') at which Sweelinck presided. [2] During a long afternoon little Constantijn, about six years of age, made no mistakes—though others made many—until one moment when he looked up, lost his place, and could not return. He burst into tears in front of the entire gathering. What music would he and other members of this Sweelinck circle [3] have been playing around the year 1603? The fashion for the 'barbitus Britannica', as Huygens called the viola da gamba, was new in the Netherlands, and no doubt 'Engelse Musijk voor de Phiool' [4] was imported as avidly as were the instruments themselves. [5] A large repertory of viol consort music (including pieces by Richard Deering) was published in Germany by the itinerant Englishmen William Brade and Thomas Simpson as early as 1609. [6] When Matthysz began printing his successful series of music for popular consumption around the middle of the century, one of his first volumes (1648) was *XXIX Konincklycke Fantasien*, consisting entirely of

---

[1] The complete works of William Brown, as well as of Peter Philips and Pieter Cornet will be edited by the author in a future volume of *MMN*.
[2] See above, p. 5.
[3] For the many English connexions of the Calandrinis and members of their circle, see Bachrach, *passim*.
[4] For the five such volumes in Huygens's library, see Bachrach, p. 57.
[5] In 1638, Huygens bought an 'accord de six violes vielle' for the then impressive sum of thirty pounds, on the advice of Nicolas Lanier, whom he had met in 1621 at the house of Lady Killigrew.
[6] Many pieces included in *Jacobean Consort Music*, ed. T. Dart and W. Coates, *MB*, IX (1955). See pp. 60 and 100 for a fantasia and a pavan by Richard Dering.

English viol fancies ('Royal' because they had come from the English court). A curious inclusion is the work of William Daman, [1] whose music had long since dropped out of fashion in England. Perhaps his fantasia had been imported at the time of Sweelinck and kept alive by such connoisseurs as Huygens, whose own boyhood viol teacher was also an Englishman, 'William H.' [2] Huygens's contact with English viol players and composers continued into his maturity. His autobiography not only tells us about his joining a consort of English gentlemen at the house of Sir Henry Wotton (who spent the winter of 1614–15 in The Hague), but also describes in detail the English manner of playing chords ('lyra way') over 3, 4, or even all 6 strings (and a later note in his index mentions the addition of a seventh string). [3]

In the musical relations between England and the Netherlands in this 'Golden Age', the Dutch were certainly not the only beneficiaries. Dutch tunes such as 'Hanskin' or 'De Rommelpot' turn up in English settings, and a small number of Sweelinck's works may be found in English manuscripts. Yet few, if any, of the native English composers appear to have been influenced by him (or by any other Dutchman). While some returning Englishmen and a few emigrant Dutch brought new elements into English music, musical influence flowed mainly in the opposite direction, across the Channel towards the Netherlands. In fact, both the influx of English players and musicians and the vogue their music enjoyed wrought profound and, for the most part, salutary changes in Dutch music.

[1] Walloon composer born in Liège, *c.* 1540, emigrated to England in 1562, died in London 1591.   [2] Bachrach, p. 57.
[3] Original Latin text in Bachrach, 212–13. Dutch translation by A. H. Kan in *De Jeugd van Constantijn Huygens door hemzelf beschreven* (Rotterdam, 1946), p. 24 f.

II

KEYBOARD MUSIC IN THE
NETHERLANDS BEFORE SWEELINCK

SOURCES for the musical antecedents of Sweelinck's keyboard style in his own land are extremely scarce. We
are forced to rely on conjecture, and shall probably never
know in detail the nature of his musical heritage. Nevertheless, in a book concerned with the origins of keyboard
music in the Netherlands up to 1630, Charles van den Borren
devoted sixty-seven pages preparatory to his study of Sweelinck (itself only forty-one pages) to what he called 'musique de
clavier conjecturale',[1] reviewing the various publications
preserved from the sixteenth-century Netherlands (particularly Antwerp), that are described on their title pages as
'accomodées aussi bien à la voix comme à tous Instrumens
Musicaux', or 'zeer lustich enden bequaem om te spelen op
alle musicale Instrumenten'. Since the appellation of 'all
musical instruments' by definition includes those various
types furnished with keyboards, Van den Borren felt justified
in devoting much of his study to these published works. As he
realized, any analysis of this music must remain on conjec-
tural grounds, for it was certainly the performer, not the composer or publisher, who made these pieces really 'accomodées'
to his particular keyboard instrument. In several instances,
Van den Borren attempted a hypothetical 'réduction en
tablature'; he could not possibly, however, have reconstructed
the half-improvised, half-composed 'intabulations'—with their
elaborate ornaments and divisions which we may be sure any
sixteenth-century keyboard performer would have played.
Without notated examples of music specifically for keyboard

---

[1] *Les origines de la musique de clavier dans les Pays-Bas (Nord et Sud) jusque
vers* 1630 (Brussels, 1914), p. 132.

from this period of Netherlands history, we can never hope to understand the sudden appearance of Sweelinck—of his brightly shining star in a musical firmament otherwise obscure, if not void. Van den Borren admits that his 'arrangements hypothétiques d'œuvres vocales' are insufficient to compensate for an apparent lacuna of keyboard sources. Evidence that they once existed is supplied by both 'la réputation acquise à l'étranger par un nombre relativement grand d'organistes néerlandais de la seconde moitié du XVIe siècle, et, d'autre part, la simple possibilité d'une apparition comme celle de Sweelinck'.

A manuscript long known to scholars (including Van den Borren) but until recently neglected and misunderstood, can throw some light, however dim, on the period preceding Sweelinck. The keyboard book inscribed 'Suzanne van Soldt, 1599' on its cover, although easily accessible in the British Museum since 1873, has been largely ignored by Continental scholars because of its presumed English repertory, while English historians have passed it by because of its Dutch connexions. In a recent complete edition of the manuscript, [1] the author identifies its owner in 1599 as having been the young daughter of a wealthy refugee Flemish merchant in London, who had left Antwerp most probably before 1574. [2] It is the author's hypothesis that only the four pieces copied at the end of the manuscript in a different hand date from c. 1599; the main body of the manuscript could have been copied in the Netherlands in the 1570s. [3] The book might have been

---

[1] *MMN* III, pp. x–xii, xxvi–xxxii, and 1–56.

[2] In that year Queen Elizabeth, because of the extraordinarily large numbers of immigrants over the past decade, and in order not to unduly offend Philip of Spain, ruled that no more members be received at the Dutch Church (Austin Friars) in London, insisting instead that they be dispersed and settle in provincial towns. For further biographical information about the Van Soldt family, see *MMN* III, pp. x–xii, to which should be added miscellaneous references (without musical significance) in *Returns of Aliens. Publications of the Huguenot Society of London*, X: 2 (1902) and X: 3 (1907).

[3] This conjecture has been generally accepted; cf. *Mens en Melodie*, XVII (1962), p. 3.

brought to England by Susanne's father, or by other of her relatives, from Antwerp or Breda. Evidence against its having originated in England is provided by the watermark, the handwriting, the inscriptions, and especially the repertory. To these strong arguments a small detail of notation also contributes. The manuscript shares with the *Fitzwilliam Virginal Book*, a source otherwise so unlike the Van Soldt book, a peculiar propensity for a redundant final chord at the end of certain pieces. Alterations must be made in order to accommodate first and second endings, and the ultimate breve chord often seems superfluous. Ferguson recently conjectured that Tregian wrote such endings merely for a decorative purpose.[1] Had he consulted the Susanne van Soldt manuscript, he would have seen that his thesis was too limited.[2] A more likely possibility is that these tautological chords were a traditional feature of Northern continental keyboard notation. Sometime after the 14-year-old Francis Tregian arrived at Douai in 1586 he adopted this trait and hence it survives in the *Fitzwilliam Virginal Book*.[3]

Even if we may assume the body of Susanne van Soldt's book to have been copied in or near Antwerp, there remains the difficulty of identifying even the approximate area of origin—a fortiori the composers—of the anonymous works it contains. Only three works are ascribed: 'Susanna Vung Jour' to 'Orlando Lasso', who wrote the vocal model but certainly not the keyboard setting, and a pavan and matching galliard to 'Bassano', who could be either an Italian or an English resident of this large family of musicians. The latter

---

[1] Howard Ferguson, 'Repeats and Final Bars in the *Fitzwilliam Virginal Book*', *Music & Letters*, XLIII (1962), p. 348.

[2] Redundant final chords appear elsewhere too in keyboard dances (cf. various German collections of the early seventeenth century). There are, moreover, places where the repetition is musically satisfying. The repeated chord may, indeed, have been meant to be played.

[3] Elizabeth Cole, 'Seven Problems of the Fitzwilliam Virginal Book', *Proceedings of the Royal Musical Association*, LXXIX (1953), p. 61, first suggested that the famous anthology was begun in the Lowlands rather than in the Tower of London. Use of the term 'Rep.' (*Reprinse*) for the various repeats may also be a Flemish feature.

would seem more likely for reasons of geography and repertory, but this is not clearly borne out by the style of the music.
Although there is an abundance of repeated chords, as in
related dance pairs from an English source (the *Dublin
Virginal Book*), the typically English 'tonic-dominant' figure
for the left hand is missing and the main-note ornaments
(trills of various lengths beginning not with the upper but
with the main note) point to Italy rather than England.
Perhaps it was written by the Giovanni Bassano of Venice
who published several volumes of instrumental fantasies and
ricercari. As for the remainder of the manuscript, the only
identifying clues are the titles and of course the style of the
pieces, the latter furnishing the most decisive proof but being
at the same time the most difficult to establish.

The eleven psalm settings are perhaps the easiest to deal
with from the point of view of style. They consist of little more
than the unadorned psalm tune neatly harmonized in four
parts, with cadences ornamented according to the following
stereotype, which may be traced back at least as far as the
1520s in Italy (Marc Antonio Cavazzoni).

Apart from this cadential figure (and the lapse in part-
writing at cadences to accommodate a sonorous five-tone
chord, as in the example above) there is little if any attempt to
transform these psalms into interesting keyboard pieces or to
exploit the medium in any way. Monotony is the inevitable
result, and the dullness is only aggravated by the use of the
cadential figure, for it recurs essentially unaltered no less than
thirty-five times in the course of these short settings. Only
twice is it varied by way of starting the trill with the upper
note: in XVIII and, approached by leap, in IX.[1] The latter

[1] *MMN* III, 33 and 12.

instance occurs in the one setting which in quality stands
noticeably above the others. Here the cadential figure is imag-
inatively extended in m. 5 to provide an imitative sequence
between treble and alto, and in mm. 13–14 there occurs
the closest thing to lively instrumental figuration in the entire
group of eleven settings. Though this psalm is marked by
greater variety and interest, it is nonetheless homogeneous
in style with the other ten.

There is no reason to conjecture that these settings might
have been copied from a foreign source, or even from a
'professional' source of any sort. They seem to be local pro-
ducts, and of a non-professional niveau. Adumbrations of
Sweelinck's style these psalms do not provide, but they give
us very probably a sampling of some keyboard clichés prevalent around Antwerp during Sweelinck's youth: the preference for four-part writing except at cadences, for wide
spacing in the bass (octaves and fifths or frequently octaves
alone), and quite pronouncedly for the Italianate and stereotyped cadential trill beginning on the main note. From such
conclusions we may proceed to draw inferences about the
more varied and artistically interesting pieces in Susanne
van Soldt's book.

After the psalms, the work which most strongly implies
local origin is the long dance-setting titled 'Brabanschen
ronden dans ofte Brand', a provincial variant of the ubiquitous
branle. The Netherlands seems to have been famous for its
round dances [1] and the present example follows the usual
pattern: a sedate duple beginning gives way to a triple section
(*proportio sesquialtera*) which is then doubled in speed for the
final lively *branle* danced by the youngest couples. This latter
section bears close resemblance, particularly in melodic
shape, to the untitled no. 12 of the *Dublin Virginal Book*. Far
from implying English influence, however, this concordance
binds the work still closer to the vicinity of Brabant. As John

---

[1] Cf. for instance 'Ain Niederlandisch runden Dantz' in Hans
Judenkünig's *Ain schone kunstliche Vnderweisung* (1523), ed. A. Koczirz,
D.T.Ö., XVIII, 37 (1911), p. 11.

Ward points out, the English piece is merely a simple version of a *branle* known on the Continent as 'Hoboken', after the suburb of Antwerp by that name. [1] It is thus not surprising that in type of keyboard texture and in ornamentation the round dance or *branle* of Brabant relates closely to the psalm settings, since both originated in or around Antwerp, *c.* 1570. The Italian cadential figure is used (thrice in the *branle simple*), though it is always followed by broken harmony in the rhythm of dotted quarter, eighth, two quarters—a figure more appropriate to the dance than the solemn static chords of the psalm cadences. This rhythm is never combined, however, with the characteristically English 'tonic-dominant' alteration as it is so often in the early works of Byrd. [2]

The other dances are considerably smaller in scope but much the same in keyboard technique, in the spacing of chords, and in ornamentation. The titles of a few suggest Flemish origin, but in the main they belong to the international repertory of dance tunes which prevailed at this time. Their international character is perhaps epitomized by the 'Pavane dan Vers'. Its title, though orthographically peculiar, certainly ties in with the Brabantine connexions already discussed. As 'Pavane d'Anvers' it graced several previous collections printed in the Spanish Netherlands. However, this pavan was known in England as 'Turkeylony' (perhaps from the Italian *tordiglione?*) and may in fact be modelled on one of Azzaiuolo's *Villotte alla padoana* (1557). Its so-called 'reprysse' in the Van Soldt manuscript is actually a separate dance known in France as 'Tintelore d'Angleterre', a name which may in turn derive from the Italian 'Tiente alora'. [3] Other dances in the book are almost as widely international; [4] yet many were especially popular in Antwerp in the 1570s, as their inclusion in the Phalèse editions testifies. Thus, while their place of origin can probably never be established, there is nothing to argue against the likelihood of the *keyboard*

[1] *Dublin Virginal Book*, 2nd ed., J. Ward (Wellesley, 1964), p. 47.
[2] See below, p. 119.   [3] See *M.L.A. Notes*, XI (1954), p. 303.
[4] Cf. *MMN*, III, pp. xxvi–xxxii, *passim*.

settings themselves having originated in the Netherlands.

A dance pair, 'De quadre pavanne' and 'De quadre galliard', present a more complex problem. They do not belong to the international repertory (they are known in no other source), and they probably reach us more or less in the state in which they were composed, in contradistinction to the 'evolved' dances which exist in countless variants. 'Quadran' or 'Quadro' pavans were common in Elizabethan England, and Otto Gombosi has plausibly suggested that the term is merely the English name for the *passamezzo moderno*, which uses B-natural (*quadratum*) as opposed to the B-flat of the *passamezzo antico*.[1] If the term does indeed derive from the Latin, there is no reason why 'quadre' need be regarded as a Flemish corruption of the English. It could also in the Netherlands have served to denote the *passamezzo moderno* (though the author knows of no other example).

There is likewise in the style of the two dances nothing compellingly indicative of English origin. The pairing of pavan and galliard in the late sixteenth century suggests England or France, and the music is closer in style to the keyboard music of England than to that of Germany or Italy. There are, however, strong stylistic ties with the pieces already discussed, and furthermore, noticeable differences from corresponding English pieces. The pavan is considerably more extended and, in general, more elaborate than any preserved English pavans before Byrd's. The galliard at the beginning of the *Mulliner Book* is comparable in scope and perhaps contemporaneous in date of origin;[2] but it is markedly different in style, full of strong six-part chords, and favours triadic figuration, repeated chords, and written-out trills beginning from the upper note. The 'quadre' pavan and galliard proceed mainly in four-part texture with occasional five-part (and thrice in the galliard, six-part) chords on

[1] 'Stephen Foster and "Gregory Walker"', *The Musical Quarterly*, XXX (1944), p. 145.
[2] The opening section of the *Mulliner Book* may be much later than heretofore assumed: see Speuy, p. 162, n. 56.

accented beats. They adhere mainly to stepwise figuration
and use exclusively main-note trills. The 'tonic-dominant'
alternation already mentioned as a feature of English keyboard
dances both before Byrd and during especially his earlier
years, is lacking in the 'quadre' pair. There is likewise no
use of the short *stretto* motives which become a constant
unifying device with Byrd, and already even with some pavans
of the *Dublin Virginal Book*. [1] The 'quadre' pavan and galliard
are thus very likely a unique example of a dance pair in
Flemish sixteenth-century keyboard music, related to corresponding contemporaneous works in England, but stylistically
distinct.

The final work from the Susanne van Soldt manuscript
remaining to be discussed is at once the longest, the most
elaborate, and the most difficult to identify of the entire collection. That the 'intabulation' titled 'Susanna Vung Jour'
dates from after 1560 is certain, for in that year Lassus published his five-part setting of Guéroult's famous *chanson
spirituelle*. It was his version, with part of the *superius* borrowed
from Lupi's tenor, which formed the basis for most of the
sixteenth-century instrumental arrangements, including that
in the Van Soldt book. More than a dozen keyboard settings
are preserved from all parts of Europe. A remarkably faithful
copy of the same piece as that in the Van Soldt book occurs in
an English manuscript. [2] The work is, however, very different
in style from the settings known to be by English or Scottish
composers, and, significantly, most (but not quite all) of the
ornaments were 'anglicized' by the English scribe: in his
manuscript, they begin on the upper auxiliary rather than,
as in the Van Soldt book, the main note. Both the ornamentation and figural style point to Italy rather than England,

[1] Cf. especially no. 26, ed. Ward. Since this pavan and its galliard, stylistically by far the most advanced pair in the book, occur near the
end, and since the final piece (variations on *Chi passa*) is the most
elaborate and forward-looking of all, the manuscript would seem to
have been compiled over a period of years. The last pieces could have
been composed a decade or so later than those opening the collection.
[2] BM, MS. Add. 30485, f. 51[v].

and there are striking resemblances to Andrea Gabrieli's setting (composed sometime between 1560 and 1586, although not published until 1605, after his death). Gabrieli's opening (the first seven semibreves) is unornamented, but thereafter the similarities to the Van Soldt version are numerous, as the following excerpt may serve to demonstrate.

In its adherence to four-part texture, with occasional five- and even six-part chords for accent, as well as in certain details of ornamentation and in the preponderance of treble figuration, the Van Soldt 'Susanna' is still closer to works like the 'quadre' pavan and the 'Brabanschen ronden dans' than to Italian keyboard styles. Perhaps it was written by a Nether- lander under Italian influence; if not, then the (originally Italian) composition was considerably altered by some Nether- lands musician-scribe. In any case, its presence in the Van

Soldt book attests an influence of Italian keyboard music in the Netherlands before Sweelinck.

A keyboard manuscript in a Swedish library, recently described by Thurston Dart, was owned around 1600 by a certain Elisabeth Eijsbock, probably the young daughter of a wealthy merchant. [1] As Dart suggests, she or her family may have had some connexion with the Netherlands, to judge by the surname and by the presence of some pieces with Dutch or Low German titles. (Perhaps they were Protestant refugees from the Spanish Netherlands.) However, the manuscript is highly international in repertory, as was typical around 1600, and could have been compiled by or for a dilettante of catholic (but Protestant) tastes in almost any of the Northern countries. There is no reason to seek further for the place of origin than the title page, which places the Eijsbock family in Frankfurt (an der Oder), [2] especially since the manuscript is in German tablature. There is also no reason to be further concerned with this collection in a study of Sweelinck. Nothing could be more removed from his keyboard style than the crude bungling of these simple settings of popular pieces of the day. Even 'Pavana Lachrima', Dowland's great masterpiece, is garbled beyond belief—and its second strain is titled 'Alter Pavana', as if it were a separate piece.

Susanne van Soldt's manuscript remains, then, as a solitary source of keyboard music in the Netherlands before Sweelinck. Although the main body of the book was probably compiled before Susanne was born, it may also—like the portion written for her—have been compiled for a young amateur. Evidence connects the collection with the region

[1] Stockholm, Kungl. Musikaliska Akademiens Bibliotek, Tablature no. 1. See Thurston Dart, 'Elisabeth Eysbock's Keyboard Book', *Svensk Tidskrift för Musikforskning*, XL (1962), pp. 5–12.

[2] Dart gives Frankfurt-am-Main, presumably because of its relative geographical proximity to the Netherlands. Linguistically, however, Frankfurt-an-der-Oder, where Low German was spoken, is closer, and therefore the more likely choice. The name Eijsbock is unknown at the archives at Frankfurt-am-Main. The author's inquiries to Frankfurt-an-der-Oder (East Germany) remain as yet unanswered.

of Antwerp rather than the North. Nevertheless, its contents help us to make speculations regarding the (now lost) Dutch keyboard music of professional level composed by Sweelinck's immediate predecessors. First of all, we may note that Italian influence was prominent, while English elements were as yet hardly felt. This balance changed radically with the arrival of Sweelinck (and of English musicians). Secondly, if a collection on the amateur's level contained such a relatively large proportion of competent and even excellent pieces, then keyboard music must have been on a high level—higher than, for instance, in Germany at that time. Certainly these pieces are much more advanced than those in such a collection as the Löffelholtz tablature (1585) and even compare favourably with pieces in the best 'professional' tablatures of Schmid or Ammerbach. Nevertheless Van den Borren's statement still holds more or less true: Sweelinck's keyboard *œuvre* 'va nous ouvrir des perspectives nouvelles et nous montrer la musique de clavier des Pays-Bas arrivée soudain à un éclat que rien de ce que nous avons étudié jusqu'à présent ne pouvait faire prévoir'. [1]

[1] *Op. cit.*, p. 131.

III

SWEELINCK'S KEYBOARD MUSIC

NEW SOURCES AND PROBLEMS OF AUTHENTICATION

BEFORE attempting to make valid stylistic comparisons between the works of Sweelinck and other composers, it is necessary to establish a canon of his keyboard compositions. In 1894, near the beginning of his career, Max Seiffert first edited Sweelinck's *Werken voor Orgel en Clavecimbel*. In 1943, near the end of his life, a second, enlarged edition was brought out in occupied Amsterdam. [1] It was augmented through the discovery of several new sources, but also by the editor's attribution to Sweelinck of many anonymous works, particularly chorale variations. In the course of the present study, the need for a new, third edition has become clear. Eleven new sources have been discovered since 1943, eight of them of major importance: Turin, National Library, Giordano volumes 1, 5, 6 and 7 and Foà volume 8; [2] Leningrad, Library of the Academy of Sciences, MS. QN 204; [3] Clausthal-Zellerfeld, [4]

[1] Reprinted in 1957 and 1962.
[2] These volumes were first cited by Walter Rubsamen, 'Music Research in Italian Libraries', *Notes*, VI (1949), p. 557. They were subsequently studied by B. van den Sigtenhorst Meyer, who visited Turin in the summer of 1951 and worked on sixteen pieces attributed to Sweelinck but overlooked six others. He passed his studies on to Alfons Annegarn who, five years after Van den Sigtenhorst's death, edited five of the seven unique works (all five spurious, as we shall see) in Uitgave XLVII VNM (Amsterdam, 1958).
[3] This source was discovered by the author in 1958 and the Dutch works it contains were published in *MMN* III.
[4] First studied and described in Breig *Sw* and *Sch*. The tablatures were discovered by Gustav Fock of Hamburg, who refused a request for permission to study the works by Sweelinck which they contain, perhaps because of his intention to edit the Scheidemann chorale settings for Bärenreiter Verlag. A microfilm was kindly secured, however, through Pastor Burose of Clausthal-Zellerfeld, who served at that time as librarian for the Calvörsche Bibliothek.

Bergakademie Clausthal Technische Hochschule Bibliothek (*ex* Calvörsche Bibliothek), $\mathcal{Z}e$ 1 and $\mathcal{Z}e$ 2; and three sources of very minor interest: Oxford, Christ Church MS. 1113; Berlin (now Tübingen) MS. 40615; and Lüneburg, Rats-bücherei, K.N. 207/15. In addition, new light has been shed on several of the manuscripts known to Seiffert, including the most important of all the sources, the Berlin MS. Lynar A 1 [1]. Finally, further study of the sources and the works of Swee-linck and his contemporaries has enabled us to see that many of Seiffert's ascriptions are no longer valid. The 1943 edition, then, admirable in its day, can no longer adequately serve as a basis for the study or performance of Sweelinck's works. Fortunately an excellent new edition is scheduled to appear in 1968, in three fascicles: I. Fantasies and Toccatas, edited by Gustav Leonhardt; II. Chorale Variations, edited by Alfons Annegarn; and III. Secular Variations, edited by Frits Noske.[2]

In the past, Seiffert's edition has been accepted almost without question. Tusler, for instance, in his lengthy study of Sweelinck's 'organ music'[3] failed even to mention the fact that twenty of the 'Sweelinck' works with which he was dealing were attributed only by Seiffert and either appeared anonymously, or were ascribed to other composers, in the seventeenth-century sources. Even Van den Sigtenhorst Meyer, in an otherwise admirable and thorough study, avoided any general discussion of Seiffert's ascriptions. An unfortunate result is that one of his detailed analyses[4] concerns itself not only with an anonymous fantasy (S. 13) but also with a related piece (S. 12) which, as we shall presently see, is actually Bull's *God Save the King*. Lydia Schierning, in her recently published dissertation, has ventured to contradict

---

[1] See *Reinken*, pp. 45–51. Cf. also an article by Werner Breig, to appear in *Archiv für Musikwissenschaft* in 1968. Seiffert's completely unfounded hypothesis that *Ly* A I was written by Matthias Weckmann has been accepted as fact by nearly every musicologist working in this area and by most recent reference works. Richard Marlow's ed. of G. and R. Farnaby's keyboard music, *MB* XXIV (1965), even makes Weckmann Sweelinck's pupil—a chronological absurdity.   [2] Cf. App. VI.

[3] R. L. Tusler, *Organ Music of Sweelinck* (Bilthoven, 1958).   [4] vdSM, 251–53.

Seiffert; but she relies wholly on bibliographical evidence without making the slightest attempt at stylistic analysis. Primarily concerned with the Lübbenau (Lynar) sources, she remarks that Seiffert's 'Inanspruchnahme aller in *Ly* A 1 enthaltenen Choralbearbeitungen muss sehr kritisch behandelt werden'. [1] However, instead of critically reviewing Seiffert's ascriptions she merely proceeds to chart bibliographically all the chorale variations, toccatas, and fantasies included in his edition, by dividing them into three categories: *Sichere*, *Fragliche*, and *Anonyme*. These divisions are based solely on the manner in which the pieces happen to have survived. In the first class are included all works accompanied in the sources by the clearly and fully spelled name of the composer (including Fantasia S. 12 which, as we shall see, is actually by John Bull). The second category arbitrarily comprises all those works marked only with initials or abbreviations (even when their meaning is as obvious as in 'M. Joan: Pet: S: Amb: Org:'). As for the third class containing the anonymous works, she concludes, solely on the basis of her charts, that these 'können aber nicht mehr Sweelinck zugeschrieben werden', adding that it is 'unhaltbar, einem Komponisten Werke nur nach stilkritischen Gesichtspunkten zuzuschreiben'. [2] This kind of purely bibliographical approach, with its total rejection of stylistic evidence as a factor in determining authenticity, should be avoided. The judgements of a modern editor can often prove more accurate than the vagaries of an ancient scribe. Problems of authentication can find their satisfactory solution only through an intelligent appraisal of the external evidence provided by the sources in conjunction with the internal evidence provided by stylistic analysis.

Limiting himself to Sweelinck's chorale variations, Werner Breig has recently made a much more penetrating study [3] of these problems. His emphasis on the placement of the *cantus firmus* and on the number and type of variations employed seems at times not totally relevant to the question of

---

[1] Schierning, *Die Überlieferung der deutschen Orgel- und Klaviermusik* (Kassel, 1961), p. 91.   [2] *Ibid.*, p. 97.   [3] Breig *Sw*, 258–76.

personal style characteristics in the music with which he is dealing. Moreover, his otherwise admirable article is impaired by a categorical rejection of Sweelinck's *Psalm 116* (S. 51 = A. 11) and *Herzlich lieb hab ich dich, o Herr* (S. 45 = 14 A*) as unauthentic. These works are attributed in the sources to, respectively, 'J.P.' and 'M. Joan Pet: Schw: [*read as* Schön *by Gombosi and Annegarn*] Ambst: Orga:'. Breig's reasons for contradicting these seventeenth-century ascriptions are insufficient and unconvincing. In spite of his refusal to accept Miss Schierning's categories, he seems nevertheless to have been influenced in these two cases by her concept of a 'fragliche' category.

The preponderant share of the new material in Seiffert's 1943 edition consisted of chorale variations. As Van den Sigtenhorst noted in the revised (1946) edition of his book, [1] the quality of these new pieces is not quite equal to their quantity. It was perhaps this fact which led Manfred Bukofzer to remark, with what seems to be veiled disparagement, on the 'severity and gravity of those "spiritual exercises" '.[2] Yet neither writer observed that of the total of twenty-four chorale variations fully one half are ascribed to Sweelinck by Seiffert only, not in a seventeenth-century source. Van den Sigtenhorst even singles out four of the variations, S. 43, 47, 55, and 57, as probably composed only to provide examples for students. The last three, he says, 'are so dry and dull' that even as pedagogical examples 'they can hardly be termed successful'. [3] He finds an exception in S. 43, which does not, however, approach the heights of Sweelinck's best work. He does not mention the fact that all four of these variations come from the same source, where they are all anonymous. Furthermore, they form, together with S. 36 (also anonymous), the only works in the Seiffert edition consisting entirely of two parts.

The four works singled out by Van den Sigtenhorst are preserved in MS. 27 of the National Museum in Budapest

[1] vdSM, 121 f.
[2] M. Bukofzer, *Music in the Baroque Era* (New York, 1947), p. 75.
[3] vdSM, 198.

where they appear between Sweelinck's *Ich ruf zu dir* and the
Passamezzo also ascribed to him. But instead of regarding them
as sanctioned by the works which surround them, we should
see them rather as separating a series of Sweelinck and
Scheidt chorale variations from a group of secular variations
by the same composers. Gombosi, who first studied the
manuscript, dismissed them as 'vier höchst unbedeutende
und primitive Choralbearbeitungen'. [1] Seiffert, on the other
hand, included them in his edition with only the following
terse defense: 'Auf die mit Sweelincks Namen signierte Nr 46
folgen Nr 57, 43, 47, und 55 anonym; ihr Kompositionsstil
weist jedoch unverkennbar auf Sweelinck hin.' [2] It is now
possible to prove that S. 55 was not written by Sweelinck
but by a lesser colleague and countryman, Henderick Speuy. [3]
With this discovery, Seiffert's assumption must be discarded,
and our credence for his attribution of the three remaining
bicinia is seriously undermined. It would, in fact, be more
logical to suppose that Speuy rather than Sweelinck was the
composer of these three also. But let us first examine the style
of the works concerned before attempting any attributions.

Probably the dullest pages in the Sweelinck *Werken* (1943)
are those occupied by the second variation of S. 47, *Nun
freut euch, lieben Christen gemein*. The chorale melody appears
crudely in the bass, as a seemingly endless chain of fifty-two
unmitigated semibreves. Even against such odds a composer
of genius could have created a florid soprano line to counter-
act in an inventive manner the utter monotony of the bass.
But not the faintest spark of genius illumines this variation. [4]

---

[1] Otto Gombosi, 'Ein neuer Sweelinck-Fund', *TVNM*, XIV (1932), p. 5.
[2] Sweelinck, *Werken* (1943), p. lviii.
[3] *Speuy*, 143–62, and the mod. ed. of Speuy's *Psalm Preludes* by F. Noske
(Amsterdam, 1962), pp. 25–27.
[4] Tusler (*op. cit.*, p. 74), however, without questioning the authenticity
of the work, outlined its structure and stated: 'This literal repetition of
phrases is rare and produces an unusually well-balanced organization.
Again Sweelinck has made the long lines of the cantus firmus independent
and contrasting with the lively figuration. In performance one must
beware of this figuration for its pleasant nature must not be overcome by
digital display; these are not toccatas.'

The fault lies not so much with the motives themselves—there is no single figure that could not conceivably have been written by Sweelinck—but with the manner in which they are employed. The 'tremolo' of broken thirds, for example, is a favourite device of Sweelinck's (as it is of his pupils, particularly Scheidt), but here (mm. 93–96) it is insensitively overdone. Not only does the figure persist too long, it also lacks even the variety it could have received within its jejune triadic framework. For an imaginative use of the same device one need only turn to the second variation of Sweelinck's *Ballo del granduca*, (S. 65 = N. 1) or the fourth variation of his *Est-ce Mars* (S. 58 = N. 3). Furthermore, the manner in which the motives are linked is exceedingly awkward and arbitrary. One overworked pattern is abruptly replaced by another, in contrast to the organically flowing lines one expects from Sweelinck. Finally, to the internal evidence of stylistic arguments may be added the external fact that this variation, at m. 81, calls for a high b", a note not available on Sweelinck's instruments and, as one might expect, not present in any of his indisputably authentic works. Van den Sigtenhorst[1] already called attention to this circumstance but concluded that Sweelinck must have composed such a work only for use by his German students, without having played it himself. A much more plausible explanation is simply that the piece was not written by Sweelinck.

Markedly different in style is S. 43, *Es spricht der Unweisen Mund wohl*, the third of these four *bicinia*. The rhythmic *cantus firmus*, slightly ornamented (*cf.* mm. 9, 18, and 33) moves mainly in half-notes, while the 'free' line employs primarily third species counterpoint. While shorter and simpler than the *bicinia* discussed thus far, it nevertheless shows more contrapuntal mastery. *Bravura* passagework is totally lacking—Breig[2] calls it 'allzu anspruchslos'—but the line is supple and sensitive, particularly in its transitions from one figure to another. The figures themselves are certainly

---

[1] vdSM, 205 f.   [2] Breig *Sw*, 268.

within the vocabulary of Sweelinck, as the following characteristic excerpts illustrate.

However, *Es spricht* lacks a companion in format among the
preserved authentic works, and since it appears anonymously among *bicinia* by other composers in its unique source,
an ascription to Sweelinck, in spite of stylistic similarities,
cannot be wholeheartedly accepted.

The remaining anonymous *bicinium* from the Budapest
source, *Wo Gott der Herr nicht bei uns hält*, was published as
S. 57, variation 1. It reappears, together with a second variation on the same chorale, in *Ly* A I. The first variation bears
little resemblance to authentic works by Sweelinck. The
'free' line comes to a halt with every phrase of the chorale.
It is, moreover, not a very highly developed or beautifully
flowing line, and the frequent cadences only tend to accen-
tuate its awkwardness. In some parts the piece has also a
curiously antique flavour, in spite of the final cadence which
stamps it as roughly contemporary with the bulk of Sweelinck's
work. The Phrygian cadential pattern at mm. 25–26, the
manner of wavering between the raised and lowered sixth
degree as in mm. 15–16, and especially the repeated cadence
formulas, mm. 6 and 11, all point to an older or at least more
conservative contemporary of Sweelinck.

The second variation, which follows without interruption
in *Ly* A 1, reveals far fewer retrospective features. The
third species contrapuntal figure involving chains of fourths
or fifths alternating with seconds (mm. 49–51) is frequent

with Sweelinck and his school. Moreover, the final cadence is of a type that could well have been written by the master himself (cf. the ending of his toccata, S. 25 = L. 22). But it is also a cliché adopted by several of his pupils—witness the ending of Scheidemann's (as yet unpublished) variations on *Kit's Almand*[1] or his *Fantasia* from the Leningrad manuscript.

Thus it is clear that such superficial resemblances (generic rather than specific) can hardly warrant the ascription to Sweelinck of a piece otherwise so unlike his authentic works.

Breig finds both variations qualitatively below the level of authentic Sweelinck works and feels that, were Sweelinck the composer, there would originally have been at least one more (climactic) variation. (The present author cannot concur with his emphasis on *number* of variations as a factor in determining authenticity.) He concludes: 'es soll nicht ausgeschlossen werden (auch die Doppelüberlieferung von V. 1 ist zu berücksichtigen),[2] dass wir hier ein Parergon in Sweelincks Choralwerk vor uns haben; die Faktur des Stückes macht es aber nicht sehr wahrscheinlich.'[3]

Following the two variations on *Wo Gott der Herr nicht bei uns hält* in *Ly* A 1 are an unusually long *bicinium* on *Allein zu dir, Herr Jesu Christ* (S. 36) and three variations on *Ach Gott, vom Himmel sieh darein* (S. 34). There follows the 'Pavan

---

[1] Preserved in the Copenhagen Adnex to Voigtländer's *Oden* and, anonymously, in WM as 'Englische Mascarata'. Breig *Sch*, 3, n. 11, errs in stating that only Var. 1 is found in the Vienna source. The setting in Lüneburg, K.N. 146, which he lists as a concordance to Var. 1, differs so extensively that it seems more reasonable to consider it an anonymous work.
[2] Why should this be of concern, since both versions are anonymous?
[3] Breig *Sw*, 266 f.

Philippi' with attribution to 'Joan Peters'. Since Seiffert had falsely assumed from its position in the Budapest source that *Wo Gott der Herr nicht bei uns hält* was the work of Sweelinck, it is understandable (though without justification) that he should have regarded the anonymous works between it and the 'Pavan Philippi' as by the same composer. Such an assumption requires the support of stylistic evidence if the two intervening works are to continue to be accepted as authentic.

Such testimony as can be brought forth in the case of the long *bicinium* is certainly not overwhelming. As pointed out by Breig, [1] it compares unfavourably with the four excellent Sweelinck variations (the second of which is also a *bicinium*) on the same melody in the Clausthal-Zellerfeld tablature (A. 2). Even without comparison, however, stylistic elements such as the unduly extended sequences or the repetitive and, for Sweelinck, rather antiquated cadence formula (cf. mm. 16, 31, 55, 57, 63, and 75) would tend to class this as either an early or an unauthentic work. Breig suggests that the piece stems from an unknown *Kleinmeister* of the Sweelinck school. Seiffert's attribution of the three variations on *Ach Gott, vom Himmel sieh darein* (S. 34) is even less credible. The work is loosely constructed, totally lacking the coherence of Swee- linck's genuine compositions, and the harmony shows charac- teristics of a slightly later period—as do the cadences, which are all rather suggestive of Scheidemann. The repetitive figuration (as in mm. 29–35), however, and the counterpoint of mere syncopated parallel motion (as at mm. 8–10) argue against an ascription to any of Sweelinck's best pupils. In any case, the work seems more properly associated with Scheide- mann, or his school, than with Sweelinck.

All the remaining anonymous chorale variations included in Seiffert's edition are taken from a single source: WM. In all the 248 extra-large folios of the manuscript, comprising a liberal international anthology of late-sixteenth and early

[1] *Ibid.*, 267.

seventeenth-century music, there is only one Sweelinck work which would be classified as 'sicher' by Miss Schierning: a 'Toccata Joh: Peter: Schweling'. Two other works are identified by initials—one of them erroneously with 'M. F. P.' instead of the expected 'M. J. P.'. Among ff. 191–224 are scattered seven other pieces without attributions but identifiable from other sources. One of these, *Wir glauben all an einen Gott* (S. 56=A. 13), has since been found in two additional sources unknown to Seiffert and will be discussed later. The five other anonymous chorale variations were entered together in a section of the codex with authentic Sweelinck works (ff. 191–224). *Nun komm der Heiden Heiland* (S. 49), however, occurs much earlier in the collection (f. 60'). This fact alone should suffice to make Seiffert's ascription highly questionable. In the *Anmerkungen*, he defends his attribution with only the modest claim of 'nächste Blutsverwandtschaft' to Sweelinck's variation style. A single hearing can confirm this obvious relationship, yet a thorough analysis only furnishes proof that these variations are the work not of Sweelinck but of his immediate school. [1]

The harmonies, the spacing, the figural techniques are all intimately connected with Sweelinck's style. However, the manner in which the figures are arranged, the successive build-up of segments or 'layers' of rhythmic patterns, and the insistent, mechanistic repetition of short, static figures (as at mm. 59–60) is quite unlike anything in Sweelinck's authentic works. Furthermore, the second variation includes purely triadic virtuoso figuration far exceeding anything of the type to be found elsewhere in works attributed to Sweelinck. These are the very differences which tend to distinguish the variation style of Scheidt from that of his master. As exemplified in the following excerpts, this type of triadic figuration, though quite alien to the works of Sweelinck, is typical of his pupil.

[1] Both Gisela Gerdes, *Die Choralvariationen J. P. Sweelinck's* (typewritten dissertation, Freiburg i Br., 1956), pp. 115 ff. and Breig, *Sw* 270, have doubted the authenticity of this work.

Van den Sigtenhorst considered this set of three variations to be incomplete because it 'suddenly' ends with twelve measures of 3/2. [1] As he pointed out, Sweelinck shows a preference for treating a variation in triple meter as penultimate rather than final. On the other hand it is quite usual for Scheidt to end a series of variations with a section in triple meter. While an attribution of *Nun komm der Heiden Heiland* to Scheidt should not be taken as more than a tentative suggestion, it seems at least better justified than Seiffert's ascription to Sweelinck.

The five sets of sacred variations (S. 39, 40, 42, 44 and 50) entered in WM among works known to be by Sweelinck share much more than a common location source. They are by far the highest in quality of all the anonymous chorale variations included in Seiffert's volume. [2] All five of these works consist of two four-part variations, unlike any authenticated Sweelinck works. Extensive sixteenth-note figuration is notably lacking, and the lines flow smoothly, while the harmonic progressions, more regulated than venturesome, suggest a period later than Sweelinck's. There are variations (cf. S. 44, *Herr Christ, der einig Gottes Sohn,* second

---

[1] vdSM, 297.

[2] Especially notable is the second variation of S. 40, *Durch Adams Fall ist ganz verderbt,* where the chorale phrase is prepared by canonic imitations in diminution in the other voices, with a sure, subtle handling of the concluding dotted rhythms (from m. 92 imitated at the interval of a quarter, and at mm. 100–101, a half). The work is found on f. 191^V, not 171 as stated by Seiffert.

variation, and S. 39, *Dies sind die heilgen zehn Gebot*, second variation) with an ornamented *cantus firmus* as solo line, foreshadowing Buxtehude, but unlike anything Sweelinck is known to have written. As has been shown in connexion with S. 34, *Ach Gott vom Himmel sieh darein* from *Ly* A 1, the cadences employ certain formulas found extensively in the works of Scheidemann. Through Gustav Fock's recent discovery of the Clausthal-Zellerfeld tablatures, it is now possible to establish that one of these paired variations is indeed the work of Scheidemann: *O lux beata trinitas* (S. 50) is found in *Ze* 1, p. 230, with an ascription to 'H. S. M.' (*H*einrich *S*cheide*M*ann). It seems logical to assume that the other four pairs, so closely related stylistically, were written by the same composer. [1]

Breig [2] has found analogies in treatment of the *cantus firmus* between Scheidemann's *Christ lag in Todesbanden* and *Kyrie dominicale* (both from *Ze* 1), and, among others, the anonymous *Durch Adams Fall ist ganz verderbt* (S. 40). He feels, however, that S. 39, *Dies sind die heilgen zehn Gebot* is too poor in quality to be the product of more than a mere imitator of Scheidemann. In view of the highly uneven quality of Scheidemann's total work, Breig's position is not necessarily valid, although both variations do have a curious modal ambiguity quite foreign to the harmonic style of the other four. The opening is clearly in the Mixolydian mode on G, but a B-flat is unexpectedly introduced in m. 15 and there follows a wavering between Dorian on G and Ionian on F, with an abrupt return to Mixolydian for the last seven measures of the first variation. In the second, this process is carried yet a step further, and the E-flat in m. 51 puts us in Aeolian on G. Two bars later, the presence of an F-sharp seems to imply G minor—an implication immediately contradicted by the

---

[1] All but S. 39, *Dies sind die heilgen zehn Gebot*, have been included in G. Fock's ed. of *Heinrich Scheidemann, Choral-bearbeitungen* (Kassel, 1967), pp. 16, 25, 50 and 110. S. 44, *Herr Christ, der einig Gottes Sohn*, has here been transposed up a tone by Fock, without any indication or justification.
[2] Breig, 270 f.

closing four-and-a-half measures in pure G Mixolydian. It is true that an alteration from Mixolydian to Dorian could easily be inferred from the *cantus firmus*. This hardly provides license, however, for the numerous, irregular, and often unprepared shifts which the composer of these variations obviously enjoyed. Until the total repertory of North German chorale variations becomes more accessible and better known, this particular work cannot be convincingly ascribed to any single composer.

The Clausthal-Zellerfeld tablatures also throw new light on works which, although attributed to Sweelinck in the seventeenth-century sources, are imperfectly preserved and therefore problematical. Unique to *Ze* 1 is a very beautiful set of variations on *Allein zu dir, Herr Jesu Christ* (A. 2), ranking with *Ich ruf zu dir* (S. 46 = A 16) and *Erbarm dich mein* (S. 41 = A. 5) among Sweelinck's finest works. Like the majority (two-thirds) of the chorale variations ascribed to Sweelinck in the sources, *Allein zu dir* consists of four variations. (The term 'Versus' is used in the Zellerfeld tablatures, but this seems merely to be a later term—used, for instance, by Scheidemann —for what Sweelinck would have called a 'Variatio'). Unlike most of the authentic chorale variations, however, *Allein zu dir* has a *bicinium* not as the opening but as the second variation, a placement rare also with other composers. The recovery of the Zellerfeld variations was seen by Breig[1] as providing confirmation for what previously had to be regarded as a very questionable sequence: the four variations on *Wir glauben all an einen Gott* (S. 56 = A. 13). Only variations two (a *bicinium*), three, and four are authentically preserved in *Ly* A 1, while variation two alone is preceded by a four-part variation in WM. Simply to join these fragments (as Seiffert did tentatively) with the resulting sequence of 4 : 2 : 3 : 3, now seems to be a solution borne out by comparison with *Allein zu dir*, both from the placement of the *bicinium* and from the triple section in the final variation.

---

[1] Breig *Sw*, 264 f.

However, it should be noted that Giordano 5, a source previously overlooked, follows *Ly* A 1 and opens with the *bicinium*.

Similar comparisons may be brought forward to argue against accepting as genuine a set of variations whose authenticity has already been disputed on other grounds: [1] the four variations on *Herzlich lieb hab ich dich, o Herr* (S. 45 = A. 14*), preserved only in the Bártfa manuscript (one of the latest and least trustworthy sources) and in the most corrupt state imaginable. Seiffert worked intensively to correct the worst errors and present an acceptable text. In spite of his efforts there still remains evidence of sections having been omitted, figuration having been altered and simplified, etc. Breig concludes that the work cannot be by Sweelinck. It is only the final variation, however, which seems stylistically out of the realm of Sweelinck's works. The preceding three are closely related to other authentic works (cf. mm. 109–110 with mm. 60–63 of *Est-ce Mars* and mm. 168–169 with mm. 114–115 of *Wir glauben all an einen Gott*) and the first, at least, ranks also in quality. It seems likely, then, that the first three are remnants from a set of variations by Sweelinck and that the variation which is at present in the third place, a *bicinium*, originally was placed at the opening or as the second variation in the series.

Similar problems of ordering and of authenticity are raised by the discovery of the variations on *Vater unser im Himmelreich* in the later Zellerfeld tablature (*Ze* 2). The first variation is the same as the second of those already published by Seiffert from the Budapest manuscript (S. 54, Var. 2 = A. 9, Var. 1); the second and the unfinished third do not correspond, however, with any of the remaining three variations from that source. Certain crudities of the opening variation in Budapest (for instance the abruptly static block semibreve chords which interrupt each phrase and the parallel fifths in m. 8) led Breig to question its attribution. These points of style,

---

[1] *Ibid.*, 262.

together with the use of an *a'* instead of a *b'* in the *cantus firmus* at m. 22, isolate this variation from the others. In all likelihood it does not belong with them, and should be regarded as anonymous. The fourth Budapest variation also, though it uses the proper *cantus*, seems unlike Sweelinck's authentic works in style. The opening is stiff, and the scalar sequence at mm. 124–126 is rigidly maintained longer than in any work known to be by Sweelinck. Moreover, the modest, overly-simple ending is unlike his usual cadences. For a final flourish it can muster no more bravura than a single descending scale—an inevitably disappointing anticlimax. The third variation, on the other hand, is one of the liveliest and freshest of all Sweelinck's chorale variations, and it ends with a typical cadence in which the syncopations of 'contrametric' five-note scales combine with a final scalar flourish. It is impossible to agree with Breig that merely because the texture differs from the usual chorale variation this piece, too, is unauthentic. For the same reason Breig calls the second and third variations of *Psalm 116* (S. 51 = A. 11), quite carefully preserved in *Ly* B 2, doubtful. But it seems much more likely that Sweelinck was in both cases applying some of the techniques of his toccatas to the chorale variation, as his students were often to do (and as he himself did) to the fantasia, particularly those with echoes.

It is unfortunate that the Zellerfeld manuscript ends after only the second phrase of the chorale in the third variation. Not only is this fine movement thus left incomplete, but we are also left in doubt as to the total structure of the set. Until more evidence is found, a musically satisfying solution is to place the third variation from the Budapest source as the final one. The resulting set of four (with third incomplete) is unusual in some respects: all variations are four-voiced and the *cantus firmus* is transposed (down a fourth to the alto) in the second and its values doubled in the third. The latter anomaly however cancels, with its variety, the monotony of the former. Moreover, precedents for both the alto transposition and the doubling of the *cantus firmus* are found, respectively, in the clearly authentic variations on *Da pacem* (S. 38 = A. 4) and *Christe, qui lux es et dies* (S. 37 = A. 3).

Having discovered that Seiffert unjustifiably included so many anonymous chorale variations in his edition, we may well proceed to examine with suspicion his attribution of other anonymous works. Let us begin with the fantasies. As Thurston Dart has pointed out, [1] the piece labelled 'Phantasia Ut sol fa mi Joann Pieters' in *Ly* A 1, p. 87 (S. 12 = L. 33*) is essentially the same composition as John Bull's ostinato-variations on *God Save the King*, preserved in an early nineteenth-century printed transcript from a manuscript now lost. Only the endings (from m. 110) differ. 'The attribution to Bull is to be preferred not only on the grounds of style, but also because of the English title "God Save the King" found only in the Pepusch-Kitchener-Clark manuscript'; and, Dart argues, 'the ostinato four-note theme fits these words perfectly, and this may well have been the traditional English acclamation of loyalty to the Crown sung at coronation and upon occasions of national rejoicing.'

Dart does not measure out his 'grounds of style' to support the attribution. While there is little in the opening *bicinium* until m. 40 that could mark the piece as distinctively Bull's, the florid line after this point becomes typically restless and quite eccentric in its virtuosity. Later (mm. 82–106) the four-note ostinato is fitted against virtuoso keyboard figurations of a type that one might encounter in Sweelinck's toccatas, but never to such a degree nor with such insistence. The rather mechanistic drive of these sequential patterns is more reminiscent of Scheidt than of Sweelinck, but there are strong traces of the erratic, capricious invention characteristic of Bull and so often lacking in Scheidt's more prosaic figuration. Thus there seems good reason to accept Bull's authorship of the first hundred and ten measures of the piece.

There remains the problem of the final measures and of

[1] 'Sweelinck's "Fantasia on a theme used by John Bull" ', *TVNM*, XVIII (1959), pp. 167–69.

the related ostinato-variations, anonymous in a Lüneburg source. [1] The latter employ the same four-note motive as 'God Save the King' and were ascribed to Sweelinck by Seiffert on the basis of the 'Ut sol fa mi' title in an index of the Lynar manuscript A 1. This was, however, before he had actually seen the source and discovered the 'Phantasia' it contains to be a different work from the Lüneburg 'Fuga'. In the article already cited, Dart presumes that Bull sent a copy of his fantasia to Sweelinck and adds that 'at some later date, probably after Sweelinck's death, Bull's piece turned up among Sweelinck's loose papers, minus its last page'. Later he speaks of 'its faulty conclusion', implying that the final page was composed after Sweelinck's death (perhaps by the copyist of *Ly* A 1 whom Dart mistakenly states to have been Matthias Weckmann). [2] In a later publication, however, Dart tacitly recants this hypothesis, for his annotation to the recent edition of the piece [3] merely states that the different ending in *Ly* A 1 'possibly represents Sweelinck's completion of a defective copy of the music'. This conjecture comes closer to fitting the evidence.

The style of these last seventeen measures certainly supports the theory of Sweelinck's authorship. The reduction of the ostinato theme by diminution to imitative eighth-notes and finally to sixteenth-note figuration is a touch characteristic of Sweelinck; so, too, are the last three measures, encompassing a sweeping scale and a solid, majestic close in C major. Not only are these seventeen measures worthy of Sweelinck; they rank with passages from some of his best works. They seem, in fact, a marked improvement over Bull's longer but less climactic ending. Bull's six-note trill-like figures at m. 111, reminiscent of his short preludes (see the *Fitzwilliam Book, passim*) are doggedly repeated fourteen times in sequence. Sweelinck (assuming the *Ly* A 1 is indeed his)

---

[1] K. N. 208A, f. 34ᵛ, where it is titled 'Fuga'.
[2] For proof that Weckmann did not copy this book, see *Reinken* 45–51.
[3] John Bull, *Keyboard Works*, MB, XIV (London, 1960), p. 167.

replaces these with flexuous, ever-changing patterns, and shortens the section of florid sextuplets by seven measures. The intensity is hardly lessened at the return to quarter-note movement and there is a continuous drive to the close. Bull's sextuplets, on the other hand, round off a section at m. 120, and are succeeded by fifteen measures of anticlimactic coda. Perhaps most significant of all, the sextuplets lead to a cadence on A minor which is, rather ambivalently, the key of the coda. The final chord of A major closes a piece in which a single ostinato figure outlining the C major triad, ever at the same pitch level, has been held tenaciously until the very end. This tonal aberration, characteristic of Bull but rare among his North European contemporaries, has a freshness particularly attractive to modern ears. But with a little historical insight, one might be able to imagine it affecting Sweelinck in quite a different manner.

Is it necessary to allege that Sweelinck somehow received a 'defective copy' of Bull's piece? A more reasonable assumption is that Sweelinck, while admiring much in Bull's work, preferred to rewrite the ending according to his taste, thereby improving *Bull*'s 'faulty conclusion'. This would provide a perfectly simple explanation for the ascription of this piece to Sweelinck in *Ly* A 1, a source otherwise so accurate and reliable. From the point of view of the copyist, this was Sweelinck's 'version' of the piece; therefore it appears under his name, just as Poglietti's 'versions' of Bull's hexachord fantasy (involving only minor alterations) appear under Poglietti's name in several sources. [1]

Following the same line of reasoning, one might speculate that Sweelinck was not entirely satisfied with the Bull fantasy even as he had rewritten it. Thus eventually he might have

[1] Cited in F. W. Riedel, *Quellenkundliche Beiträge zur Geschichte der Musik für Tasteninstrumente in der zweiten Hälfte des* 17. *Jahrhunderts* (Kassel, 1960), p. 149. Dart's list in *MB*, XIV (London, 1960), p. 160, is incomplete and neglects to mention that the *Musica Aulica* edition is no longer owned by the Minoritenkonvent. It was purchased in 1934 from a dealer by the Vienna Stadtbibliothek and is now Musiksammlung Mc 10774 of that library.

been stimulated to compose a new piece of his own (the anonymous setting S. 13) [1] retaining the same four-note theme Bull had chosen, still employing it as an endless ostinato much in the manner of Bull, and using the last eight measures (with the ingenious diminutions of the theme) from the ending he had composed for Bull's piece. Unfortunately for this hypothesis, the Lüneburg piece is simply too dull to merit an attribution to Sweelinck. The figuration is square and repetitive and the C major implications of the theme are followed so slavishly, without recourse to modulation or to contrasting freer sections, that there are, in fact, only two accidentals in the entire piece: C-sharp once, merely as a neighbouring tone, and F-sharp at a cadence point, serving the function of a secondary dominant. The anonymous composer followed Bull's example by repeating the ostinato without transposition and at regular intervals, avoiding rhythmic transformations until the very end and remaining largely in the soprano at the same pitch level. Nowhere in Sweelinck's works is such an ostinato technique employed. As a result of this device, there are sections of the piece (for instance mm. 90–110) that sound in many ways closer to the style of Bull than to that of Sweelinck. However, considering the piece as a whole, it is probably a work from the (German?) school of Sweelinck. The closing eight bars, identical to those we have attributed to Sweelinck, could then be explained as a conscious emulation of the master.

Fantasias number 7 and 11 of Seiffert's edition are preserved anonymously in a sole source, the Berlin (*ex* Lübbenau) Lynar tablature designated by Seiffert as *Ly* B 2. Except for variations on Psalm 116 bearing the initials 'J. P.' (Sweelinck) and some works by Sweelinck's pupil, Melchior Schildt, the contents are anonymous. [2] The beginning of the manuscript

---

[1] See p. 62, n. 1.
[2] Anonymous variations on Psalm 140 ('Die zehn Gebot Gottes', f. 21), overlooked by Seiffert, correspond to those attributed to Sweelinck in the *Fitzwilliam Virginal Book* (S. 52 = A. 12).

is badly damaged. It opens with a barely legible piece whose title is beyond deciphering; but the work can be identified from another source as Sweelinck's 'Praeludium' (S. 33 = L. 27). Immediately following it is the Fantasia, S. 7. As Seiffert mentioned, the opening theme of this work resembles that of the C major echo fantasia (S. 18 = L. 14) indubitably by Sweelinck. More important, the treatment of both themes in augmentation and diminution is similar. The figural techniques are all more or less within the same vocabulary as those of Sweelinck. Masterful large-scale organization is lacking, however, as are the smooth, organic transitions from one section or motive to another, typical of Sweelinck's authentic works. The deceptive cadence at the end of the exposition (m. 24) is clumsy, and the strong sectional divisions at, for instance, m. 136 or mm. 51–52 are, at best, uncharacteristic. The immediate repeat of mm. 52–60 an octave lower with a third voice added above has no counterpart in Sweelinck's authentic works, and the playful sequences of falling thirds at m. 91, the 'octave echoes' at m. 149, and the excessively long sequence beginning at m. 30, all seem too light, loose, and almost casually assembled to belong with those masterpieces of concentrated expression which comprise his indubitably authentic fantasies. The exposed fifth in m. 115 and the B natural in m. 72 are further anomalies, although the latter of these might be a mere scribal error.

More strongly assured on stylistic grounds is the attribution to Sweelinck of a Fantasia (S. 11 = L. 32*) which occurs later in the same manuscript. Indeed, it contains a veritable catalogue of the figural patterns and contrapuntal devices most typical of the composer. The skilful contrapuntal handling of a slightly chromatic theme, and a powerful imitative section treating the subject in diminution, are equal in quality and resemble in style the traits we have come to associate with the very best of Sweelinck, and with the works of no other contemporary keyboard composer. This Fantasia is on a par with, and indeed resembles, such a work as the unquestionably authentic Fantasia (S. 5 = L. 4) ascribed to Sweelinck in all three early sources.

There remains one further anonymous Fantasia which Seiffert chose to include in his edition: S. 19, from *Ly* B 3, a tablature devoted to works by Sweelinck and his pupils. At first glance, he seems perfectly justified in doing so. It is a 'Fantasia auf die Manier eines Echo' (as others of this type are called in the German sources) and as such it represents a genre generally supposed to have been invented by Sweelinck. Tusler, for instance, says 'the "echo fantasia" is always associated with Sweelinck and rightly so, for I have been unable to find any of this type of composition for organ in his predecessors or contemporaries'.[1] Datable predecessors are indeed lacking, but a glance, however superficial, at the music of his contemporaries will yield proof that Sweelinck was hardly alone in the field. Even the famous *Tabulatura Nova* by Scheidt contains a lengthy essay in this genre. [2] Examples of 'octave echoes', i.e. the repeat of a short motive at the upper or lower octave, are plentiful in Elizabethan virginal music. The device was undoubtedly adapted to the keyboard from the 'paired imitations' characteristic of vocal writing throughout the sixteenth century, especially by imitators of Josquin. A typical example by Janequin may be compared with a French *chanson* by Sweelinck which resembles it. As the excerpts show, the same device became incorporated into English keyboard style already by the late sixteenth century. Peter Philips used it in his 'Passamezzo Pavana' (in the *Fitzwilliam Virginal Book*) composed in 1592, the year before his trip to Amsterdam. As one of his best pieces composed up to that time, we can easily imagine that he would have played it for Sweelinck during his visit.

[1] *Op. cit.*, p. 64.
[2] Printed in *Tabulatura Nova*, II (1624); modern ed. in *D.D.T.*, I (1892), p. 95; new ed. in *Werke*, VI (1953). Since confusion has arisen concerning the manner of performance proper for Sweelinck's echo fantasies, it is well to point out that Scheidt clearly desires his 'Echo' to be played on an organ with two manuals, loud and soft. He marks only the *forte* passages, but it is nevertheless perfectly simple for the performer to determine where the echoing *piano* should occur.

One often finds similar writing in Italian and especially
Spanish keyboard music. [1]

Neither in Southern Europe nor in England, however, did a
particular echo genre develop, and in both countries echo
devices in keyboard music were limited to 'octave echoes'.
Byrd's 'Eccho paven & galliard ... in gamut' mentioned
by Tomkins, though now lost, [2] was probably so named
because of changes in register rather than volume. Byrd may
never have known a two-manual keyboard instrument
capable of dynamic echoes, *forte* and *piano* at the same pitch

[1] See Almonte C. Howell, Jr., 'Paired Imitation in Spanish Keyboard
Music of the Sixteenth Century', *The Musical Quarterly*, LIII (1967),
pp. 377–92. However, the exclusivity which the author accords to Spain
both in matters of 'paired imitations' for keyboard and in the use of divided registers for the organ is open to dispute.

[2] In Paris, Bibl. du Cons., MS. Rés. 1122, p. iii. Stephen Tuttle, in *MB*,
V, p. 158, n. 39, suggests that Tomkins might have been referring to
The Seventh Pavan: Canon, but the difference in key, as well as this pavan's
lack of association with a galliard in either source (Tuttle neglects to
mention the *Fitzwilliam Virginal Book*, no. 275, as a second source) make
his hypothesis unlikely.

level, and he certainly never knew such a two-manual harpsichord.

It seems to have required access to large two- and three-
manual organs [1] (practically unknown in Italy or England)
to bring into being the type of echo fantasy based on purely
dynamic echoes. That this genre was current throughout the
Netherlands by the early seventeenth century is proved by a
number of 'echo' pieces in the Liège *Liber fratrum Cruciferorum*,
dated 1617 at the end of the last page. [2] In addition to an
'Echo D'Jean Piere Sweelingk' (S. 14 = L. 11) and another
(S. 15 = L. 34* and 34 A*) without inscription, [3] it contains
an 'Echo' identified at the end as by 'Fr. Gerardus Scronx', [4]
an anonymous 'Echo pour Trompette', [5] and five other anonymous works titled 'Echo'. [6] Of these only the Scronx,
S. 15, and another of the anonymous pieces [7] at all resemble

---

[1] Sweelinck's echo fantasies, with their rapid alternation of *forte* and
piano could not have been played on the harpsichords of the period nor
on the single-manual organs which seem to have prevailed in England
as in Italy. An interesting hypothesis is set forth by J. H. van der Meer
in his article 'Per Ogni Sorte di Stromenti da Tasti', *TVNM*, XIX
(1960–61) pp. 71–73. He suggests that some of Sweelinck's echo fantasies
were performed on a 'mother and child' double virginal, the *piano* echoes
being played on the *ottavina* (thus sounding an octave higher than written).
The musically infelicitous results, however, can hardly serve to sub-
stantiate his meager organological evidence. Nevertheless, one can
hardly disagree with his meek concluding sentence: 'I only mean to say
that a performance of these works on a "mother and child" is certainly
not an impossibility'.
[2] University Library, MS. 888. Modern ed. by A. Guilmant in *Archives
des maîtres de l'orgue*, X (Mainz, 1914).
[3] Attributed to 'J. P.' in Berlin, Staatsbibliothek, MS. 340 of the former
Amalienbibliothek des Joachimsthalschen Gymnasiums, f. 30′, the least
reliable of all Sweelinck sources. Gustav Leonhardt feels this piece is an
arrangement of a work for two choirs and, in spite of the attribution, not
by Sweelinck (see the commentary in his 1968 edition).
[4] Guilmant ed., p. 79. Other works by this composer are not known, nor
has he been otherwise identified. The 'Fr.' before his name would seem
to imply that he was, like the copyist and/or owner of the manuscript,
a Crutched Friar (member of the *Fratres cruciferi*) at Liège. It is not
impossible that he might have been a student of Sweelinck's, though
there is no documentary evidence yet discovered.
[5] *Ibid.*, p. 66.   [6] *Ibid,.* pp. 34, 68, 81, 103 and 105.
[7] *Ibid.*, p. 81.

the Sweelinck echo fantasia style. [1] In all three, as in the echo attributed to Sweelinck in the same source, the contrast between the repeated motives is made clear in the notation by the use of red ink. [2] The red undoubtedly represents the *piano* echo, though occasionally a motive in red precedes a repeat in black, thus (unless a scribal error) denoting an effect of 'anticipated' echo.

Another anonymous work in similar style and probably from the same period is found in WM as 'Echo à 2 claver 5 toni' (f. 218). The work begins in an imitative style similar to that of Sweelinck, with a cadence of scalar brilliance closing the first section. There follows a portion employing short motives, but in sequence rather than echo. The next section consists entirely of brief two-bar phrases, each literally echoed—even the left–hand is repeated exactly. Finally, a section of still shorter motives, echoed in the right hand only, and a cadential flourish in the manner of Sweelinck ends the piece. With its stiff figuration and square melodic ideas, it ranks in quality far below the four such Sweelinck fantasias whose authenticity is assured.

To return to the anonymous fantasia in *Ly* B 3 (S. 19), we see that the notion of Sweelinck as unique composer of echo fantasias, as implied by Seiffert, Tusler, and others, is false. Thus S. 19 cannot qualify as a work of the Amsterdam master merely by being in the 'manner of an echo'. The harmony is extremely static, if not boring (symptomatically, only 17 of the 129 measures have any accidentals whatever); and the melodic ideas are excessively simple. Of the echo fantasias

---

[1] The others are 'echoes' in name only, and it is difficult indeed to find a logical reason for their title. Sequences occur (but not obtrusively) and there are occasionally motives repeated with only slight variation, but never in a manner that would suggest an echo. Sometimes the upper manual (*bovenwerk*) was called the 'echo'; it is just conceivable that these were simply untitled works which the owner of the manuscript preferred to play on the upper manual. However, this explanation is less than satisfactory, particularly in the case of the 'Echo pour Trompette'.

[2] Seiffert's edition gives no acknowledgement of the presence of such notation in the Sweelinck echoes in the Liège source. Cf. vdSM, 212 f.

mentioned thus far it most resembles the 'Echo à 2 claver 5 toni' in WM.

Thus, to review the works falsely ascribed to Sweelinck by Seiffert: S. 55 is by Speuy, S. 12 by Bull, and S. 50 by Scheidemann, as are probably S. 39, 40, 42, and 44. S. 49 might be by Scheidt, and S. 43, 36, 13, and 7 are probably also from the immediate school of Sweelinck. S. 19, 34, 47, 57, and Variations 1 and 4 of S. 54, whether by pupils or imitators, are inferior works.

The discovery since Seiffert's 1943 edition of several new sources has brought with it new problems of authentication. The Turin manuscripts supply conflicting attributions for two toccatas and provide the unique source for six very dubious works: three ricercars, two fantasias, and one 'Fuga'. A late and untrustworthy source in Celle ascribes two spurious works to 'M.G.P.S.' and 'M. Jean Piterson'. Finally, *Ly* B 2, although known to Seiffert, supplies some fine works which he probably overlooked and which might plausibly be ascribed to Sweelinck.

The first Giordano volume in Turin ascribes Toccata S. 23 (L. 31*) to Hans Leo Hassler and S. 26 (L. 30*) to Jakob, his younger and less famous brother who also studied in Italy. A comparison with Hassler keyboard works preserved elsewhere [1] yields no conclusive results. The works of both Hasslers share with Sweelinck's own authentic toccatas a strong dependence on late sixteenth-century Venetian models. The two works in dispute seem if anything still more Italianate than those toccatas assuredly by Sweelinck. The figuration (for instance, mm. 30–35 of S. 23) is freer, more melodic, and the harmonic sequences, in chains of fifths (mm. 60–64 of S. 23 or mm. 37–40 of S. 26), are more obvious and direct than is usual in Sweelinck's compositions. The Turin source for L. 30* is much more accurate than the mangled version (S. 26) ascribed to 'Schweling' in WM (cf. Figures 4 and 5),

---

[1] Ed. E. v. Werra, *D.T.B.*, IV/2 (Leipzig, 1904); and the unpublished works in Berlin (now Tübingen) MS. 40615.

which might be an argument towards accepting the Turin ascription to Jacob Hassler. Further study of both Hasslers' complete works might throw new light on the problem— which remains, meantime, unresolved.

A 'Ricercar a 4 voc.' in Turin, Giordano 7, ascribed to 'Johann Peterle',[1] was overlooked by Van den Sigtenhorst and Annegarn.[2] Except for the undoubtedly genuine variations on Psalm 36 (A. 10), this ricercar (L. 35*) ranks highest in quality among the unique works ascribed to Sweelinck in Turin. However, it shares with the other five published by Annegarn many elements foreign to the style of Sweelinck as known from more reliably attributed works. Certain details may remind one of the master's works, but the over-all form is weak and ambling by comparison. The same contrapuntal devices may be employed—augmentation, diminution, stretto— but they are never handled with the convincing ease and refinement known from the genuine fantasies. For example, the stretto imitation at m. 35 of L. 35* leads to clumsy but unavoidable direct fifths in m. 37. The gratuitous dissonance which follows at the end of m. 41., or that at the end of m. 11, is typical of the careless composer(s) of the other five Turin works. The awkward part-writing also leads often to unconvincing dissonance treatment, as in the handling of six-four chords in L. 35* or the approach to the bass dissonance in m. 38 of L. 36* (Annegarn's 1958 ed. no. 1). Citing further crudities would be both tedious and pointless: these works were not written by Sweelinck, or any other composer of interest.

It may seem rash to dismiss as unauthentic an entire group of six works attributed in a seventeenth-century source to either 'J.P.S.' or 'Johann Peterle'. If the young Sweelinck did after all study in Venice (see p. 85), could these not be early

---

[1] Misread as 'Pecerle' by Schierning, op. cit., p. 131. An inventory of the Turin volumes, more accurate than Schierning's, may be found in Oscar Mischiati, 'L'Intavolatura d'organo tedesca della Biblioteca Nazionale di Torino', L'Organo, IV (1963), pp. 1–154.

[2] See above, p. 46, n. 2.

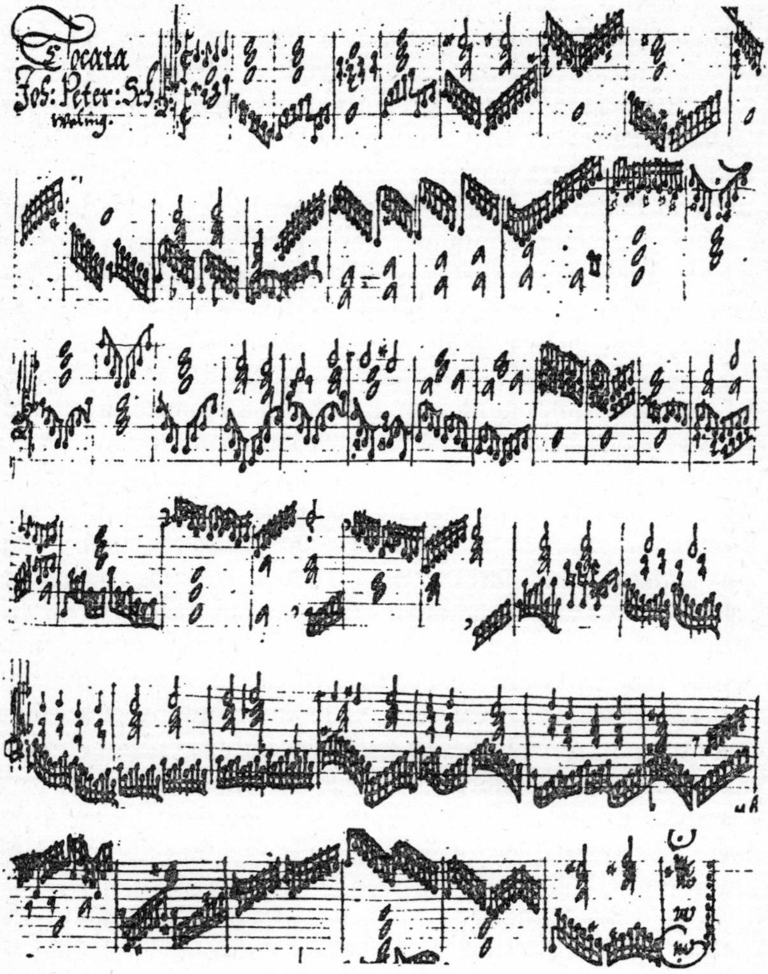

Figure 4. Toccata L. 30 (S. 26), the Vienna version, by 'Joh: Peter: Schweling' (WM fol. 88^v–89^r). Note: In this and the next figure the staves of the original right-hand pages have been inserted between those of the left-hand ones to facilitate reproduction.

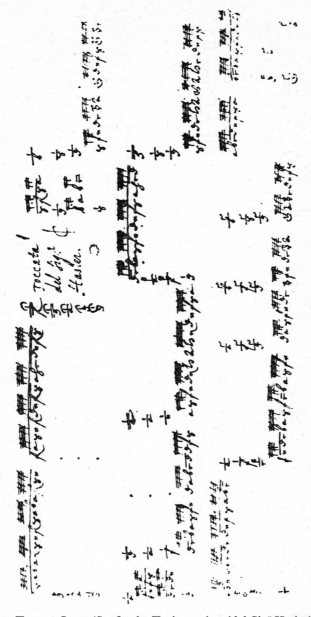

Figure 5. Toccata L. 30 (S. 26), the Turin version, 'del Sig^r Hasler' (Tor G 1, fol 37–38).; continued on the two following pages; see note to figure 4).

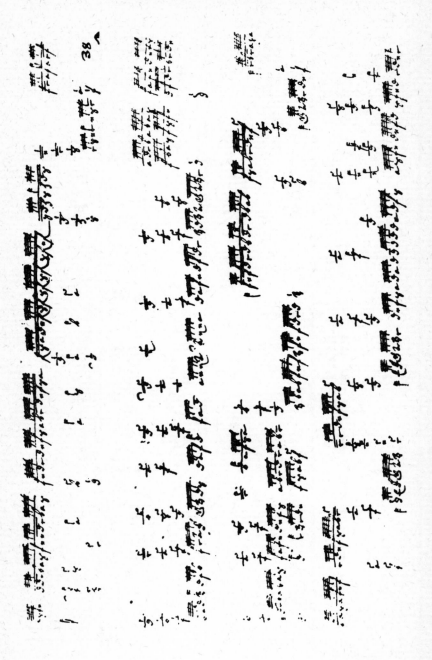

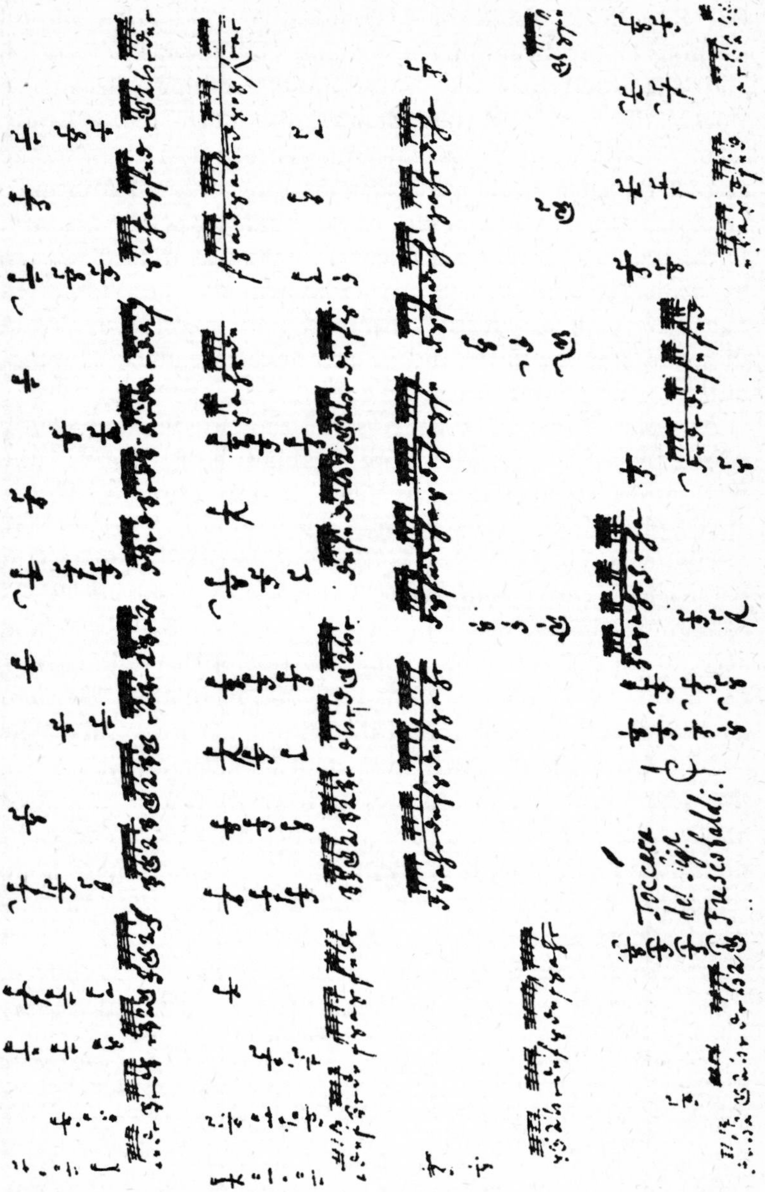
Toccata del Sig. Frescobaldi.

works preserved via H. L. Hassler, another Venetian student?[1] But Sweelinck would have received a solid contrapuntal training before beginning any study of Venetian virtuosity, and it is exactly in basic contrapuntal handling where these works fail most miserably. Besides, the Turin pieces would seem to date from the seventeenth century and even, in the case of the curious chordal ricercars (L. 39*–40*, Annegarn 1958 ed. nos. 4–5), from the second quarter of the century. Perhaps the 'Ricercar a 4 voc.' (L. 35*) was indeed written by some 'Johann Peterle', little-known and best forgotten South-German organist. A simpler, and more likely hypothesis, is that the scribe did indeed have Sweelinck in mind, but was merely mistaken.

As pointed out by Frits Noske,[2] the two works recently edited by J. H. Schmidt[3] from a tablature of c. 1662 in the Bomann-Museum, Celle, are also highly dubious, if not apocryphal. This is true particularly of the 'Bergamasca' attributed to 'M.G.P.S.'. It is conceivable that the first eight bars (which correspond to the versions set by Bull and Frescobaldi, for instance) might be a fragment by Sweelinck and account for the attribution; but the rest of the eight tedious variations is the work of a silly, unimaginative German keyboard player from around the middle of the century. The second Celle piece, 'Alemande de Chapelle', attributed to 'M. Jean Piterson', would appear from its title to be based on a work of Champion de Chapelle, father of Chambonnières, and presumably a friend of John Bull.[4] There is no reason to assume that he wrote anything more than the original allemande, however, for the style of the variations is quite Anglo-Dutch and not at all French. It is, indeed,

[1] Both the Turin sources and the related Padua tablature (University Library, MS. 1982) seem to be South German in origin.

[2] 'Een apocrief en een dubieus werk van Sweelinck', *Mededelingenblad VNM*, XX (September, 1966), pp. 27–30. An expanded version in English will be published in *Notes*. Cf. Schmidt's reply in the same journal, XXV (April, 1968), pp. 58–64.

[3] *Exempla Musica Neerlandica*, II (Amsterdam, 1965).

[4] See Thurston Dart, 'John Bull's *Chapel*', *Music and Letters*, XL (1959), pp. 279–82.

possible that they were written by Sweelinck (variation 2 even has faint echoes of 'Mein junges Leben' in mm. 18–20). However, the third and final variation is such a clumsy mixture of keyboard clichés that, in view of the late date and untrustworthy nature of the source, it seems likely these variations are corrupt if not inauthentic.

It has been suggested by Breig [1] that a set of four variations on 'Wie schön leucht Unss der Morgenstern' from *Ly* B 2 (ff. 10^V–12) might be attributed to Sweelinck on grounds of style. He was unaware, however, that the opening 'Variatio' corresponds very closely to the vocal setting by Sweelinck's son Dirck from the *Livre septiesme* (Amsterdam, 1644). [2] Whether Dirck made a vocal setting of his father's keyboard piece, or himself wrote variations very much in his father's style, it will probably never be possible to tell unless keyboard compositions by him should come to light. Meanwhile, we may with considerable certainty attach the surname of Sweelinck to the piece. [3]

As Breig points out, the appearance of the *cantus firmus* in half and quarter rather than whole notes, and always in the treble, points to the secular rather than the chorale variations. Similarly indicative are the number of variations—five rather than (with the majority of chorales) four, the extremely free ornamentation of the *cantus*, the lack of strict adherence to the same number of voices within a given variation, and the preponderance of purely instrumental devices. Not that similar devices are absent from the chorale variations—they are not. But in no authentic chorale variation is there such an extensive display of triadic figuration, scales in parallel tenths, and 'tremolos' of repeated notes or

[1] Breig *Sw*, 273.
[2] See the ed. of this work by F. Noske in *Six Seventeenth-Century Carols from the Netherlands* (London, 1965), pp. 17–20.
[3] Unfortunately, it will not be included in the 1968 Sweelinck edition. The author, who hopes to edit it in *MMN*, cannot agree with Frits Noske (commentary to his fascicle III of the 1968 ed.) that simply because Dirck published a vocal version under his name the keyboard piece could not possibly be his father's.

broken thirds. All these devices are, on the other hand, present in much the same manner in Sweelinck's secular variations. This curious circumstance—a sacred melody found treated in Sweelinck's secular manner—has a simple explanation. Nicolai's tune became extremely popular in Holland during the seventeenth century. Since it could have no connexion with the Calvinist service, it is only natural that the melody was known not only in serious settings of the translated hymn but also in popular Dutch songbooks as a tune for such secular texts as 'Arm Blindeman' or 'Ay, ouden, kouden, Klappertant'. [1] This also accounts for two Dutch keyboard settings (the only two extant, excepting the present set of variations) in collections otherwise totally given over to secular music: the Leningrad manuscript (*c.* 1650) [2] and the G. H. Broekhuijzen manuscript (1668–69). [3]

Another work from *Ly* B 2 has also been cited by Breig [4] as a probable Sweelinck composition: the two *bicinia* on *Psalm 60* (A. 16*). His comparison of the *cantus firmus* treatment with that of the two opening *bicinia* in Sweelinck's *Psalm 140* (S. 52 = A. 12) is especially apt, since there are also similarities in figural design (cf. particularly the alternating 'tremolo' of thirds and the two-octave sweeps of 'zig zag' patterns outlining a triad plus the equivalent of an 'added sixth'). His suggestion that these two seemingly isolated *bicinia* originally formed the opening of a larger set like *Psalm 140*, (S. 52 = A. 12) is also plausible. Only the quality of the second *bicinium* casts doubts on its authenticity. Especially in the counterpoint to the second and third phrases it tends to employ sequential figures longer and with more rigid severity than was Sweelinck's custom. As an isolated piece it would strongly suggest Scheidt as composer. Since, however, it is coupled with the first *bicinium* very much like Sweelinck's authentic work, and since it is based on a psalm, not a chorale, Scheidt is less likely than Sweelinck to

[1] *MMN* III, xxxvi.   [2] *MMN* III, 64 ff.
[3] Published in *Weekblad voor Muziek*, 3 and 10 January 1903.
[4] Breig *Sw*, 273.

have been the composer. In any case, it would add little
lustre to his adopted canon if proved to be genuine.

Four variations on 'Es spricht der unweisen Mundt woll'
(ff. 23'–25), the last with pedal, form the third and final
work which Breig attributes (more hesitantly) to Sweelinck.
Unlike *Psalm 60* (A. 16*) it certainly does not lack in quality.
In style, however, there are several elements, in addition to
those Breig describes, which point to the generation of
Sweelinck's pupils rather then the master himself. Nowhere
in Sweelinck's authentic work do we find, for instance, a
broken dominant seventh to resemble the following example,
where also the added *f'* violates the otherwise consistent three-
voice texture.

Anon., *Es spricht der unweisen Mund* :

The presence of variation 1–3 in *Ze* 2 with an attribution to
Scheidemann is pointed out by Breig to be indecisive since
that source also names him as the author of variations on
Erbarm dich mein (S. 41 = A. 5) known to be Sweelinck's.
Nevertheless, since some stylistic details also suggest Scheidemann rather than Sweelinck, there seems little reason to
dispute the ascription.

A final work from *Ly* B 2, a set of three variations on *Psalm
23*, 'Mein hütter Vundt mein hirtt' (ff. 19'–21), may be
added to the list of anonymous works probably by Sweelinck.
The work was disregarded by Breig for no stated reason. He
mentioned the close resemblance between the first and third
(the final) variations of this work and numbers three and
four of *Psalm 116* (S. 51 = A. 11) by Sweelinck;[1] but he
considered the latter a work of dubious authenticity and
cited the relationship to the anonymous *Psalm 23* in support

[1] Breig *Sw*, 261, n. 3.

of his point. Since, as we have shown, there is no valid reason to discount the attribution of *Psalm 116* (in *Ly* B 2) to 'J.P.', the connexion with the first and last variations of *Psalm 23* argues instead for acceptance of this set as a work by Sweelinck or his immediate school.

A study of the middle variation, a *bicinium*, provides confirmation of such a tentative ascription. Already in the third and fourth measures there appears the 'zigzag' pattern of the 'added sixth', typical of Sweelinck, and his characteristic subtle shift from one figure to a related one, welding the lines into an organic whole. Comparison of this *bicinium* with that by Henderick Speuy on the same psalm tune yields conclusions similar to those reached by comparison of Sweelinck's and Speuy's *bicinia* on *Psalm 116*.[1] Speuy's setting alternates the *cantus firmus* between upper and lower voices, while the free voice runs almost uninterruptedly in sixteenth or eighth notes. The anonymous *bicinium* has far greater rhythmic variety and a clearer demarcation of the phrases of the psalm melody, even though the *cantus firmus* remains entirely in the treble. The free line builds toward cadences at the end of the psalm phrase and then starts afresh with quarters, then eighths, and gradually sixteenths. The result is a sense of direction and of formal clarity characteristic of Sweelinck's *bicinia* but lacking in the psalms of Speuy or other lesser composers of the period.

Finally, a less important series of compositions from another manuscript, KN 208/1, has been attributed to Sweelinck by John R. Shannon. In his edition of these works [2] he states that 'numbers 32 through 37 are possibly by Jan Pieterszoon Sweelinck'; but in his master's thesis, on which this edition was based, he had been more cautious and singled out only numbers 32, 33, 36, and 37.[3] Certainly there is no

---

[1] See the discussion of these two works in *Speuy*, 143–62.
[2] *The Free Organ Compositions from the Lueneburg Organ Tablatures* (St. Louis, 1958), p. 3.
[3] *The Free Organ Compositions from the Lueneburg Tablatures* (unpublished master's thesis, Univ. of N. Carolina, 1956), p. 43.

reason to connect either the crude 'Praeambulum oder Fuga'
[*sic*] no. 34, or the fragmentary 'Praeambulum' no. 35 with
Sweelinck's name. Toccatas 32 and 33 are quite another
matter. Except for the opening four measures of no. 32, they
are very much in the style of Sweelinck's toccatas. The ill-
fitting opening was probably added later, like the first three
bars of another anonymous toccata in the Lüneburg tablature
which is actually by Sweelinck. [1] Like that work, too, these
toccatas might be mere portions of Sweelinck originals—as
might also the toccata from the Leningrad MS. They are
nevertheless quite attractive pieces—especially no. 33 which,
as Shannon points out, begins almost exactly the same as the
Toccata L. 31* (S. 23) attributed to Sweelinck in one source,
but to H. L. Hassler in another. The case for nos. 36 and 37
is much weaker. Some slight resemblances to Sweelinck's
toccata style are generic rather than specific and merely
stamp these works as of his school or from his milieu. Neither
the opening of no. 36 nor the endless stereotyped 'octave
echoes' of no. 37 resemble anything written by the Amsterdam
master. If they stem from Sweelinck originals, they have been
marred beyond recognition. They resemble the Scheidt
toccatas from the Daniel Schmidt Organ Book and the
Berlin Graues Kloster MS., which may also be imperfectly
preserved.

There are no other works in the known keyboard literature
of this period for which even a tentative attribution to Sweelinck seems justifiable. This situation may change as new
sources are uncovered and old ones better understood. Some
of the many works we know to be lost might yet be found:
the 25 variations on 'Den lustelijken Mey' which he played
for Baudartius, the works in the G. W. Scharffe tablature of
1673 (burned in 1870),[2] or the 'Fuga' upon which Bull
composed a 'Fantazia' a few weeks after Sweelinck's death
(S. 71). We may add a *Tablatura* announced by the printer
Melchoir Oelschlegel of Halle for the Herbstmesse at Leipzig

---

[1] L. 16 (S. 21) in KN 207/15, no. 27.   [2] Cited in S., p. xlviii.

in 1630 and described as 'Fantasien m. 3. St. d. alle 8. Tonos von J. P. S. Organisten zu Amst. komp. u von Samuele Scheid Hallense kolligirt'. [1] Riedel has suggested these might be the anonymous fantasies in the Leipzig MS., City Music Library, II, 2, 51. [2] The thought of recovering in a manuscript this lost printed work of Sweelinck is certainly exciting. There are, however, decisive arguments against his hypothesis. The Leipzig fantasies are indeed in three parts, but they are not limited to '8 Tonos'; the last is in '9. Toni ex A la mi re'. Moreover, the first of them is found in WM f. 209' with the ascription 'Fantasia à 3 Paul Sivert'. For this reason Seiffert, without knowing of the lost Sweelinck edition, published the anonymous fantasies as the work of Paul Siefert (1586–1666), a pupil of Sweelinck. He seems to have been perfectly justified in doing so. From the point of view of style, these fantasies are certainly homogeneous. They appear to be by a single composer and intended as one group. They seem later, and more suave, than Sweelinck's fantasies, and employ more limited resources, lacking his lively contrasts. They are, in short, restrained, well-balanced, and slightly dull.

To summarize the conclusions reached in this chapter, let us briefly classify the works discussed. S. 7, 12, 13, 19, 34, 36, 39, 40, 42, 43, 44, 47, 49, 50, Variations 1 and 4 of 54, 55, and 57 were all wrongly ascribed to Sweelinck by Seiffert. Toccatas S. 23 and S. 26 may be by Hans Leo and Jacob Hassler respectively . Newly discovered works to be added to the Sweelinck canon include *Malle Symen* (N. 5), a fantasia (L. 10), and a toccata (L. 26) from the Leningrad MS.; variations on *Psalm 36* (A. 9) from *Tor* G 5; on *Allein zu dir* (A. 2) from *Ze* 1, and on *Onse Vader in hemelrijck* (A. 9) from *Ze* 2. In addition, 4 variations on *Hoe schoon lichtet de morghen ster*, three variations on *Psalm 23*, and two *bicinia* on *Psalm 60*, all from *Ly* B 2, may, in the author's opinion, be attributed to Sweelinck.

---

[1] See A. Göhler, *Verzeichnis der in den Frankfurter und Leipziger Messkatalogen der Jahre 1564 bis 1759 angezeigten Musikalien* (1902), I, p. 915.
[2] F. W. Riedel, *op. cit.*, p. 48.

IV

SWEELINCK'S KEYBOARD MUSIC

TOWARDS A CHRONOLOGY

EVEN more difficult to date than to authenticate, the key-board works of Sweelinck defy any attempt at precise chronological ordering. With neither printed nor autograph sources, much less dated ones, and with no manuscripts traceable from earlier than the last decade of his life, it seems hopeless to try and separate his work into chronological categories—unless, perhaps, into 'late' and 'still later' periods. Nevertheless, the few relevant facts, when assembled together, provide at least some ground for hypotheses about chronology. These, in turn, give some support to our succeeding chapters, in which Sweelinck's works are compared with English music of an earlier date.

Sweelinck's earliest studies in composition, as well as in organ playing, must surely have been with his father, Peter Swybertszoon, organist of the *Oude Kerk*,[1] about whose music or musical training nothing at all is known. He could in any case have hardly exerted a very profound musical influence on his son, for he died when Jan was only eleven. His successor as organist of the *Oude Kerk*, Cornelis Boskoop, may also have taught the young Sweelinck, but he, too, died in that same year. His fifty four-part polyphonic psalm-settings, 'lustich om singen ende speelen op verscheiden instrumenten', published in 1568 when he was organist of the Oude Kerk at Delft, have been preserved and were edited by Seiffert in 1899.[2] The five- and six-part settings mentioned in Boskoop's preface probably never reached print; those in four parts bear suffi-

[1] vdSM, 63 f.   [2] Uitgave XXII. *VNM.*

cient testimony to his conservative style and to his craftsmanship, polyphonic skill, and total lack of genius. This man
could have given Sweelinck some excellent training in counterpoint during the few months before his death, but he
could not have left much of an imprint on the young organist's
keyboard idiom.

We are even more at a loss for reliable information concerning the important formative years which followed.
Although the Alteration establishing the Reformed Church
was accomplished in Amsterdam in 1578 by relatively peaceful
means, this was still a turbulent period of change. How
Sweelinck acquired his musical education in the midst of
this turmoil will perhaps never be securely established. We do
know that by 1 May 1581, he was city organist at the Protestant *Oude Kerk*, the same edifice where his father had been
the Catholic church organist. Most probably he had occupied
this post earlier, for in 1580 a certain 'Maria pieters de Zuster
van de organist' was buried, and it is hardly likely that Sweelinck would have been preceded in his post by some other
'Pietersz'. [1] In addition, we have the posthumous remark by
C. G. Plemp [2] (who knew him) that Sweelinck served as
organist for 44 years. If we accept this at face value, we could
infer, as does Van den Sigtenhorst, that the 15-year-old
Sweelinck assumed his life-long post at the *Oude Kerk* in 1577—
thus as *Catholic* organist one year before the Alteration. (Surely
it cannot be coincidence that our source for this information is
the Catholic Plemp.) If we were to accept also the remark in
a document [3] of 1680 that Sweelinck learned 'his art' from
Lossy in Haarlem, then we can easily dismiss the widely
accepted hypothesis that he studied in Venice with Zarlino.
The notion of a Venetian trip stems, after all, only from the

---

[1] vdSM, 39.

[2] *Poëmata* (Antwerp, 1631), p. 184, according to vdSM, 284, n. 66. This
passage has never been reprinted and was available only in the unique
copy in the library of the Academy of Sciences, Trippenhuis, Amsterdam.
Since that library's recent move to ostensibly more efficient quarters, this
rare and important volume cannot be traced.

[3] Discovered by A. Bredius in 1914, see vdSM, 30, n. 73.

notoriously inaccurate *Grundlage einer Ehren-Pforte* of Mattheson (1740). But can we be sure that the document of 1680 is any more accurate? It declares only that Jacob van Noordt, successor to Sweelinck's son Dirck, had several times heard that Sweelinck had learned his art from 'Jan Willemss.' (Jan Willemszoon Lossy, *c.* 1545–1629), who is referred to elsewhere in the same document as 'organist tot Haerlem'. Repeated searches through Haarlem archives have failed to turn up any information about Lossy as a composer or keyboard player. If Sweelinck had studied organ or keyboard composition at Haarlem as a young boy, it would more likely have been with Floris van Adrichem, organist of the St. Bavo Kerk from 1575 to 1578, who was called to the St. Cassiusmünster in Bonn where he 'summa cum laude, cum sit expertissimus in ea arte, in organis lusit'. [1] Compared with van Adrichem, Lossy seems to have been a rather minor figure, who is mentioned as a 'hoechconter' (countertenor) from Dordrecht, paid 30 stuivers per month in 1568, [2] and given a raise in 1577 for helping out by doubling the lower voices on his bass shawm. That Sweelinck would really have learned 'his art' from such a man is difficult to believe. A Venetian sojourn is made credible by the fact that Sweelinck gave his pupils Zarlino's treatise to copy, [3] and by the strong stylistic resemblance of his toccatas to similar works by well-known Venetian students such as H. L. Hassler. In any case, with no proof of study in Venice, and with so little known about Jan Willemszoon Lossy, Sweelinck's background remains a mystery.

For attributing works stylistically to Sweelinck's early

---

[1] See J. Schmidt-Görg, 'Musikgeschichtliches aus den ältesten Kapitelakten des Bonner Münsters', *Bonn und sein Münster, Festschrift für J. Jinsenkamp* (Bonn, 1947), p. 187. Quoted in M. A. Vente, 'Sweelinck en de traditie', *O.K.W. Mededelingen*, XVIII (14 May 1962), p. 205. Cf. *Bouwstenen* (1965), 85 and 91.
[2] See Jos de Klerk, 'Sweelincks leraar ontdekt na een duik in de archieven', *Gregoriusblad*, LXXXII (1961), p. 141.
[3] *Werken*, X.

years there is thus no sound basis other than judgements
regarding the maturity or immaturity of particular pieces.
His works are certainly varied in quality, as they are in technique, yet seldom do they seem immature. A possible exception is the 'Capricio', relegated to the *Anhang* in both the 1943
(S. 70) and the 1968 (L. 29*) editions, a work which will be
discussed later under 'Chromatic Fantasies and Meantone
Tuning'. This might be regarded as a preparatory study for
the greater and more mature chromatic fantasy. It is so
imperfectly preserved, however—we have it only from the
hands of an incompetent bowdlerizer (cf. p. 68, n. 3)—that
judgement must be reserved. The fourteen undisputably
authentic fantasias (counting L. 10, the little Leningrad
'Fantazia', but not S. 7, 11, 12, 13, 15, or 19) show a variety
of styles, but a fairly uniform degree of maturity. Even the
Leningrad 'Fantazia' is in its way a fairly polished example
of Sweelinck's art, resembling in style certain of his *Rimes
françoises et italiennes* (1612).

Of the echo fantasias, S. 18 (= L. 14) may be earlier than the
others: its repetitive but exuberant sequences are a little less
masterfully controlled than elsewhere in his work, but this
fantasia stands alone among the six 'echoes' in that its repeated
motives are echoed by a change of register ('octave echo')
rather than a change of dynamics only. Since the echo
fantasia probably grew out of earlier keyboard forms in which
'octave echoes' were prevalent (which, in turn, grew out of
the 'paired imitations' of Renaissance vocal music), it seems
reasonable to assume that L. 14 may represent a transitional
stage. Nevertheless, in their play with dynamic space, the
echo fantasias were essentially a forward-looking and novel
genre in Sweelinck's day, a genre created perhaps no earlier
than the first years of the seventeenth century (though most
likely before 1609, when Scheidt left Amsterdam). Thus in
terms of Sweelinck's total creative accomplishment L. 14 is
not necessarily an early work.

Van den Sigtenhorst singled out the variations on *Fortune
my foe* (S. 64 = N. 2) and on *The Spanish Pavan* (S. 68 = N. 9)

as being rather stiff, lacking the mastery and expansion ('ver-wijding') of the others. [1] He believed that these must either be remnants of early work, or else that they were written for the 'classroom', i.e. for young or inexperienced pupils. The latter hypothesis seems the more likely in view of the charming simplicity of these pieces and the ease with which they may be performed. 'Stiff' is certainly not an apt description here, and their lack of 'expansion' or display of contrapuntal mastery is probably only the result of their brevity and of the purpose for which they were written, not of their having been composed early in Sweelinck's life.

To these two sets may be added a third work of similar level, the variations on *Moll Sims* (N. 5) from the Leningrad MS., which seems also intended for pedagogical use. Since Sweelinck's professional activity (and personal pleasure) during the last two decades of his life was largely concerned with teaching, it can be assumed that he wrote many small pieces for his less accomplished pupils, and that some of these should have survived. Except for Willem Janszoon Lossy (son of Sweelinck's own presumed teacher), who came to Amsterdam about 1598, there is no record of any pupils, either Dutch or German, before the early years of the seventeenth century. During the second decade they became numerous. Pedagogical works, therefore, are more likely to date from after 1600 until 1621 than from the sixteenth century.

In his only attempt to place any of Sweelinck's keyboard works chronologically, Van den Sigtenhorst chose to divide the toccatas into two groups, one distinguished from the other by its 'much greater variety and much more colourful mixture of figures'. [2] The group thus described, representing a 'higher step' and therefore a later period, includes S. 20–22 (= L. 15–17,) and S. 30–31 (= L. 19–20); the others he believed to be earlier. His choice, however, was obviously influenced in the main by length and excellence, not by style. It is true that the splendid toccata in *a* (S. 21 = L. 16) pre-

---

[1] vdSM, 194.   [2] vdSM, 174.

served in a larger number of sources than any other piece by
Sweelinck—seven, including the discriminating *Fitzwilliam
Virginal Book*—makes such a work as S. 32 (= L. 25) seem
somewhat mediocre by comparison. There is however no
essential *stylistic* difference between the works, nor does the
inferior one seem immature. Moreover, Van den Sigtenhorst
did not know that two of the works he considered early
(S. 26 = L. 30* and S. 23 = L. 31*) may not be by Sweelinck
at all but by Jacob and Hans Leo Hassler respectively (see
p. 70 f.). A comparison of L. 30* with the superior, more carefully preserved version attributed to J. Hassler shows that
most of what Van den Sigtenhorst found awkward, and
therefore 'early', was the responsibility of the compiler-
scribe, not the composer.

The extent to which the state of preservation can influence
opinions of a work—extending to notions of chronology—is
illustrated further by the case of Toccata S. 29 (= L. 24).
We might expect this work to have survived in an authoritative
condition, for it is found in three sources, one contemporary
with Sweelinck [1] and another nearly so. [2] But such is not the
case. The London version, probably copied shortly after
1618, [3] calls this toccata a 'Fantasia' (a not infrequent inter-
change at this period) and contains one obvious error: a
wrong chord in m. 30. These two facts, together with some
frequent but minor discrepancies from the Berlin source, led
Seiffert to exaggerate in describing the manuscript as careless,
full of wrong notes, deleting whole measures, and arbitrarily
altering the figuration. On this basis he omitted the source
from consideration—his non-collated text thereby losing even
the valuable ornament symbols which were probably used by
Sweelinck. Having uncovered Seiffert's exaggerations, Van
den Sigtenhorst wrote an article in 1931 [4] describing the

---

[1] BM MS. Add. 29,486, *c.* 1618 (see below, n. 3.).
[2] Berlin, Gymnasium zum Graues Kloster, MS. 52, which Seiffert dates
c. 1625. The third source is Tor G 1, f. 61.
[3] The preceding page is inscribed 'finis Tonorum 27 Septembris 1618'.
[4] 'Naar aanleiding van een toccata van J. Pz. Sweelinck', *TVNM*, XIII
(1931), pp. 161–65.

London source and including a facsimile of the complete
piece as it appears there. Since he felt both versions had merit,
he concluded that the Berlin 'Toccata' represented Sweelinck's
own 'enrichment' of his earlier work, the London 'Fantasia'.
In his 1943 edition, Seiffert referred to this article but refused
to alter his previous opinion of the London source. Van den
Sigtenhorst was equally adamant in the 1946 revision of his
book. Both writers failed to recognize that both sources—as
well as the third, unknown to them—provide nothing more
than an approximation of Sweelinck's original. All three
manuscripts contain errors and passages that Sweelinck could
not possibly have written. The Berlin source is on the whole
to be preferred, but it should be regarded neither as an
exclusively authentic source, nor as a later improvement by
the composer of an earlier toccata. Only one fact relevant to
chronology can properly be derived from a study of these
sources: that the toccata in question must have been written
some time before *c.* 1618.

Let us turn now to other manuscripts, as a means of determining external factors of chronology. We might reasonably
expect to find abundant indications of dating among the
numerous and widely dispersed sources. Twenty-eight different manuscripts provide us with over a hundred instances in
which these works might have been dated. Yet in only two
cases are dates to be found; in one, the year is almost certainly incorrect. The Vienna Bull manuscript (National
Library, MS. 17771) dates the famous chromatic fantasy as
1621, but it also attributes the piece to 'Doctor Johan Bull'.
The scribe seems to have confused the work with a (rather
chromatic) fantasy by Bull, composed shortly after Sweelinck's death, in 1621. The second, more trustworthy, date
comes from a source that is in general very reliable, the
Fitzwilliam Virginal Book. At the end of the Amsterdam master's
long hexachord fantasy, Francis Tregian neatly wrote 'Jehan
Peterson Swelling. 1612.' It is unlikely that this date records
when Tregian finished copying the piece or when he obtained

access to it: his custom was to date the works themselves—cf. earlier in the manuscript, where he placed '1562' and '1564' at the end of the two *Felix namque* settings by Tallis. In any case, 1612 is a *terminus ante quem* for Sweelinck's hexachord fantasy. The 'Praeludium Toccata' (S. 21 = L. 16) copied in the same collection must be earlier than 1619, the date of Tregian's death. These two pieces are an excellent sampling of Sweelinck's best and maturest work, with two of his most important genres represented: the fantasy and the toccata. This testifies to the full development of his creative powers as a keyboard composer at least a decade before his death.

Later in the *Fitzwilliam Virginal Book* appear variations on the hundred-and-fortieth 'Psalme' (S. 52 = A. 12) found also in *Ly* B 2 as 'Die zehn Gebot Gottes'. Still later the noble 'Fantasia' is inscribed (S. 3 = L. 3), one of Sweelinck's best works and at the same time, with its inversions and augmentations, one of his most complicated and austerely contrapuntal. Tregian would have copied these at some time between 1612 and 1619.[1] There are no other dates inscribed in the book after the '1612' already mentioned. However, some further hints may be obtained from four works by Richard Farnaby scattered through the latter half of the book after the entry of Sweelinck's 'Psalme'—two of them before his 'Fantasia'. Young Richard, who was born in the mid-1590s (probably 1594)[2] and married in 1614, is not likely to have written a piece as good as 'Nobodyes Gigge' (also in *Ly* A 1 as 'Flet Street') before the second decade of the century. Moreover, the second of his works in the *Fitzwilliam Virginal Book* is a setting of 'Fayne would I Wedd' from Campion's *Fourth Booke of Ayres* (1617).[3] Sweelinck's fantasy L. 3 would then have been copied between 1617 and 1619. Intermediary for the excellent selection of pieces by Sweelinck was possibly

---

[1] Cf. Elizabeth Cole, 'Seven Problems of the Fitzwilliam Virginal Book' *Proceedings of the Royal Musical Association*, LXXIX (1953), p. 56.
[2] Wilfred Mellers (article 'Farnaby' in *MGG*) errs in assuming that the son of Giles Farnaby baptized at St. Mary-le-Bow's in 1599 was Richard.
[3] It is not impossible that he got access to the air prior to its publication, but this does not seem very likely.

Tregian's friend and one-time associate at Douai, Peter Philips. If, as seems plausible, Philips obtained copies of these works directly from Sweelinck, then this fantasy may have been composed only shortly prior to 1619. Sweelinck's best-known work, the chromatic fantasy, present in no fewer than five later sources, is conspicuously absent from Tregian's otherwise select sampling; this omission could just possibly mean the work was composed sometime during the last two years of his life.

Another *terminus ante quem* is provided by Liège MS. 888, dated 1617 at the end of the last piece. Two echo fantasies, S. 14 (= L. 11) and S. 15 (= L. 34* and 34A*), and a toccata, S. 30 (= L. 19), would thus have been composed before that time. S. 21 (= L. 16), also found in the Liège source, has already been mentioned as dating from before 1612. All other sources for Sweelinck's keyboard works seem to be posthumous in date of origin and thus offer no clues for chronology.

There are, however, some few other relevant factors. Dowland's ever popular 'Flow, my teares' was composed and probably widely known in manuscript several years before he included it in his *Second Booke of Songes or Ayres* (1600), and even before 1596 when William Barley published a lute transcription in *A new Booke of Tabliture*.[1] When in 1595 Dowland entered his name underneath a short canon in the Album Amicorum of Johannes Cellarius of Nürnberg,[2] he wrote 'Io. Dolandi de Lachrimae his own hande'. Thus the eponymous pavan must have been known in Germany already by 1595. It seems unlikely, however, that Sweelinck would have encountered the piece (and composed his 'Paduana Lachrimae') much before the end of the century. Joachim van den Hove's *Florida* (Utrecht, 1601) included a beautiful

---

[1] Surprisingly, vdSM, 192, knew only Dowland's editions of 1605, *Lacrymae or Seven Teares figured in seven passionate Pavans* and thus erred in dating Sweelinck's setting after 1605.
[2] BM, MS. Add. 27,579. Reproduced in Georg Kinsky, *History of Music in Pictures* (Leipzig, 1929).

and elaborate lute setting which Sweelinck might have known
and even played. In any case, he would certainly have known
the pavan by 1603, when his Amsterdam colleague, Willem
Swart (*c.* 1575–*c.* 1640), who lived near the Oude Kerk at
75 Warmoesstraat, published a polyphonic version with
Dutch text in his *Lust-hof der Nieuwe Musycke*.

Swart's book also contains a five-part setting of Peter
Philips's famous pavan, skilfully underlaid with a Dutch text
beginning 'Wy Engelen goet'. The *superius* (the only part
preserved) begins exactly like the upper line of Sweelinck's
setting; both differ considerably from the various other Continental and English versions. Without documentation to the
contrary we can only assume that the lesser composer imitated
the greater, which would date Sweelinck's 'Pavan Philippi' as
before 1603.

Another musical connexion between Sweelinck and Philips
has previously been overlooked. Peter Philips's five-part
ensemble setting of the 'Aria del Gran Duca Ferdinando di
Toscana'[1] is harmonically identical with Sweelinck's well-
known 'Balleth del granduca' from the Bártfa tablature.
Whether they realized it or not, both composers were writing
variations on a vocal dance elaborately set by Emilio Cava-
lieri[2] for the marriage of Grand Duke Ferdinand of Tuscany
with Christine of Lorraine in 1589. The 'Granduca' variations
must thus be subsequent to the 1589 wedding. The *ballo*
remained popular far into the seventeenth century, however.
As 'Laura soave'—does 'Laura' refer to Signorina Lucchesini?[3]—it appeared in Caroso's influential *Nobiltá di Dame*
(1600, and again in 1630).[4] As 'Ballo di Firenze' or 'Aria di

---

[1] New York Public Library, Sambrooke manuscript, ff. 522'–523.
[2] 'O che nuovo miracolo', with text by Laura Lucchesini, ed. D. P.
Walker, *Les Fêtes de Florence. Musique des Intermèdes de 'La Pellegrina'* (Paris,
1963), p. 140.
[3] Cf. Angelo Solerti, 'Laura Guidiccioni Lucchesini ed Emilio del Cava-
liere'. *Rivista di Musica Italiana*, IX (1902).
[4] It was from this version, transcribed from lute tablature by O. Chile-
sotti (*Biblioteca di Rarità musicali* I, p. 22) that Respighi made his transcription for orchestra.

Firenze' it gradually spread throughout Europe and was used for sets of variations by many seventeenth-century composers including Frescobaldi. [1] Although Sweelinck might have learned the piece from Peter Philips during his 1593 visit, he could also have picked it up later from any number of sources. Thus Sweelinck's variations are definitely after 1589, probably after 1593, and might very well be seventeenth-century.

From the above survey we can see that in cases where it has been possible to establish at least an approximate date, it is always a seventeenth-century one. None of Sweelinck's preserved works can be shown to have originated in the sixteenth century—i.e. during his first 38 years. To strengthen the implications of this observation, there is the strong possibility that Sweelinck's chorale variations were written for his German pupils, since few of these works (probably only the psalms and *Onse Vader in hemelrijck*) could conceivably have been destined for use in the Calvinist Oude Kerk. Thus they, too, would date from the last fifteen years of his life. Furthermore, the lack of autographs and the preservation of only three sources dating from Sweelinck's lifetime (among the twenty-eight known at present) means that our knowledge of his keyboard music must derive almost entirely from his pupils and followers. Only the music that he wished, for one reason or another, to pass on to students is likely to have survived, and there would naturally be more late than early works involved.

Perhaps Sweelinck's early years were occupied mainly with the composition of vocal music. His first printed works were the now lost *Chansons* of 1592; his earliest preserved book, the important five-part *chansons*, appeared only two years

---

[1] 'Partita sopra l'aria di Fiorenza' in Rome, Bibl. Apostolica Vaticana, Codice Chigiano Q. IV, ed. A. Santini, *Musica Veterum*, III (Rome, 1940), pp. 1–3. Further concordances are discussed in R. Casimiri, 'Girolamo Frescobaldi, autore di opere vocale sconosciute ad 8 voci', *Note d'Archivio*, 1933, pp. 1–32. Cf. also the anonymous keyboard settings in K.N. 146, no. 162 and in the former Berlin MS. 40316.

later. [1] His creative powers at the keyboard during this period may have been manifested through improvisation rather than composition. If this was the case, Sweelinck can be contrasted with a figure such as William Byrd, who composed much of his instrumental music in his youth, and later turned more to vocal music. Most of Byrd's important keyboard pieces were completed before the end of the sixteenth century —*My Ladye Nevells Booke* was finished in 1591. These works, then, along with related music by Byrd's countrymen, could well have been familiar to Sweelinck at a fairly early age and have strongly influenced him.

[1] vdSM, following the preface in which the date 1584 was misprinted for 1594, praised the volume as the work of an extraordinarily 'begaafde leerling' ('gifted pupil'), aged twenty-two. The misprint had already been pointed out by P. Bergmans, *La biographie de Corneille Verdonck* (Académie Royale de Belgique, 1915–1918), p. 145. See Frits Noske, 'Sweelinck na vier eeuwen', *TVNM*, XIX, (1962–63), p. 128.

V

SWEELINCK'S KEYBOARD MUSIC

STYLE

i. *Works based on English pavans*

THE most tangible evidence of English elements in Sweelinck's keyboard music is naturally to be found in those works based directly on English models. Here the aspects of the original that Sweelinck chose to adopt can be clearly seen in contrast to his personal alterations and transformations. Several of his secular pieces are closely related to specific English works. Of these, two stand apart: the 'Pavan Philippi' and the 'Paduana Lachrimae'. These two pavans are patterned so closely after specific models (Philips's 1580 pavan and Dowland's famous *Lachrimae*) that they must be considered as paraphrases or varied restatements of the English originals. 'Collorirt' would have been the proper contemporary German description, and this word is actually added to the title in the sole source for the Sweelinck-Dowland piece, the Bártfa tablature.

To call these two works sets of variations, as many writers have done, is misleading. By a remarkable coincidence, both are pavans; Sweelinck retains the traditional AA' BB' CC' structure, adding more elaborate divisions for the repeats A', B', and C'. In his 'pavan Philippi' he added a second, more ornamented version (still following the same scheme of three strains, with repeats more elaborate than the first statements). In this he adumbrated the French practice of adding an ornamented *double* after a completed piece. [1] The

---

[1] This should be contrasted with the 'Reprinse sequitur' which follows the complete (A A' B C B' C') 'Pavana Lachrime' in Van den Hove's *Florida* (1601)—a retrospective rather than a forward-looking element. It resembles a triple-meter 'Nachtanz'. Sweelinck's practice may be found carried a step further, however, in the pavan with its related galliard by Ferdinando Richardson (alias Heyborne) in the *Fitzwilliam Virginal Book*, each followed by a separate 'Variatio'.

Figure 6. 'Pavan Philippi' (Ly A 1, pp. 188–89).

source (*Ly* A 1) places a number '2' before this second ornamented version, and Seiffert printed it as '2e Variatie' as
though the work were two variations on a theme. He should
have distinguished it from Sweelinck's true sets of variations
which are grouped with this piece in the same part of his
volume—from the 'Pavana Hispanica', for instance, which
immediately precedes the 'Pavan Philippi'.

According to Tregian's inscription in the *Fitzwilliam Virginal
Book*, Philips's pavan was composed in 1580 and was 'the first
our Phi[lips] mad[e]'. It is paradoxical that his first pavan
(and earliest known piece), composed before he had left
England, should have become his best-known work, in spite
of a long and productive life abroad. Probably Philips recog-
nized the merits of his early work and himself contributed to
its wide dissemination on the Continent, where it can be
traced still today in no less than six different versions. [1] The
two elements which contributed most to its popularity may
have been the memorable cross relation of the opening phrase
—the leading tone immediately contradicted by a major
triad on the flatted seventh—together with the striking
'*cantus firmus* effect' of the last strain. This effect involves an
introductory chord [2] followed by a melody of repeated semibreves, presented on the downbeat but heard against shifting
block chords on beats two, three, and four. Philips used the
same device again in the last strain of a later pavan, no. 5 of
Christian Hildebrand's *Ausserlesene Paduanen und Galliarden*
(1607). [3] Sweelinck liked the device so well that he not only
adopted and elaborated it in his setting, but also incorporated
the technique in other compositions. For instance, the following excerpt from his fourteenth fantasia appears to owe its
impetus to Philips's pavan.

---

[1] See p. 99 f.
[2] Misplaced by Seiffert at the end of strain 2 instead of the beginning of
strain 3 in Sweelinck, *Werken*, p. 252, m. 49, and p. 254, m. 127.
[3] See B. Engelke, *Musik und Musiker am Gottorfer Hofe* (1930), p. 71.

In the recently discovered 'Fuga 7. Toni' from the Turin collection (probably a very corrupt version of a lost piece by Sweelinck, the technique is carried still further.

In England, Philips's 1580 pavan was widely known as a consort piece, in the familiar instrumentation for treble viol, flute, bass viol, lute, cittern, and pandora. The excellent arrangement printed in Morley's *The First Book of Consort Lessons* (1599 and 1611), with related versions in various manuscript parts at Cambridge University and Mills College,[1] may be by Philips himself. The accompanying 'Galliard to Phillips Pavin', found only in this source, stylistically resembles his 'Galliardo' in the *Fitzwilliam Virginal Book*, especially in rhythmic contour. (This is a strong argument for his authorship of the consort arrangement.) In addition to the consort versions the work is known from English sources as a solo for lute (twice in the *Dallis Pupil's Lute Book*, 1583, Dublin, Trinity College Library, D 3. 30, and once in the *Wickhambrook Lute Book*, Yale University Library) and for cittern (in Robinson's *New Citharen Lessons*, 1609). There are no English keyboard versions, apart from Tregian's copy in the *Fitzwilliam Virginal Book*, which probably was given to him personally by Philips, and represents the 1580 original.

On the Continent the piece was widespread in the most elaborate lute settings. Johann Rudenius, in *Flores Musicae*

[1] See Sydney Beck's critical notes to his edition of Morley (New York, 1959), p. 187, where he identifies and describes these parts.

(Heidelberg, Voegelin, 1600),[1] called it merely 'Pavana Anglica'.[2] It was doubtless the most popular 'English pavan' on the Continent, until surpassed by Dowland's *Lachrimae*. That Sweelinck set the pavan, then, was not necessarily the direct result of personal contact with Philips, as most writers have assumed. The two undoubtedly met in Amsterdam in 1593 and perhaps again in Antwerp in 1604 (see p. 28f.), but even without these contacts Sweelinck would have known Philips's famous piece from the many English, German, and even Dutch editions. As an amateur lutenist he must have played, or at least attempted to play, the rather difficult 'Pavan Pietro Filippi' set by Joachim van den Hove in his *Florida* (1601). In spite of the difference of media, there is some relationship in figural technique between Van den Hove's and Sweelinck's settings (cf. the opening of the ornamented second strain in Van den Hove with mm. 100–103 in Sweelinck); the *Florida* pavan may even have stimulated Sweelinck to compose his setting of the same piece. However, he must have known it in other versions as well, for Van den Hove's divisions entirely disintegrate Philips's 'cantus firmus effect' (except for a solitary measure), while Sweelinck preserved it, even in his ornamented 'double'.

The crude setting by Valerius in the *Neder-Landtsche Gedenck-Clanck* (1626) plagiarizes (and badly corrupts) Van den Hove's version of twenty-five years earlier; but it also restores the semibreves and chords of Philips's third strain. Swart's devotional five-voice setting of 1603, 'Wy Engelen goet',[3]

[1] A copy unknown to bibliographies may be found in the library of the Austin Friars Dutch Reformed Church, London. Wolfgang Boetticher lists a first edition of 1598 as located at Brussels, Bibl. du Cons., in his article 'Laute' for the encyclopedia *Die Musik in Geschichte und Gegenwart*, and in his unpublished 'Habilitationsschrift', *Studien zur solistischen Lautenpraxis* (1943). However, no such work is listed in *RISM*, *Recueils imprimés*, I (1960). There are many errors in Boetticher's bibliography.

[2] This concordance was missed by Beck, *loc. cit.*, who also overlooked the versions in the *Wickhambrook Lute Book* at Yale University and in *Elisabett Eijsbock's Keyboard Book* (Stockholm, Royal Academy of Music Library).

[3] I.e. 'We Angels good'. This title was misprinted as 'Wy Engelen gret' in *Grove*, 'Philips', a mistake carried over by both Sydney Beck, *op. cit.*, p. 187, and John Steele, article 'Philips' in *MGG*.

also appears to have retained the third strain intact, to judge from the single preserved part, a *superius*. Swart was so adept at fitting the Dutch text to a pre-existent piece that the word 'vroolick' comes appropriately at a syncopation, and 'hoogen toon' is nicely underlaid at the leap to a high G, the climax of the series of semibreves. The resemblance between Swart's opening line and Sweelinck's has already been noted in the previous chapter. It is not impossible that Sweelinck used Swart's setting as a model; but the reverse is a more likely assumption, until evidence can be found to show that Sweelinck, like Handel, borrowed from minor composers.

One of the most striking differences between Philips's and Sweelinck's pavans is the strict four-part contrapuntal style of the latter. There are hardly half a dozen places in all of Sweelinck's double setting in which a fifth note is added to the harmony; these few are all cadential or otherwise accented tonic or dominant chords. Philips, on the other hand, uses five- and even six-part chords freely and in a manner very idiomatic for the keyboard, particularly for the virginals. For the sake of sonority he tends especially to add the fifth above the bass G, A, or d, with disregard for 'voice-leading'. In contrast, Sweelinck maintains the framework of a four-voice texture even when it might seem unimportant to the essence of the music, as in the '*cantus firmus* effect' of the third strain:

An important reason for the difference in texture is certainly Sweelinck's inheritance of the Netherlandish penchant for strict polyphony. From the very first measures we are in the presence of a more consistently contrapuntal mind. The alto, for example, entering late rather than directly as part of the opening chord, continues through to the fifth measure as a contrapuntal line. With Philips, the alto line is already lost in the second measure, if indeed it is heard to emerge at all from mere chordal accompaniment.

The opening of the second strain is one of the more polyphonic moments in the Philips pavan. At this point the melody seems intended to accommodate imitation at the fifth. Philips employs a loosely imitative four-part texture here, and at the reprise reduces the contrapuntal lines to two, adding a typical English cross-relation. Sweelinck maintains four parts strictly and at the reprise heightens the counterpoint, sacrificing even the harmonic variety of the original for the sake of strict imitation over a D pedal.

Consistency of four-part counterpoint is matched in Sweelinck's pavan by consistency of figuration. Motives present in Philips's original are adopted by Sweelinck, but expanded and developed in a thorough and coherent manner, quite in contrast to the casual freedom of the Philips piece. For example, in the opening of the reprise of strain 1 Sweelinck adopts the eighth-note motive of Philips's second measure as well as the eighth-notes of the left hand in bar 4. However, he abandons Philips's variety of motives, the poignant cross relation in bar 3, and the static opening. Already in the first measure he converts the tonic — leading-tonic — tonic turn of the melody into an eighth-note motive which runs uninterruptedly throughout the four-bar phrase. Alto and tenor are also given parallel eighth-note movement: Philips's essentially chordal support is thereby converted (through the extensive use of his own motives) into a contrapuntal web which is distinctly Sweelinck's own. The consistent parallel sixths, a feature of all four measures and a frequent occurrence in many of Sweelinck's works, are quite unlike the open, almost fragmented texture of Philips's pavan. They are not uncharacteristic of other English keyboard music, however. Byrd employs very similar figuration, notably in variations 10–11 of 'Hughe Ashton's Grownde' (before 1591).

In making Philips's figuration more consistent and unified, Sweelinck is sparing of sixteenth-note figuration, at least in his first setting of the pavan. This restraint not only heightens contrapuntal intensity but also prepares, by contrast, for the extensive display of the second (elaborated) version which consists largely of sixteenth-note runs. These are introduced gradually, however, and the second setting opens with imitative parallel sixths related to passages in the first.

As Sweelinck's sixteenth-note figuration gradually becomes more florid, a new rhythmic element is introduced, a motive of three sixteenths. At the reprise of strain 1, the upper line still resembles the more rapid parts of Philips's reprises.

Philips:

Sweelinck:

By the beginning of strain 2, the three-note motive hinted at earlier—see the brackets in the above example—has become predominant. Through sequential repetition, this motive shifts the rhythmic impulse of the upper line unavoidably into short, lively, syncopated triple patterns. A metre of 3/16 is temporarily superimposed on the basic 4/4 patterns. The result is far from the calm dignity of the original pavan; yet, if we turn again to the works of Byrd, we find the same effect employed in abundance—and in a pavan probably composed when Sweelinck was ten. [1] The 'Pavana. Sr Wm Petre', well-known from its inclusion in the famous *Parthenia*, as well as in *My Ladye Nevells Booke* and other manuscripts, was most likely written in 1572, the year Sir William Petre died. [2] In the *Nevell* source, the contemporaneous fingering is even preserved, providing evidence that the cross-rhythm of the three-note figure would have been accented in performance through articulation. The passage from Sweelinck's pavan would probably also have been fingered in this manner.

Sweelinck:

[1] The same device appears also in Tallis's *Felix namque*, composed the year of Sweelinck's birth. See *Fitzwilliam Virginal Book*, I, p. 431.
[2] As pointed out by Thurston Dart in his Notes to the recent edition of *Parthenia* (London, [1961]), p. 39, this work was probably composed as a 'funeral pavan' to commemorate the death of Sir William. Cf. also F. G. Emmison's *Tudor Secretary, Sir William Petre at Court and Home* (Cambridge, Mass., 1961), p. 213.

Sweelinck adopts Philips's unusual phrase lengths in each strain (A is thirteen measures, B is eleven, C fifteen) and for the most part faithfully duplicates his harmonic scheme. The few discrepancies in accidentals are, for this period, insignificant. Chromatic alterations tend to vary even in the same piece from manuscript to manuscript, depending on the location, the date, or the mere caprice of the scribe. Cross relations are less prominent in the Sweelinck settings. This might be a Continental trait, though it is more likely due to the later date of Sweelinck's work. In any case, they are by no means absent (cf. mm. 38, 80, and 84); only the simultaneous cross relations (cf. Philips, mm. 9 and 15) are avoided. Probably the treble c-sharp of Sweelinck's m. 88 would not have been considered necessary by Philips.

Sweelinck's 'Paduana Lachrimae', his other English pavan setting, is likewise known from only a single source. But while the setting of Philips's pavan comes from the most reliable of all the manuscripts, *Ly* A 1, Dowland's 'Flow, my teares' 'collorirt' by Sweelinck is preserved only in the late and very corrupt Bártfa tablature. Sweelinck's variations on *Ich ruf zu dir* and *Soll es sein* are present in both sources, and a comparison shows how badly mangled these works had become by the time Zacharias Zarewutius, organist, compiler, and copyist, transcribed them in the Bártfa tablature. Further evidence may be found by comparing *Wie nach einem Wasserquelle* (no. 55) with the original *Psalm 42* by Speuy.[1] Even without the aid of such comparisons we can readily discern wrong notes, arbitrary deletions or simplifications, and general carelessness. According to Seiffert,[2] 'es ist unvorstellbar, wie ein Abspielen solcher Vorlage einigermassen einwandfrei verlaufen könnte'. Many corrections in the text were made by

---

[1] *Speuy*, 146; and the plates facing 147.   [2] *Einleitung*, xlviii.

Seiffert, but we must still be wary of accepting this piece as anything more than an approximation of Sweelinck's original.

In addition to Seiffert's thoroughly justified alterations in the corrupt text, there remain several awkward places, capable of improvement, which he overlooked. In the sixth and seventh measures, comparison with Dowland's own settings and with the various versions of his work by other composers (including Sweelinck's pupil, Schildt) clearly shows that the following alterations bring us closer to the original state of Sweelinck's composition.

At the opening of the second strain, the descent of the alto and tenor in the second measure coincides clumsily, giving accent to an exposed fourth on the second half of the second beat — a crudity quite foreign to Sweelinck's usual smooth contrapuntal handling. Altering the rhythm in the tenor avoids this defect and creates an imitation of the soprano, probably restoring Sweelinck's intention.

Similarly, the addition of a half-note *b* in the tenor, replacing the rest in the second half of m. 37, both corrects the faulty intervallic structure (the fourth above a 'bare' octave) and gives continuity to the tenor line. Dotting the first half note of the tenor and making the second a quarter note in m. 66 likewise restores the imitation between tenor and soprano present in Dowland's and probably also Sweelinck's original. Other awkward spots (for example, the end of m. 75 or the last eighth note in m. 86) are less easy to improve without extensive rewriting, but are no less assuredly corruptions or simplifications of Sweelinck's work.

A comparison of Sweelinck's 'Paduana Lachrimae', as preserved in the Bártfa tablature, with Melchior Schildt's setting of the same pavan further provides strong indirect evidence of the corrupt state of Sweelinck's work in that source. Schildt's setting is preserved in an accurate and reliable, though not autograph, manuscript. [1] Although it may well have been composed after Sweelinck's death, it is not impossible that it was done, or at least begun, under his tutelage. It bears some resemblance in technique to Sweelinck's setting, but far exceeds it in virtuoso passage-work and in abundance of excellent and original figuration. The Schildt setting does, however, relate very closely to more elaborate (and better preserved) works by Sweelinck. Schildt's work probably stands in relation to Sweelinck's Bártfa pavan much like a beautifully preserved painting by a minor artist compared to a mediocre copy of a great master's lost painting. Although the latter once inspired the former, it is now the minor artist's work which paradoxically seems superior. In music it is much more difficult than in painting to determine the extent to which a copy falsifies the original. Nevertheless, it should be clear from the preceding discussion that the Bártfa tablature provides us with no more (and probably less) than a mediocre version of Sweelinck's 'Paduana Lachrimae'.

[1] Copenhagen, Royal Library, MS. Adnex to Gabriel Voigtländer's *Oden* (1642). Modern ed. of the Schildt pieces by H. Panum in *Monatshefte für Musik-Geschichte*, XX (1888), pp. 37–41.

This fact is important to consider when comparing Sweelinck's setting with related works by Byrd, Morley, and
Farnaby, in the *Fitzwilliam Virginal Book*.

Even if Sweelinck's pavan were known in its original,
unsimplified form, it is unlikely that it would equal Byrd's
setting in elaborateness. In the latter, florid figuration is
extraordinarily plentiful, spilling over even into the cadences.
Every rhythmic crevice is filled with brilliant motion, and
not a moment of repose remains. Little survives of Dowland's
dark, sombre, sustained harmonies, which in his song embod-
ied the 'shadowes that in darknesse dwell'. The same chords
are present in Byrd's setting, of course, but they are illuminated by the brilliance of his figuration. An ever-changing series
of short, imitative motives passes in rapid, kaleidoscopic
fashion. If, as it seems, Byrd's pavans became more restrained,
unified, and introspective in later years (cf. the Earl of Salisbury's pavan of 1612), then his *Lachrimae* setting would be
among the earliest of its kind and could very well have been
known to Sweelinck. The essentially four-part writing, the
snatches of imitation permeating the texture, and the consistent working-out of a rhythmic motive are all elements in
common with much of Sweelinck's writing. Little of these
attributes remains in the present state of Sweelinck's pavan;
but where elaborate (original?) figuration is present, there
are close resemblances to Byrd's setting. With both composers
an occasional passage of scalar sixteenth-notes sweeps up or
down, temporarily replacing the contrapuntal texture even
though still notated in pseudo-polyphonic fashion.

Although it is usually classed with Byrd's and Farnaby's, Morley's 'Pavana' [1] is not based strictly on the famous song. It is, rather, a free paraphrase in the manner of Dowland's own six 'Passionate Pavans' which follow the best-known one in his published *Lachrimae* of 1605. The first seven notes of Morley's melody coincide with those of the famous pavan, but already in the second measure the harmony is altered. Reminiscences recur at the beginning of the second strain, but its close differs. (Morley stays in the relative C major while the Dowland song and its settings close on the dominant E major.) This strain is extraordinarily monothematic for a pavan, the cliché motive G-A-G-C recurring insistently in imitation. In the paired 'Galliarda', also remotely connected with the *Lachrimae* song, Morley uses a related motive not in the second but in the third strain. Curiously enough, the same motive occurs in Farnaby's *Lachrimae* setting, also at the opening of the second strain. The motive is not derived from Dowland, nor is it present in any of the other settings, and Farnaby's use of it is probably a reference to Morley's pavan. The latter would have been written before the turn of the century, whereas Farnaby's piece seems to be a later work. It is certainly his best and most extended essay in a dance form, and represents his singular, eccentric style in an advanced stage. It is among the last things copied by Tregian into the *Fitzwilliam Virginal Book*, probably in 1619, and could certainly have been newly composed then, considering the close ties between composer and copyist, and between the Farnaby and Tregian families. [2]

---

[1] A lute version in Cambridge, Univ. Lib., MS. DD 9. 33, ff. 11'–12 (dated 1600) is inscribed 'A Paven Mr Birde set to Lute by fr[ancis] Cutting', a detail overlooked by Thurston Dart in his recent edition of Morley's *Keyboard Works* (London, 1959). There is little reason, however, to doubt the *Fitzwilliam Virginal Book*, a source more trustworthy in its attributions. The presence in this pavan of cross relations contrary to *dicta* in Morley's treatise is, as we shall see, no evidence against his authorship.

[2] The various hypotheses concerning Farnaby's death early in the century (cf. entry 'Farnaby' in *MGG)* must be abandoned in light of the late J. L. Boston's discoveries, which included the record of the burial of Giles Farnaby on 25 November 1640 (see *Grove*, entry 'Farnaby').

In any case, even if it were chronologically possible, it is unlikely that Farnaby's setting would have influenced Swee- linck's. The piece resembles Sweelinck's general style (though not his *Lachrimae* in its present state) in being more consis- tently contrapuntal than most English keyboard music. Never- theless, Farnaby's bizarre and capricious figuration, with its nervously dangling melodic fragments and its near crudities, is a far cry from Sweelinck's calm reserve and masterful, refined dignity.

Morley's pavan, on the other hand, is much closer in spirit to Sweelinck's. Both composers maintain a similar balance between florid scalar figuration or idiomatic chordal writing and a contrasting stricter polyphonic style involving short motives in stretto. Like Sweelinck, Morley is also fond of figuration in parallel sixths (cf. also the third strain of Morley's 'Quadro Pavan' in the *Forster Virginal Book*).

Among many other resemblances, perhaps the most inter- esting to note is a similar use of a cadential cross relation. This point of likeness is the more remarkable since Morley speaks so vehemently against cross relations of various types in his treatise *A Plaine and Easie Introduction to Practicall Musicke* (1597). One can only conclude that his pavan was composed some years earlier than 1597, and that his taste had changed—or he had grown tired of the device—in the meantime. However, there is a lack of consistency between much of his music and his theoretical writings, as a number of scholars have pointed out. [1] The inconsistency is the more curious since there is no great disparity in years between his

[1] Cf. Lowinsky, Kerman, R. Alec Harman.

treatise and his music, and Morley was no more than forty at the time the *Introduction* appeared. Thus in the 'Second Part' of his book he says of the following example (with its simultaneous cross relation) that

it is an unpleasant harsh music; and though it hath much pleased divers of our descanters in times past and been received as current amongst others of later time, yet hath it ever been condemned of the most skilful here in England and scoffed at amongst strangers, for, as they say, there can be nothing falser, and their opinion seemeth to me to be grounded upon good reason however it contenteth others. [1]

Morley (1597):

Nevertheless, something 'falser' does occur, not in an early descanter, but in Morley's own keyboard pavan, the one here under discussion. The following clash between D and D-sharp is unabatably harsh; the *Fitzwilliam Virginal Book* editors' attempt to soften the dissonance by adding a sharp to the treble D misfires, for the passage is only worsened by the creation of an augmented fourth and an accented doubled leading tone. A more recent edition by Thurston Dart [2] justifiably adds an unequivocal natural to the treble D.

Morley, Pavan:

---

[1] Modern ed. by R. Alec Harman (London, 1952), p. 177.
[2] Thomas Morley, *Keyboard Works* (London, 1959), I, p. 18.

Sweelinck's final cadence includes a similar dissonance—less harsh, because unaccented, but still stronger than in works of his less closely related to English models.

Sweelinck, Paduana Lachrimae:

In the 'Third Part' Morley again condemns a cadential cross relation, this time in an unidentified Kyrie by Taverner: 'Although Master Taverner did it I would not imitate it'. [1]

Taverner, Kyrie :

Explaining what he considers to be faulty in the Taverner excerpt, Morley expounds on the harshness of the music and claims that

the close in the Counter part is both naught and stale, like unto a garment of a strange fashion which being new put on for a day or two will please because of the novelty, but being worn threadbare will grow in contempt; and so this point, when the lesson was made, being a new fashion was admitted for the rarity, although the descant was naught as being only devised to be foisted in at a close amongst many parts for lack of other shift; for though the song were of ten or more parts yet would that point serve for one, not troubling any of the rest, but nowadays it is grown in such common use as divers will make no scruple to use it in few parts whereas it might well enough be left out, though it be very usual with our organists.

[1] *Ibid.*, p. 259.

To the latter observation the eager student, Polymathes, adds his corroborative comment: 'That is very true, for if you will but once walk to Paul's Church you shall hear it three or four times at the least in one service if not in one verse.' As the modern editor points out, it is clear from this gibe that Morley was no longer organist at St. Paul's though he had held that post as recently as 1591. The editor also quotes a passage from the thirteenth of Morley's madrigals for four voices, containing a cross relation similar to the one Morley criticized in Taverner's Kyrie. Edward Lowinsky in his study of 'English Organ Music of the Renaissance'[1] refers to the editor's 'brave footnote-battle against Morley's "surprising" criticism' and contributes the following explanation of his own.

Aside from the fact that a minister's sermon against sin cannot be invalidated by the observation that he is not free from sin himself, Morley's 'sin' is actually of a different order entirely. True, in the passage quoted the tenor runs against the discant as the alto ('counterpart') does in Taverner's example. However, this passage occurs not at an ending but in the middle of a piece, and more important: Morley does not go to a cadence on G, he nimbly leaps off the suspended dominant on G and moves on to C, thus giving the false relation every aspect of a mere passing dissonance divesting it of the power to compromise the finality of a cadence through the unresolved conflict between F and F-sharp. [2]

Other works by Morley, however, provide more exact analogues to the Taverner passage. It would be hard to imagine a closer parallel than the following excerpt from Morley's 'Galiarda' in the *Fitzwilliam Virginal Book*.

Morley, Gallarda:

[1] *The Musical Quarterly*, XXXIX (1953), pp. 373–95 and 528–53.
[2] *Ibid.*, p. 381.

The accompanying pavan has similar cadential patterns, and in both works there are striking parallels to corresponding passages in Sweelinck's 'Paduana Lachrimae'.

Paradoxically, in spite of Morley's expressed aversion to this cadential pattern it may have been through him that Sweelinck came to include the same mannerism in his own keyboard music. Sweelinck could also have acquired this cadential cliché from Morley's teacher, William Byrd, or from Byrd's and Morley's friend Ferdinando Richardson (alias Heyborne). Similar passages are not infrequent even in the later keyboard pieces of Bull, and may be found here and there in works by others, such as Dowland and Peerson. [1] Nevertheless, since the pattern occurs more often in the 'Paduana Lachrimae'

[1] Cf. *MB*, XIV, p. 7: m. 9, p. 12: m. 82, p. 13: m. 33, p. 14: m. 73; etc.; Dowland's 'Farewell', mm. 20–21; Peerson's 'Alman', end of second strain. The same pattern was used rather early in Italy (cf. Malvezzi's music for *La Pellegrina*, 1589, ed. D. P. Walker, *Fêtes de Florence*, 1963; and cf. also the toccata in Venetian style by either Jacob Hassler or Sweelinck, L.30*, m. 44); and, apparently at a later date (early seventeenth century), in Spain. See the 'Falsa' (so-called because of the cross relations) by S. Aguilera de Heredia from the Escorial manuscript (in Pedrell, *Antologia*, I, p. 64, m. 35; p. 65, m. 53. Cf. also p. 67, fifth from last measure). Cf. also a rare French example in Richard's 'Gigue', Bauyn MS. (Paris, Bibl. nat., Rés. Vm⁷ 674, f. 61). Perhaps the latest examples of all are to be found in Purcell's string fantasies (*c.* 1680).

than elsewhere in Sweelinck's compositions, [1] and since this piece is in other ways closely related to Morley's pavan, the examples quoted above may show a direct influence of Morley on Sweelinck—one which Morley, in 1597 at least, would have regretted.

ii. *Variations on English tunes*

In the two pavans just discussed, Sweelinck adopts the harmonic, melodic, and formal structure of pre-existent English pieces. Certain other works of his are less intimately connected, while still closely allied to specific English compositions. These range from such a work as his 'Malle Sijmen'—with exactly the same length, identical structure, similar figuration, and the same melody as various English settings of 'Moll Sims'—to works where little more than the tune and the general technique of discant variation is shared with the corresponding English sets. All are variations on secular melodies and of about the same length, except for the shortest, 'Malle Sijmen', which lasts a mere forty semibreves.

It is very likely that the 'Malle Sijmen' setting had suffered some corruptions and simplifications by the time it was copied in the Leningrad manuscript some thirty years after the composer's death. However, it does not necessarily follow from the apparent corruptions in the figuration that there were alterations or deletions in the overall structure of the piece. The modest formal scheme (eight-bar phrase with its ornamented repeat and twelve-bar phrase with still more elaborate variation), though unique in Sweelinck's production, need not be the result of arbitrary cuts. Although we know that sections of longer works by Sweelinck were cut during the course of the seventeenth century, there are so many simple pieces of this

---

[1] Cf. a solitary instance in Fantasia S. 8 (= L. 6), m. 160, and a variant of the same formula in m. 87 of his 'Onder een linde groene', another work closely related to English variations (Farnaby's 'Lord Zouche's Maske'; cf. the discussion below, pp. 122–24).

same type (two strains, each with ornamented repeat) in the English sources that the discovery of one by Sweelinck should not be looked upon with doubts of its authenticity, but with satisfaction at the recovery of a lost genre of his work. Most convincing is the fact that of no fewer than nine different English settings of the 'Moll Sims' tune preserved, [1] none exceeds this same limitation to two strains with ornamented repeats.

The tune itself has its roots in England, traceable to the sixteenth century but dating perhaps from a still earlier period. The 'Moll' of its title had passed into obscurity already by the late sixteenth century—or so it seems, since not even a fragment of text identifying her survives from that or any other later period. The tune was used for many ballads both in England and the Low Countries; and it passed also to Germany, presumably by way of the English comedians. The wide popularity of 'Moll Sims', particularly as an instrumental piece, is probably due largely to an anomaly of its second strain. Between two four-bar phrases is inserted an extension of four bars, consisting of a simple five-note pattern with a scalar ascent and a triadic descent. The pattern appears in minor, with an echo at the lower octave, and is followed by a sequential repetition in the relative major, likewise echoed an octave lower. The presence of these repeats at differing octave levels led naturally to the tune's being used in songbooks for dialogues, between an upper and a lower voice. It seems likely, however, that the pattern had an instrumental rather than a vocal origin, [2] and it may represent an early

---

[1] See the listing in *MMN* III, xxxviii. To these may be added a 'Mall Sims' in Paris, Bibl. Nat., Rés. 1186, f. 118', and a 'Canzon' by William Brown in the former Berlin MS. 40316, destroyed in World War II, but preserved on microfilm at Isham Library, Harvard University. Another related version, the 'Pavan' in Elisabett Eysbock's book (see p. 44), f. 59', may also be an English setting.

[2] This hypothesis is substantiated by the appearance of 'Moll Sims' in all surviving sources as two simple strains with varied repeats like the dance forms of the period and unlike the popular (vocal) tunes, which were set as consecutive variations. The title may have been acquired through association with the dance of some theatrical personage.

example of the characteristic English 'octave echo' already discussed in connexion with Sweelinck's echo fantasias. The piece was in fact widely known in Holland as 'd' Engelsche Echo'.

The echo motive is present in all known settings, [1] though each has its individual version and its own varied repeat. Sweelinck's (as preserved in Leningrad) first presents the pattern in its simplest shape, adorned with only a single ornament. Likewise Leonard Woodeson's variations, a simple anonymous setting in New York Public Library MS. Drexel 5609 (p. 92), and the 'Pavana M.S.' in the *Fitzwilliam Virginal Book* all preserve the simplest form of this motive, each with its variant in ornamentation.

The Drexel version, an example of the simplest possible setting, is otherwise unlike Sweelinck's. In the excerpt quoted, the *Fitzwilliam* 'Pavana' (improperly so titled, probably only because it is a measured, duple, dance-like piece) is nearly identical with Sweelinck's setting. Its varied repeat also hits upon nearly the same division that Sweelinck chose:

[1] Its absence in a piece called 'Wanton Season' (in *Schott's Anthology of Early Keyboard Music*, III) whose melody is otherwise related to that of 'Moll Sims', makes the editor's assertion that it is another version of the same tune very questionable.

It differs quite markedly from Sweelinck's 'Malle Sijmen' in other respects, however. There is a very strong contrast between the chordal, rather unadorned strains and their repeats with almost uninterrupted sixteenth-note figuration. Sweelinck, on the other hand, introduces figuration already in the first measure, and his reprises are only moderately more elaborate than the strain they repeat. Certain measures are even identical in both the strain and its repeat (cf. mm. 5 and 13). Like the anonymous *Fitzwilliam* setting, a version in the same collection by Farnaby is also chordal and lacking in figuration in its first strain. [1] He uses more varied figuration in the reprises, and his second strain, with its dotted figures, is somewhat freer and less chordal than the first.

Leonard Woodeson's and William Brown's settings are still closer to Sweelinck's in technique. [2] Brown's is rather advanced in style and may be later than Sweelinck's. It shares with Farnaby's setting a preference for pronounced triadic figuration more characteristic of Scheidt than of Sweelinck and even exceeds Farnaby in the use of broken chords at cadences.

---

[1] The lack of ornament symbols is surely only Tregian's omission, however, and is characteristic for the series of Farnaby pieces copied at the end of the *Fitzwilliam Virginal Book*.
[2] There is no evidence to prove that Woodeson ever left England, but his single known keyboard piece survives only on the Continent: in *Ly A* 1, the prime Sweelinck source. For William Brown, see above, p. 32 f.

The Woodeson setting, on the other hand, employs exactly the same figural techniques Sweelinck's does. In similar fashion, too, it lessens the contrast between 'unornamented' strain and ornamented repeat by introducing some figuration into the first statement as well as its reprise. The similarity of approach is best illustrated by comparison of the opening measures of the second strain.

In the left-hand accompaniment, Woodeson varies the texture more than Sweelinck, adding a few syncopations and making use of the cadential formula established by Byrd some decades before.

Both compositions make extensive use of a primarily chordal bass, with emphasis on fifth and octave, and (except for the 'octave echo' of the second strain) eschew any figuration for the left hand such as may be found in Farnaby's and Brown's settings. It is impossible to date the work of Woodeson. His birth date is unknown, and he died later than Sweelinck, in 1641. There is therefore a possibility that his setting was subsequent to Sweelinck's and did not influence it but rather derived from it, or from the same English sources. In any case Sweelinck's 'Malle Sijmen' belongs unquestionably to a category of composition intrinsically English and does not differ in essence from any of the preserved examples of this category. It is also worth noting that of the ten surviving specimens of what was once presumably a very large group of

works based on the same prototype, Sweelinck's is the only
one known to have been written by a non-English composer.

The shortest of Sweelinck's variation sets (as distinguished
from his *settings*, such as 'Malle Sijmen') is a group of three,
found in their German source [1] under the title 'Von der Fortuna ward ich getrieben'. It is surely only because the manuscript is of German origin that the title survives in this form.
The melody came from England where it was known variously
as 'Fortune my Foe', 'Farewell Delight', or 'The Hanging
Tune'. It would have been familiar to Sweelinck in many
English and, of course, Dutch versions.[2] If he had given his
variations a foreign title it would have been English, not
German; but most likely they were called 'de Engelsche For-
tuijn'.

Of the many English keyboard settings preserved [3] none
compares to Sweelinck's in size and scope except William
Byrd's. Although Byrd's 'Farewell Delighte: Fortune my Foe'
consists of four rather than three variations, it is nevertheless
remarkably like Sweelinck's in structure. Both composers
begin with a simple statement (simpler than most opening
variations of the period), then proceed with predominant
eighth-note figuration essentially in four parts, and close with
a brilliant variation, full of scalar patterns of sixteenth-notes.
Like Byrd, Sweelinck tends to alternate such sixteenth-note
passages between the right and left hands, repeating in
slightly modified form a pattern that spans a single measure.
The following excerpts are taken from the same point in both
sets, i.e. the middle of the final variation. Sweelinck seems
almost to have adopted Byrd's technique of figuration and
even some of his figural patterns.

---

[1] Berlin, Gymnasium zum Graues Kloster, MS. 52. They are also, with
some preferable variants, in Tor F 8 f. 132–4 as 'Sonata prima J. L. H.'
The initials refer to Hans Leo Hassler, but this attribution is probably
a scribal error, as is the designation 'Sonata'.
[2] For a list, see *MMN* III, xl f.
[3] See *ibid*. To this list may be added an anonymous setting in Oxford,
Christ Church MS. 431, f. 20.

Whereas Byrd tends to repeat figures in a static fashion, Sweelinck often alters them through a sequential change of harmony or by some other means of forward propulsion. He also gives his work direction by beginning the final variation in eighth-note movement, shifting gradually through a subtle transition to sixteenth-note motion, and returning to eighth-notes at the end. Byrd rigidly maintains a steady, but less driving, flow of sixteenth-notes, quite without interruption (except for ornamentation and a solitary eighth-note breathing space in the thirteenth measure). Such perpetual motion is typical of late sixteenth-century English keyboard music, whereas Sweelinck, along with other seventeenth-century keyboard composers, tends to alter rhythmic patterns more frequently within the same variation. Sweelinck's technique is more rigid in other respects, however. Within his shorter spans the figural patterns are strictly and consistently maintained. Stretto imitations are rigorously carried out, and four-part texture, once established, is more stead-fastly maintained. Byrd's freer style is conceived more idioma-tically for the virginal and would adapt less well to the organ than Sweelinck's more sustained and austere polyphony. This is partly due to the profuse and apt ornamentation, however, and comparison with Sweelinck's variations in this regard is probably inappropriate. Whatever ornament symbols Sweelinck might have included in his (lost) autograph were deleted by German organist-scribes, and we can only guess at the nature and extent of his original ornamentation. [1]

Since Byrd's 'Fortune my Foe' variations were not copied in *My Ladye Nevells Booke*, they cannot be dated firmly before 1591. Stylistically, however, they resemble his earliest works. The cadential formula (see p. 119) common to his oldest keyboard music (but less frequent in works composed after 1591) appears thrice in the first variation alone. The *Nevell* collection is a very select group of forty-two of Byrd's best pieces; perhaps the 'Fortune' variations had been composed by 1591 but were simply excluded intentionally. In any case, their priority to Sweelinck's seems assured.

Preceding Sweelinck's 'Fortune' variations in the Berlin source [2] is a longer set also bearing a German title, 'Unter der linden grüne'. The same piece was copied in the Berlin Manu-script 40,316 under the simpler designation of 'Allemande'. [3] The tune does indeed resemble an almand of the period; there are two strains of nearly equal length, the first comprising the usual eight semibreves, in a deliberate duple meter. The piece was more famous as a song than as a dance, however. Again the German title is misleading, for this song was well known in Holland as 'Onder een linde groene', and there is

[1] The recent discovery of a second source for this work (see p. 120, n. 1 and the notes to N. 2) confirms this, for it adds some further ornamentation approaching Sweelinck's original.
[2] Graues Kloster MS. 52, f. 25.
[3] This source was destroyed in the last war but has been preserved on microfilm (see p. 116, n. 1).

no reason why Sweelinck should not have chosen this title
for his work. The tune was in fact so popular in the Netherlands that a number of widely varying versions circulated
under the same title. One found in the secular songbook
d' Amsteldamsche Minnezuchjes (1643) is nearly identical to the
English tune 'Lord Zouche's Maske'. [1]

The resemblance between this English tune and the one
used by Sweelinck reveals an interesting parallel between
Giles Farnaby's variations on 'Lord Zouche's Maske' from the
Fitzwilliam Virginal Book and those by Sweelinck on 'Onder een
linde groene'. The following examples attempt to reconstruct
(by eliminating added ornamentation) the varying tunes
known to each composer. The Sweelinck version has been
transposed for purposes of comparison.

The Sweelinck melody, even in its simplest, abstract form,
has more harmonic motion and bears its own particular
emphasis on the subdominant triad. The second strain also
offers melodic variety. The five-note motive common to the
end of both strains is altered and extended in Sweelinck's
version, whereas with Farnaby the final four measures of
both strains are identical. Since Sweelinck wrote four variations on the tune and Farnaby only half as many—curiously,

[1] Cf. C. van den Borren, *The Sources of Keyboard Music in England* (London,
1913), p. 330.

with a second reprise for the second strain of the first variation —it is only natural that the former's work has much more variety. But apart from the matter of length, Sweelinck's set is far richer in highly distinctive figurations and unexpected harmonies. Farnaby's persistent and nearly monotonous adherence to C major (with only six B-flats and four F-sharps in the entire piece) is in contrast to Sweelinck's remarkable shift from G to B major in m. 65, or his cross relations in mm. 56, 69, 86, 128, 138, etc. But the playful rhythmic displacement—one might call it 'contrametric figuration'—found so often in Sweelinck's variations and toccatas is present in Farnaby as well, and probably was adopted by Sweelinck from English music (see p. 128 f.).

Sweelinck's skilful transitions from one distinctive figure to another are absent in Farnaby's work. Although the Dutch composer learned much from the virginalists' use of short stretto imitations, his backgrond of training in Netherlandish polyphony shows through again and again. At the opening of the fourth variation, the tune, relatively unaltered, is integrated into an ingenious polyphonic texture woven from a single five-note motive—the very motive that appears, extended, in the latter half of the second strain. Farnaby's effusive *strettos* seem aimless by comparison with Sweelinck's restrained, terse polyphony.

Three further sets of Sweelinck's variations on secular tunes have parallels in English keyboard music, but in each instance resemblances (other than the shared tune) are minimal and comparison is hardly fruitful. The French melody widely known on the Continent as 'Est-ce Mars' was familiar in England as 'The New Sa-Hoo', but Farnaby's simple setting of the tune can hardly be compared with Sweelinck's seven variations of dazzling brilliance. Bull's variations titled 'Revenant' in the Vienna MS. 17,771 are based on a French *contrafactum* ('En Revenant de Saint Nicolas') of the drinking song ('More Palatino') employed in an anonymous set of variations titled 'Allemand' and attributable to Sweelinck; and Bull's seven variations on 'The Spanish Pavan' are based on a version of the same extremely popular piece [1] as Sweelinck's 'Pavana Hispanica'. Decided differences in scope, however, and problems of authenticity, especially in the case of the pavan, vitiate against a useful comparison of the two composers' settings.

[1] For a brief and not altogether complete history of the tune, and a list of concordances, see Diana Poulton, 'Notes on the Spanish Pavan', *The Lute Society Journal*, III (1961), pp. 5–16. For some further sources, see also *MMN* III, xxxviii. The piece was probably marked by a livelier character and faster tempo than the prevailing (Italianate) pavan, 'a kind of staid music ordained for grave dancing' (Morley, 1597). This would certainly have been one of the reasons for its becoming a popular ballad-tune, and might account for its always being called the '*Spanish* Pavan', in distinction to the more usual type of the same dance-form, though the term may also derive from the presence of the *folia* bass.

iii. *English figural techniques*

In European keyboard music of Sweelinck's time many elements of style were shared by composers of all nations. One
stylistic trait, however, clearly distinguished the English
school of the late sixteenth century. It was in purely instrumental figuration—triadic leaps, rapid scales, and other
patterns more perfectly suited to keyboard instruments than
to voices—that English composers were most forward-
looking. They established, as Manfred Bukofzer remarked,
'one of the essential elements of baroque music, namely
patterned figuration that relied on rhythmic consistency and
the abstract interplay of patterns and lines'. These specifically
instrumental devices 'mark the final emancipation of instrumental music from vocal style'. [1] Less apt is Bukofzer's subsequent description of this patterned figuration as 'non-
expressive', and his frequent use of the word 'mechanical'—
terms which he tries to invest with non-derogatory meanings.
One cannot help feeling, however, that his terminology can
apply to the music only in the case of rigid, 'non-expressive',
and therefore faulty performances. In the less interesting works
by Sweelinck's pupils a specific figural pattern is sometimes
applied in such arbitrary and overly consistent fashion that
one might justly speak of it as mechanical. Yet this is almost
never true of Sweelinck or the great English masters. The
preference for organizing a work around the repetition of
rhythmic patterns (though not necessarily mechanically)
seems to be a Northern trait, as opposed to the free, almost
amorphous flux of motives in, for instance, Frescobaldi.
Bukofzer errs, too, in associating 'mechanical severity' with
Calvinism. The 'mechanical elaboration in abstract rhythmic
patterns' to which he refers is characteristic more of Sweelinck's Lutheran pupils than of their master. Besides, he had
many Catholic friends, and could even himself have remained
a Catholic for all that we know of his personal beliefs. His

---

[1] *Music in the Baroque Era* (New York, 1947), p. 73.

figuration was Northern, not Calvinistic, and it derived, as
we shall see, from both sacred and secular music in England.

Perhaps the most basic of all types of figuration is that
which outlines a triad. Vocal lines, too, are occasionally based
on a triad; but they retain their entity as a line, whereas the
new instrumental figuration can only be regarded as 'broken
harmony'. This new development must have begun early in
the sixteenth century in England. A piece in *The Mulliner
Book*,[1] very probably by Redford (d. 1547), provides a remarkably early example of the figuration of triads in the relationship of the lower fourth, later to become the cliché of tonic
and dominant.

Redford, *Te per orbem terrarum* :

Toward the end of the century triadic figuration becomes
still more frequent. The following excerpt by Tallis, remarkably similar to a passage in Sweelinck's best-known toccata, [2]
was composed when Jan Pietersz. was an infant.

Tallis, Felix namque (1564):

Sweelinck, Toccata# 21 :

---

[1] *MB*, I, p. 47. Other examples from the same source may be found,
especially in the works of Blitheman (d. 1591).
[2] Best-known also in the seventeenth century, apparently, for it is preserved in seven sources—more than any other piece by Sweelinck.

Even closer parallels may be found among the works of
Sweelinck's English contemporaries. Bull's virtuoso variations
on *Walsingham* which open the *Fitzwilliam Virginal Book,* and
which were probably composed before he left England, contain passages which seem to carry triadic figuration to its
ultimate limits. They are matched—in style, if not in virtuosity—by sections in several of Sweelinck's compositions.

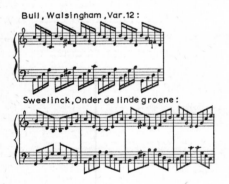

A special treatment of the triadic figure characteristic of
Sweelinck seems also to have originated in England. In the
preceding section 'contrametric figuration' was discussed—
short rhythmic shifts in the figural pattern, usually motives of
three notes in a prevailingly duple fabric. Along with nearly
every other aspect of sixteenth-century instrumental music,
this has its roots in Renaissance vocal music. In the hands of

English instrumentalists, however, it is developed to extremes
unknown in vocal works. Not only is it used in scalar patterns
(as cited on p. 124 in examples by Sweelinck and Farnaby)
but also in triadic figures. The three notes of the chord are
intentionally exploited rhythmically to create a jerky syncopation offsetting the basic duple beat. Sweelinck adopted this
device, especially in his toccatas, though he did not normally
carry it to such extremes as did the English. He transmitted it
also to his pupil, Samuel Scheidt, in whose toccatas the figure
is further modified and simplified, seldom occupying more
than a single measure at a time.

Rhythmic displacement in larger groupings may also be
effected through the irregular use of a repeated figure. This,
too, is an English trait in Sweelinck's work. The ending of his
Toccata S. 28 (= L. 18), as well as the example below from

his Fantasia S. 8 (= L. 6), may be compared with the considerably earlier Blitheman excerpt from *The Mulliner Book*, or the *Felix Namque* by Richard Farrant (d. 1581) from the same source.

Related to the breaking of triads is a common figure involving neighbouring tones in rapid alternation with chord tones:

— a device so idiomatic for the keyboard and so frequent in Northern keyboard music of this time that it might almost be termed the 'Alberti bass' of the early seventeenth century. The interval between the first and second note varies, but the second, third, and fourth invariably form a mordent pattern (in the idiomatic left-hand sequence of thumb–second finger–thumb).

A similar device involves what might be termed the 'zigzag' pattern. Various intervals consonant with the *cantus firmus* are used to make up a line with consecutive alternation between upward and downward motion. If conceived in terms of broken harmony, this figuration would often appear to involve seventh chords or triads with 'added sixth', but of course it was never thought of in such terms. The pattern must have originated simply as a means of providing a rapid counterpoint of consonances to a given slow-moving *cantus*. It then evolved into purely triadic figuration. An example of the 'zigzag' may be found already in the work of Richard Carleton. It was developed by Bull, and the excerpt from his work below represents an advanced harmonic usage.

A further manner of breaking harmonic patterns into instrumental figuration is the rapid alternation of chord tones, notated as if an inner voice were moving in syncopation. This device, which seems to have first been used extensively by Tallis, became a favourite with Bull, Sweelinck, and Scheidt and was used by them in a great variety of ways.

Related to this device of alternation, and often employed with it in the same piece or even the same variation, is the rapid 'tremolo' of intervals, usually thirds or sixths, occasionally octaves. This technique Sweelinck and his school developed more extensively than did the English; nevertheless, it may originally have come from across the Channel. There are no clear-cut examples of it from the works of the older generation, but there are some in the works of Bull. Since settings of the *Miserere cantus firmus* were so popular in England (and not elsewhere), it is probable that the following passage was written before Bull left his homeland.

We come, finally, to the common denominator of all figuration, the simplest manner of activating harmony and of creating motion: the repetition of a single note. There can be no strong proof of English priority in this case, since note repetitions play no prominent role in sixteenth-century English keyboard music. Bull does make extensive use of this technique, however, in all his various types of keyboard music. The earliest datable work to employ repeated notes is his alman for the Duke of Brunswick, probably written during his eighteen-month trip to the Continent in 1601. He could possibly have visited Sweelinck at this time; [1] the two men could also have invented the device quite independently. In any case it seems to have grown logically out of the techniques already discussed. It was probably also meant to imitate, by means of an idiomatic invention for the keyboard, the expressive tremolos characteristic of other instruments, and especially the *trillo*, or 'goat-trill', popular in vocal ornamentation of this same period. In the two-part fifth variation on *Ach du feiner Reiter* from the *Tabulatura Nova* (1624), Scheidt describes his *bicinium* as 'imitatione Tremula Organi' and recommends changing fingers on the repeated notes: 3 to 2 for the right hand, 2 to 1 for the left. Since the *Tabulatura Nova* was intended for organists, why should a work contained therein imitate the tremulant of the organ? The answer is probably that the work in question, as well as those similar ones by Bull or Sweelinck, could be played on either organ or harpsichord (or clavichord, with the effect of *Bebung*). In either case the 'tremolo' would be of a new and more agitated character than the various tremulant stops included in the organs of the day. This novel use for repeated notes was only one of many by-products of the new figural techniques born in England, adopted and enriched by Sweelinck, reworked and transformed by his successors.

iv. *Chromatic fantasies and meantone tuning*

The origins of chromaticism in the sixteenth century have interested scholars for more than half a century, from Seiffert and Kroyer to Lowinsky. [2] As these writers have shown, the

---

[1] See above, p. 27.
[2] Max Seiffert, *Geschichte der Klaviermusik* (Leipzig, 1899), p. 67; Theodor Kroyer, *Die Anfänge der Chromatik im italienischen Madrigal. Publikationen der Internationalen Musikgesellschaft*, Beihefte, IV (Leipzig; 1902); Edward Lowinsky, *Tonality and Atonality in 16th-century Music* (Berkeley, 1960), p. 41 f., as well as in various articles.

chromaticisms of early keyboard music—for example the eccentric *Consonanze stravaganti* of De Macque—have their roots in experimental vocal music, particularly the expressive chromatic madrigal. A key work influencing later madrigals was De Rore's Latin ode for four basses *Calami sonum ferentes*, almost certainly composed before 1554, the year Lassus left Italy. [1] Famous in the sixteenth century and known even in the eighteenth—Burney printed the piece in the third volume of his *History*—it may very well be the earliest piece to use the six notes of the chromatic scale which comprise the interval of a perfect fourth as a point of imitation. This subject, both ascending, as in the De Rore piece and in Sweelinck's (imperfectly preserved) 'Capricio', and descending, as in his 'Fantasia Crommatica', was to become a contrapuntal cliché in the seventeenth century and to linger on even into the eighteenth. Adopted as a ground bass motive, it became an ubiquitous harbinger of grief and, as late as Mozart, the very stereotype of sorrow.

The origins of this particular theme—used by countless composers during at least two and a half centuries of our musical heritage—have never been the subject of a systematic investigation. Musicological terminology cannot even supply a consistent name for it. If one speaks of a 'chromatic tetrachord' some musical scholars will think first of the chromatic *genus* of ancient Greek musical theory; and the purist could object that the term 'tetrachord' can hardly be applied to a series of *six* notes. To call this series a 'chromatic hexachord' is also confusing, for musicians firmly associate a hexachord with the interval of a sixth. [2] To avoid confusion on both

[1] As demonstrated in an unpublished paper on Lassus' *Sibyls* by John Roberts of Berkeley.

[2] For this reason the author chose to adopt the Italian term 'tetracordo cromatico' in his article 'L'Opera Cembalo-organistica di Tarquinio Merula', *L'Organo*, I (1960), pp. 141–51. Charles van den Borren, *Les origines de la musique de clavier dans les Pays-Bas* (Brussels, 1914), p. 141, uses the term 'tetracorde chromatique' with reference to the theme of Sweelinck's Fantasia. However, 'chromatic fourth' would seem to be a preferable term.

counts, the term 'chromatic fourth' will be adopted here. This chromatic fourth would have originated in vocal music, most plausibly around the middle of the sixteenth century, along with the first chromatic experiments to involve extended degree inflection. But in examining such early chromatic works one cannot help wondering how, by the last decade of the century, such a systematic use of successive chromatic scale tones had evolved. How did the chromatic fourth become crystallized as an entity, extricated from the maze of degree inflections and cross relations which often accompany the harmonic meanderings of that age? Most important, why did the fourth become established as the all-important interval, the almost inviolable boundary of chromatic subjects? Examples from seventeenth-century keyboard music, naming only those works which employ a chromatic scale consistently as principal theme, would include the two Sweelinck pieces already cited; Luython's 'Ricercar'; [1] Erbach's 'Canzona Cromatica'; [2] Bull's 'Fantasia' from the Vienna tablature; [3] Scheidt's *Fuga quadruplici* [*sic*] on 'Io son ferito lasso'; T. Merula's 'Sonata cromatica';[4] E. Soncino's 'Cromatica'; [5] Fasolo's 'Magnificat II. Toni 3. V.'; Froberger's 'Capriccio' and second toccata; Pachelbel's 'Fuga'; [6] Joh. Christoph Bach's 'Fuga' in E-flat; [7] W. C. Briegel's 'Fuga tertii toni'; Gottlieb Muffat's 'Fuga'; and two anonymous fantasias and a 'Ricercar cromatico' in Munich, Codex 262. The few seemingly rebellious exceptions to the rule of the fourth, such as Hans Leo Hassler's 'Ricercar II. Toni' and Merula's 'Cromatico overo Capricio', in fact only provide further confirmation. In the former the subject runs from the first to the fifth scale degree in g minor, but it is chromatic only from degree two to five. (Cf. Frescobaldi's 'Capriccio sopra Ut, Re, Mi, Fa, Sol, La' for a similar example.) With

---

[1] *MMB*, II, no. 126, p. 49
[2] Cf. *id.*, titled 'Fuga' (by Kerckhoven?), *MMB*, IV, no. 8.
[3] *MB*, IV, no. 2.
[4] Monumenti di Musica Italiana, I (1961), ed. A. Curtis, pp. 2–7.
[5] *Ibid.*, pp. 38–40.   [6] *D.D.T.*, 2e Folge, IV, i, p. 42.
[7] Included in Bischoff's ed. of J. S. Bach, (Leipzig, 1888).

Merula, the shock of the opening chromatic ascent through the interval of a ninth is followed by a reduction to the octave in the next two (dominant) entries; thereafter the fourth prevails throughout the piece. Even when a chromatic subject appears only briefly within the fabric of a larger work, it always seems to consist of a chromatic fourth. Examples may be found in Jacob Hassler's 'Toccata IV. Toni'; the last strain of Philips's 'Pavana dolorosa' 1593 (called 'Cromatica Pavana' in its lute version) and its accompanying galliard; the last strain of Tomkins's single 'Pavana' in the *Fitzwilliam Virginal Book* (and its setting by Philips in the Andreas Düben tablature in Upsala); Frescobaldi's *Capriccio sopra l'aria di Ruggiero*; an anonymous 'Fantasie' in the Liège manuscript; [1] and Anthoni van Noordt's second *Fantasia*. After the establishment of the chromatic fourth as a traditional point of imitation at the end of the sixteenth century, its intervallic boundary seems to remain intact even when adopted for chaconnes, passacaglias, and operatic laments.

To the average musician of the Baroque, the chromatic fourth must have served as an ideal emblem of grief, combining all the altered tones between the dominant and the tonic in the newly ascendant minor mode, and still carrying over, via humanist theory, some aura of ancient Greek pathos, some semblance of the chromatic gender. Already at the end of the sixteenth century a musical theorist had warned against this pseudo-tetrachord masquerading as Greek. In the 'Annotations to the First Part' of his treatise *A Plaine and Easie Introduction to Practicall Musicke* (1597), [2] Morley begins by describing the Greek 'genders' as he understood them—ascending rather than descending, in retrograde to our presentday interpretation. 'Diatonicum is that which is now in use, and riseth throughout the scale by a whole note, a whole note and a less half note'. Here he gives the example: G, A, B, C. 'Chormaticum is that which riseth by "semitonium minus" (or the less half note), the greater half note, and three half

---

[1] Guilmant, *Archives*, X, p. 30.
[2] Ed. R. Alec Harman (1952), pp. 101–103.

notes', and he gives two examples: B, C, C-sharp, E, and E, F, F-sharp, A. He goes on to explain that 'this point which our Organists use', and he here inserts the series E, F, F-sharp, G, G-sharp, A, 'is not right *Chromatica*, but a bastard point patched up, of halfe *chromaticke*, and halfe *diatonick*.' Morley thus implies that musicians with a less thorough knowledge of Greek music would confuse this 'bastard point' with the legitimate Greek *Chromatica*. He also clearly shows that the chromatic fourth was already well established in England in the late sixteenth century, at least among organists. Yet, curiously enough, it is precisely in the field of organ music where examples of the chromatic fourth from this period are lacking today. (Bull's short, turbulent 'Fantasia' already mentioned probably dates from his continental period.) Examples from sixteenth-century pavans and galliards have already been cited; solo lute pieces will be discussed presently; and in vocal music one could turn to Morley's own *Come sorrow, come*, the ending of Campion's *Author of light* from his first book (at the words 'mist and darkness'), or to John Danyel's very self-conscious setting of the text 'No, let chromatic tunes, harsh without ground, Be sullen music for a tuneless heart, Chromatic tunes most like my passions sound', in the second part of his *Can doleful notes*. Joseph Kerman cites several examples from madrigal literature, including Byrd's grimly obvious setting of 'sourest sharps and uncouth flats' [1] from *Come woeful Orpheus* (1611).

It is probably only through a loss of sources, then, that examples from organ literature are missing. If they were to be discovered, they would certainly provide interesting comparisons with Sweelinck. In the meantime, English chromatic fantasies for the lute may serve as examples for comparison with Continental works of this genre for the keyboard.

Max Seiffert described what he believed to be an important difference between the chromaticism of the Italians and that of the English:

[1] *The Elizabethan Madrigal. A Comparative Study* (American Musicological Society, New York, 1962), p. 261; p. 309, example 62.

With the former, it was repeatedly arrived at by means of appropriately illustrating a text, in which the meaning depended upon a particular stress. For the instrumental-minded English, on the other hand, who connected chromaticism with only the general concept of heightened affect, it was an instrumental resource. As soon as they use a chromatic passage, normally spanning the interval of a fourth, they link it with an accompanying figure, which brings with it a certain harmonic character to the chromatic line, and makes it adaptable to the musical context. [1]

His generalization is only partly true. The 'instrumental-minded English' did use chromaticism in their vocal music much the same way as the Italians, though certainly with more restraint and to a much lesser degree. [2] On the other hand, purely instrumental chromaticism existed also in Italy, with accompanying figures much the same as in English works. Most of the surviving examples are unfortunately from a later period: Merula, Soncino, Fasolo, Rossi, etc. Only two preserved fantasies for keyboard are known to date from the sixteenth or *early* seventeenth century, and thus to be contemporary with or prior to similar works by Sweelinck. Both, significantly, are by South Germans under Italian (Venetian) influence.

Hans Leo Hassler studied with Andrea Gabrieli in 1584–85. His 'Ricercar II. Toni' [3] makes extensive use of the chromatic fourth and is approximately the same length as Sweelinck's large fantasia—about eight minutes. In structure and in detail, however, the two works are markedly dissimilar. Paradoxically, the Hassler piece is closest to Sweelinck's style in its ending, where it differs most in specific detail from his chromatic fantasy: Hassler's final twelve measures strongly resemble passages in certain of Sweelinck's toccatas, both composers having borrowed motives from the Venetian school. But Hassler's work is much closer to the transitional late sixteenth-century Italian style than is Sweelinck's. His

[1] *Op. cit.*, pp. 67 f.
[2] See the excellent discussion of this in Kerman, *op. cit.*, pp. 212 ff.
[3] Padua, University Library MS. 1982; in *D.D.T.*, 2e Folge, IV, ii, p. 55.

use of short sections of irregular length, including a brief
section in triple metre, gives the piece an uneasy, restless
shape. It lacks, moreover, Sweelinck's consistent figuration
and his sense of climax, slowly building up through increased
motion and added contrapuntal complexity. Except in the
toccata-like ending, Hassler writes rapid figuration only at
the irregularly spaced cadence points. These sudden bursts
of brilliance seem at times unmotivated, full of clichés, and
rather archaic; they were cadence formulas common already
at mid-century. Coloratura is for Hassler a superficial addition, not an integral part of the composition as it is with
Sweelinck. Furthermore his harmony is less tonal than Sweelinck's, and he employs more two-part, note-against-note
writing. Often there is a diatonic scale in contrary motion as
countersubject to the chromatic point, a device never used by
Sweelinck, possibly because it lacks clear tonal implications.
In short, although Hassler was an almost exact contemporary
of Sweelinck, his piece seems to be of an earlier age.

Christian Erbach (*c.* 1570–1635), a younger colleague of
Hassler's, may also have studied in Venice; but very little is
known of his life before the last years of the century, by which
time he had settled in Augsburg. Erbach's work was well
known in the Netherlands—witness its inclusion in the Berlin
MS. 40,316 (compiled by a pupil of Cornet) and in *Ly A 1*
(written in the Netherlands, probably by someone directly
connected with one of Sweelinck's pupils [1]).

Indeed, the presence of much of Erbach (and of no other
contemporary German) in the latter manuscript would seem
to indicate not only Sweelinck's acquaintance with the works
of his younger contemporary but also his admiration for them.
However, the work that concerns us at present, Erbach's
Canzona cromatica, shows little relationship to the Dutchman's
style—though the theme is exactly the same in Sweelinck's
large fantasy, and in length the piece corresponds closely
to both Sweelinck's and Hassler's. Erbach's is an extremely

[1] See p. 47, n. 1.

homogeneous, rhythmically unified work, constantly flowing, without the sectionalism of Sweelinck, much less the restless interruptions of Hassler. Harmonically, it is close to Hassler and to the Venetians, though it is clearly of a later date. In its steady rhythmic flow, its lack of sectionalism, and its restraint in the use of figuration, it more nearly approaches the chromatic fantasy of Sweelinck's pupil, Scheidt, than that of his master. It might very well date from the same period as the Scheidt piece (published 1624). Like the latter it is a carefully unified and thoroughly tedious piece. Both works suffer by comparison with the brilliant figuration, the ever-changing yet logically successive rhythmic patterns of Swee-linck's truly inventive fantasy. Apart from the use of the chro-matic fourth itself, then, neither of Sweelinck's chromatic fantasies seems to have drawn on such Italian or South Ger-man models as have survived today.

In spite of their smaller scope and certain differences caused by the dissimilarity of medium, four English lute fantasies—at least two of them by Dowland—have striking stylistic bonds with the Sweelinck works under discussion. A 'Farewell' and a 'Forlorne Hope' fancy are both attributed to Dowland in Cambridge University Library MS. Dd. 5. 78. 3 (ff. 43ᵛ-44) and Dd. 9. 33 (ff. 16ᵛ-17). The Euing lute books of the Glasgow University Library also contain the 'Farewell' fancy, without attribution, followed by another anonymous chroma-tic fantasy. [1] A fourth such piece is found with no attribution in Jane Pickeringe's lute book in the British Museum, MS. Eg. 2046 (ff. 23ᵛ-24). [2]

---

[1] All three works published by David Lumsden, *An Anthology of English Lute Music* (London, [1953]), pp. 33–41. Of the anonymous Euing fancy Lumsden says: 'the quality of this piece, its style and the pieces surround-ing it in the MS. (all anon.) suggest Dowland as its composer.'

[2] The Pickeringe piece has unfortunately never been published. An attribution to Dowland is less assured than in the case of the Euing piece, for it is not paired with a known Dowland fancy in the manuscript source, and the copyist seems, furthermore, to have been profuse and conscientious with ascriptions, including several to Dowland. R. Newton, in 'English Lute Music of the Golden Age', *Proceedings of the Musical Association*, LXV (1939), p. 63, asserted that 'it may be assigned to him

These four fancies employ the chromatic fourth in both ascending and descending forms, on the tonic and dominant levels (D and A, or G and D), as do most chromatic fantasies for keyboard. In Dowland's 'Forlorne Hope', however, as in Sweelinck's fantasy, a modulation to the fifth above occurs soon after the exposition, and the subject is sounded at the level of the secondary dominant. Dowland inverts his subject and treats it in diminution. So does Sweelinck, though his statements in augmentation require the sustaining power at least of the harpsichord if not of the organ, and would be futile on the lute. Dowland uses the device of *stretto* in much the same way as Sweelinck, namely to recoup rhythmic energy after a period of extended figurations: the movement suddenly slackens but the tension remains, thanks to the excitement of the *stretto*. (Cf. mm. 17 ff. of 'Forlorne Hope' with mm. 57 ff. of the larger Sweelinck Fantasia.) Like Sweelinck, Dowland maintains a constant drive toward the final climactic cadence; and near the end of 'Forlorne Hope', and of Sweelinck's shorter fantasy, two statements of the chromatic fourth unite, contributing to the effect of climax by forming a continuous eleven-tone chromatic scale.

With both Sweelinck and Dowland the presence of the chromatic fourth is nearly always felt, but interest is concentrated on the ever-changing counterpoints to the theme and on the constantly shifting rhythmic design, with one fresh and ingenious new pattern following another. In spite of the difference in medium, some of these lute patterns are strikingly similar to Sweelinck's keyboard figuration, as the following two pairs of examples indicate:

[Dowland] without hesitation since it is so obviously a companion piece to the *Farewell*, and has numerous close resemblances to it that could scarcely be accidental.' But he did not know the Euing lute book, and was thus unaware of the fact that it was not the Pickeringe piece but another similar fancy which is there paired with the 'Farewell'. Until more English lute music is made available for study, ascriptions solely on the basis of style are bound to be tentative. The piece might even be an arrangement for lute of a fantasy by a leading keyboard composer, the original of which has been lost.

Since Sweelinck is known to have been an amateur lutenist and even a composer of works for the lute, [1] it is more than likely he would have known the lute music of his English colleague. Whether he was influenced by Dowland or vice versa can be decided only after the respective works in question have been dated. The manuscript sources of the lute fancies all date from *c.* 1600, with the exception of Jane Pickeringe's book which bears the year 1616 on its cover. The earliest of the Sweelinck sources involved is a German organ tablature now in Vienna (National Library MS. 17,771) where his

[1] See F. Noske, 'Luitkomposities van Jan Pieterszoon Sweelinck', *Orgaan der K.N.T.V.*, XII (1957), pp. 46–48; 'Remarques sur les luthistes des Pays-Bas (1580–1620)', *Le Luth et sa musique* (Paris, 1958), pp. 179–92; and a brief notice about an unknown lute setting of Psalm 23 in *Mededelingenblad, V.N.M.*, April, 1967.

large fantasia is ascribed to 'Johan Bull' and dated 1621, obviously in confusion with the (somewhat chromatic) fantasy Bull wrote the year of Sweelinck's death. The date, then, along with the ascription, must be a mistake and should be disregarded. Nevertheless, the chromatic fantasy does seem to belong to Sweelinck's later years, both as regards its unified, consistent style, and its mature craftsmanship. The fact that Tregian did not include this outstanding work in the *Fitzwilliam Virginal Book*, which otherwise provides such a choice sampling of Sweelinck's best productions, might also argue for a late date of composition. Tregian copied four of Sweelinck's finest works between the years 1605 and 1618 (the hexachord fantasy bears the date 1612): had he (or his friend, Peter Philips) known the chromatic fantasy, one would expect him to have included it. In any case, until we can be more certain of Sweelinck chronology, and until the lute fancies can be more accurately dated than merely 'before *circa* 1600', the question of Dowland's influence is left inconclusively answered.

Before closing the subject of chromatic fantasies, an important related problem should be touched upon: the question of *temperament*. It is a widely accepted thesis that fretted instruments always sounded in equal temperament, while keyboard instruments of the sixteenth and seventeenth centuries were generally tuned in some form of meantone temperament, i.e., with acoustically pure major thirds (representing the ratio 5 : 4) and flat fifths. Assuming this thesis to be correct, there would have been a rather puzzling difference between chromatic fantasies for lute and those for keyboard. One wonders how the same ears could have listened with pleasure to works so similar in style with such discrepancy in temperament. Tuning systems were, however, far more flexible in the sixteenth century than now, and the listener presumably adapted himself more readily to variations in temperament and tuning. Furthermore, it is not quite correct to assume that all fretted instruments sounded in present-day equal temperament. [1] Equal semitones do not necessarily imply equal temperament—although Vincenzo Galilei's 18 : 17 ratio was remarkably close: equal semitones of 99 cents gave an octave of 1188 instead of 1200—and it would seem that the best and most intelligent players, as well as all the theorists, were ever devising means to avoid the unsatisfactory compromises of equal temperament. Certainly Dowland was one of these, and it is interesting to note that his chromatic fantasies would have sounded, in his hands, in a system of temperament involving unequal semitones. In his son's printed lute book (1610) Dowland expounds his manner 'Of Fretting the Lute'. According to J. Murray Barbour, [2] his chromatic semitone C to C-sharp comes out 33 : 31, or 108 cents, and the diatonic semitone from D to E-flat is 22 : 21 or 80 cents. His third, C to E, is closer to the pure third (as in meantone temperament) than the Pythagorean (as in Ornithoparchus, whose *Micrologus* Dowland translated into English).

Though we are fortunate in possessing in detail Dowland's desires in these matters, we know nothing whatsoever of Sweelinck's preferences, nor of how the instruments on which he played were tuned. [3] The conventional meantone tuning of the time would, in its strictest interpretation, ill serve either of Sweelinck's chromatic fantasies, for both works call for D-sharp as well as E-flat. [4] The presence of both enharmonic tones within the same piece is actually the intensifi-

[1] Here the theoretical temperament is meant and not the very individual and constantly varying pitches which lutes and gambas actually assume in practice.

[2] *Tuning and Temperament* (East Lansing, 1951), p. 153.

[3] The organs of the *Oude Kerk* were not actually tuned by him but by the 'Beyerman' (*carilloneur*) and harpsichord maker Artus Gheerdinck, concerning whom see *Dutch HM*, 50, and B. Bijtelaar, 'De Kooromgang van de Oude Kerk', *Jaarboek Amstelodamum*, LVII, (1965), p. 47, where his burial is recorded on 9 June 1624. Pieter Fischer, in *O.K.W. Mededelingen*, XVIII (14 May, 1962), p. 201, gives Sijbrandt van Noordt de Oude as *carilloneur* of the Oude Kerk. Perhaps he preceded Gheerdinck, who accepted the post in 1594 and was succeeded, after his death in 1624, by his son Herman.

[4] *Werken*, I, no. 1, contains D-sharps throughout and a single E-flat in m. 176. No. 70 includes a D-sharp in m. 48 and an E-flat in m. 67.

cation of a problem already inherent in Sweelinck's other works. E-flat is naturally in common use, as it is with other composers of this period, but he also uses a D-sharp in several works besides the chromatic fantasies already mentioned: Fantasia S. 11 (= L. 32*) where it forms an augmented sixth with F,[1] *Onder een linde groene* (S. 63 = N. 8), measure 65, and *Allein zu dir*, variation 2, from the Clausthal-Zellerfeld MS. Although Tallis and Redford had used D-sharps in certain pieces and E-flats in others, only two cases of the use of both tones within the same keyboard piece by a composer older than Sweelinck are known. Both cases occur in the works of Byrd: his hexachord fantasy,[2] and a fantasy in A.[3] In the hexachord fantasy he uses G-sharps and E-flats in several places, and A-flat and D-sharp each occur once.[4] The fantasy in A has a D-sharp in m. 5 (in one of the two sources) and an E-flat in m. 190.

Enharmonic tones in different pieces could easily be accommodated by re-tuning, or by performance on a different instrument. For a performance on stringed keyboard instruments, the D-sharps required for one piece could be quickly and easily changed to the E-flats needed for another, and vice versa—as they undoubtedly were, even into the eighteenth century. But the presence of enharmonic tones in literature for the organ, as well as within the same piece, can only be explained by one of the following possibilities: 1. a harshly out-of-tune note was tolerated occasionally, in passing, i.e. an E-flat could function temporarily as a (sharp) D-sharp; 2. the work was intended for an instrument with split keys, i.e. the accidental between D and E would be divided,

---

[1] This work, though anonymous in its source, is probably by Sweelinck (see p. 65). Chords containing an augmented sixth are rare but by no means unknown in keyboard music of this period. For an unequivocal instance, see Morley's 'Fantasia' in the *Fitzwilliam Virginal Book*, II, p. 61. With meantone tuning, the augmented sixth sounds less dissonant than a minor seventh. Since it functions, nevertheless, as a dissonance, it would hardly matter if an enharmonic substitution were made, or if equal temperament were employed.

[2] *Collected Works*, XX, p. 123.   [3] *Ibid.*, XVIII, p. 4.

[4] Measures 154 and 227 respectively.

one half operating a string or pipe sounding D-sharp, the other half E-flat, forming acoustically perfect thirds with the tones B and G respectively; 3. some form of equal temperament was applied to keyboard instruments, at least for chromatic pieces; 4. some modification of meantone tuning was employed, as for instance the irregular system of Arnolt Schlick. [1]

The first alternative is of course possible, but it would hardly have been tolerated by sensitive musicians. There is no documentary evidence for the second: [2] split-key instruments seem to have been common in Italy [3] (where they persisted even into the eighteenth century) but were rare in the North. [4] There is overwhelming evidence against the use of equal temperament for keyboard music of the early seventeenth century, [5] and only one small piece of evidence arguing

---

[1] Cf. Barbour, *op. cit.*, pp. 137 f.

[2] See Appendix I. VdSM, 111, believed Sweelinck's instruments had keys for both E-flat and D-sharp; but he did not go into the problem of other composers' works or of the evidence—and lack of it—among preserved instruments and contemporary documents.

[3] Cf. J. Rousseau, *Traité* (1687), p. 50.

[4] However, the organ of the St. Laurenskerk, Alkmaar, (1638) had split keys until it was rebuilt by Frans Casper Schnitger. M. A. Vente, in *Die Brabanter Orgel* (Amsterdam, 1958), p. 181, printed Bull's recommendation to the churchwardens of St. John's in 's-Hertogenbosch, that the four-octave keyboard of their large new organ should be completely chromatic, i.e. without the usual short octave. It is hard to see any logic whatsoever behind Vente's contention that this recommendation shows Bull's acquaintance with and preference for equal temperament. His view was reiterated, however, and concurred with by Lady Susi Jeans in her review of Vente's book in *Galpin Society Journal*, XIII, (1960), p. 103.

[5] Tendencies toward equal temperament were rejected even by those few musicians who were aware of its existence. A good example is provided by Jean Denis, a professional keyboard tuner, whose *Traité de l'Accord de l'Espinette* (augmented ed., Paris, 1650) is soon to be reprinted with a preface by the author. Denis was present at an assembly of 'honnestes gens', where the new system of equal semitones was being demonstrated. Upon being told that it sounded false only because he was unaccustomed to it, he replied: 'si on leur presentoit un festin de viandes ameres et de mauvais goust, et qu'on leur donnast du vinaigre à boire . . . si on leur disoit qu'ils n'y sont pas accoustumez, ce ne seroit pas une bonne raison et bien recevable.' (p. 12).

for it: Bull's hexachord fantasy. [1] This unique piece includes statements of the hexachord on each of the twelve tones and at one point involves an enharmonic modulation. [2] But, as J. Murray Barbour has said, one should not try

to build up a theory of the use of equal temperament in England during Queen Elizabeth's reign on the basis of Dr. Bull's composition. Remember that it stands practically alone. It seems almost as if Bull had written a Fancy for four viols, and then led by some mad whim, had transcribed it for virginals and tuned his instrument to suit. [3]

The fourth alternative thus seems the most likely solution for works like Byrd's and Sweelinck's. Modified meantone systems, with the most frequently used thirds more in tune than others, and with the 'wolf' confined to remoter keys (F-sharp and G-flat, etc.) persisted as late as the nineteenth century. [4] Even a man so continually identified with equal temperament as Werckmeister appears to have had such a modified system rather than equal temperament in mind when he used the phrase 'wohl temperiert'. To Werckmeister ' "well-tuned" meant "playable in all keys—but better in the keys more frequently used"', according to Barbour, who quotes Werckmeister's own explanation that 'it would be very easy to let the thirds Db-F, Gb -Bb, Ab -C beat less than a full comma; but since thereby the other, more frequently used thirds obtain too much, it is better that the latter should remain purer, and the harshness be placed upon those that are used the least'. Thus, to return to Sweelinck, the E-flat of the Oude Kerk organs could have been slightly lower than required by strict meantone temperament in order to function occasionally as D-sharp. The most frequently used thirds, such as C and E, would still have been almost perfectly in tune.

---

[1] *MB*, XIV, p. 53.
[2] The following progression occurs at the fourth entrance of the hexachord: E major, A major (notated A, D-flat, E), F-sharp major (notated as G-flat major).
[3] *Op. cit.*, pp. 190 f.
[4] Cf. William Crotch, *Elements of Musical Composition* (London, 1812), p. 112.

VI

DUTCH KEYBOARD MUSIC AT
MID-CENTURY

Were we to judge only from extant sources, we might assume that after the death of Sweelinck keyboard music in the United Provinces disappeared as abruptly as it had risen to prominence with him. The abundant literary and documentary references to skilled keyboard artists throughout the century, however, as well as the numerous and familiar paintings of dilettantes at the virginals, assure us that hundreds, even thousands, of Dutch keyboard manuscripts must have existed in the seventeenth century and subsequently been lost. In the first half of the century much of the contents of these manuscripts would have been Dutch or English, and surely some of the collections must have contained works by followers of Sweelinck. Nevertheless, his Dutch students stand in sorry contrast to his prolific and illustrious German pupils, much of whose music is preserved. The Dutchmen are no more than names to us today, for not a single keyboard work of theirs has survived.[1] We must refrain from inferring their relative lack of merit or of productivity, remembering that Sweelinck, too, would be an obscure, almost unknown composer if we were dependent solely on sources in the Netherlands. That his Dutch pupils' works are no longer extant implies only that they were not well known outside the United Provinces. Dutch keyboard sources from before the eighteenth century are extremely scarce: a solitary edition, Speuy's *Psalmen* (1610), is all that

---

[1] For a list of names, see vdSM, 273. Egbert Hedding, organist at Hasselt in 1627 (d. 1658), is erroneously classed there as a dilettante.

exists[1] prior to the recently discovered Leningrad MS., dating from after 1650. [2]

Probably the most important of Sweelinck's Dutch pupils was his eldest son, Dirck, who assumed the post of organist at the Oude Kerk from his father's death in 1621 until his own in 1652. He filled this position very well, if we may judge from the high praise of his music in poems by the most cultured of his contemporary countrymen, Hooft and Vondel. [3] His four extant choral works support this esteem, in particular the *Cecilia Liedt* and a three-part canon on *Oculus non vidit*. [4] These closely follow the style of his father's music, and it is probable that his keyboard compositions did likewise. This would be confirmed if the set of anonymous variations on Nicolai's 'Wie schön leuchtet' should turn out to be attributable to him. [5]

We can only speculate, then, on the nature of Dutch keyboard music during the interim years 1621–c. 1650. Presumably the style of Sweelinck and of the English virginalists held sway during this period. When the scene is again illuminated in the 1650s by the survival of three keyboard sources, we find that remarkably little essential change has taken place in musical style. The repertory of a non-professional keyboard player, as represented by the Dutch portion of the Leningrad MS., still included pieces by Sweelinck, along with popular tunes and dances, many of them English and all of them set in a simple style derived from English virginal music. The 'Engels Voishe' ('English Tune'), although unidentified as yet, sounds like a masque tune from c. 1610–25. [6] The melody is ornamented completely in the English manner, and the left-hand accompaniment, primarily chordal, shows little change in texture from that of the simplest dances of the sixteenth century. Strongly tonal harmonic patterns, regular sequences of short motives, and the frequent use of

---

[1] Unless *Ly A 1* should prove to date from before 1650. See Reinken.
    [2] Cf. *MMN* III.   [3] See vdSM, 49–53.
    [4] All four are available in modern editions; see vdSM, 258.
    [5] See above, p. 77.   [6] See *MMN*, III, 65 f.

sixth-chords mark the work as Jacobean rather than Elizabethan in origin. The style of keyboard writing—the one
aspect of the piece which might be mid-century Dutch—
shows little advance over the past fifty years or more.

Still more retrospective is the sprightly little piece titled
'Rosemont'. [1] The tune, the structure of the work, and to an
extent even the keyboard setting are all closely related to
Giles Farnaby's *Tower Hill* (before 1609) from the *Fitzwilliam
Virginal Book*. [2] Even the key is the same. *Rosemont* is more
regular and uniform than Farnaby's work: steady eighth-note
motion prevails, three-part texture is more consistently
adhered to, and F-sharp appears throughout, in contradistinction to Farnaby's ambiguous but pleasant shifts to F-
natural. All of these traits would tend to date *Rosemont* later
and suggest that it might well have been written around the
middle of the century, only a few years before the manuscript
was compiled. If so, the resemblances to Farnaby are all the
more remarkable. In the repeat of the first strain the anonymous *Rosemont* setting employs a motive different from Farnaby's, but an identical technique. Moreover, even the motive
with its *stretto* imitations in parallel thirds has a precedent in
Farnaby's work, as shown by the last example below (note
values doubled for purposes of comparison).

---

[1] *Ibid.*, 64.
[2] A simpler version is in BM, Add. 30,486, f. 20, titled merely 'A Gigge'.

Farnaby, Lord Zouche's Maske:

The second strain, too, is much in the style of Farnaby. At the close, however, a somewhat more original scalar flourish rises to the upper G. Since it occurs also in the *Wilhelmus* setting in the same manuscript, it may be a peculiarly Dutch cadential pattern of the period. Even so, it could hardly be said to represent any very significant departure from a style thoroughly permeated with English elements.

The Camphuysen MS.[1] differs considerably in character from the Leningrad collection, although it was probably compiled at the same time. It, too, appears to be the notebook of a dilettante; but whereas the Leningrad MS. was wholly secular, this collection is almost exclusively given over to settings of sacred or devotional melodies. Of the 36 pieces it contains, only *Daphne*, based on an English tune 'When Daphne did from Phoebus fly', and *Brabantse Dragonders Mars* ('March of the Brabantine Dragoons') have no evident religious connexions. Other secular tunes are present, but they are given titles taken from Camphuysen's *Stichtelycke Rymen* where these tunes are coupled with devotional poems. This is not to say they are treated any differently, however, for there is no apparent divergence in style between settings of sacred and of secular melodies. The tune for Camphuysen's 'Moet m'in alles sich verzaken' ('One must renounce one's self in all things') is none other than the popular 'Est-ce Mars', and the anonymous setting resembles that by Farnaby which bears the English title *The New Sa-Hoo*. However, since the presence even in this short simple setting of *stretto* imitations is clearly a Dutch trait, the work may hark back to the first variation of Sweelinck's *Est-ce Mars* rather than to Farnaby.

[1] See a description of the MS. and edition of six works from it in *MMN* III, xvii–xix, xl f., and 73–82.

By far the most interesting and important of all the works in the Camphuysen MS. is the set of variations on *Daphne*.[1] In quality, difficulty, and length it so far exceeds the other pieces that one cannot help wondering why it was included in the collection at all. Since it does not resemble the Camphuysen settings, and since Dutch sources frequently transmit an international repertory, we cannot even be sure that the work originated in the Netherlands. Yet certain stylistic elements do point in this direction. In general, the work seems later in style than comparable variation sets by the English school: motives are more consistently and congruously employed, and they are often extended in long, merging series of sequences. These traits we have found distinguishing Sweelinck's works from those of the Virginalists, and they were developed—sometimes to extremes—by his pupils, particularly Scheidt. There is also a tendency in the *Daphne* variations toward maintenance of two- and three-part texture with only incidental use of four-part chords, a tendency which gains ground in the keyboard music of nearly all countries as the century progresses.

The work would therefore appear to date from approximately the middle of the century. Among the Virginalists, only Tomkins might come into question as possible author. The variations on *Daphne* are, in fact, not essentially dissimilar in technique to those by Tomkins on *Barafostus' Dream* (after 1612); but Tomkins, as is well known, returned to an ever more conservative style in his later years, and the presence of a relatively early work of his as a *unicum* in a Dutch mid-century source is most unlikely. More probable chronologically would be Scheidemann, but the work is of a much lighter, lilting character than anything we know of his. Only his variations on *Kit's Almand*[2] are comparable to *Daphne* in technique, and they are stolid by comparison. Finally, two

---

[1] Recorded by Gustav Leonhardt (Telefunken, 1967) and, on a Couchet harpsichord from The Hague, Gemeente Museum collection, by Marijke Smit Sibinga (Dutch Columbia, 1963). Ed. MMN III, pp. 79–82.
[2] See above, p. 53, n. 1.

small details may argue in favour of Dutch origin for the *Daphne* variations. The version of the tune here employed, with octave leaps in the second strain, is found in nearly all the Dutch sources, but in none of the English. Also, significantly, the cliché used at cadences—a drop from the fifth to the third—is present throughout the Camphuysen MS., and in some contemporary Dutch sources. [1] If *Daphne* is indeed a Dutch work, then its anonymity is all the more regrettable, for it could have given a voice at last to one of those many composers from this muted age, known to us only by their names.

The third and most important mid-century Dutch keyboard source is the *Tabulatuur-Boeck* (Amsterdam, 1659) by Anthoni van Noordt (d. 1675). [2] In this engraved tablature book, van Noordt said,

[I] tried to demonstrate some samples of several Psalms, in various verses, varied as well in the Superius and Tenor as in the Bassus, along with some Fantasies: for which I believe the Practitioners of this art will therefore be the more pleased; because such Tablatures (which cannot be published in the usual manner of printing, but must be printed with plates engraved especially) have up until now been issued in print by no one in our Country (although there has been here no lack of outstanding Masters [*Geesten*] in this art). [3]

[1] Cf. Van Noordt or the works of Steenwick in Anna Maria van Eyl's book (*MMN*, II). The ending of Steenwick's 'Allemand' is very similar to the end of 'Vers 2' of *Daphne*. This provides further reason for considering the latter to be Dutch, though an attribution to the mediocre Steenwick is out of the question.
[2] Seiffert's edition (1896) was reprinted in 1957 with an introduction by R. Lagas. An edition by Pidoux (1954) includes all the psalm settings but omits the six fantasies.
[3] '... getracht hebbe te vertoogen eenige proeven van etlicke Psalmen, door verscheyden versen, soo in de Superius, Tenor als Bassus verandert, beneffens eenige Fantasijen: dewelcke ick houde dat de Oeffenaers deser konste daerom te aengenamer sullen zijn; om dat dusdanige Tabulaturen (terwijlse niet op de gewoonlicke wijse van drucken konnen gemeen gemaekt, maer met platen hier toe afsonderlick gesneden, moeten ghedruckt worden) tot noch toe van niemand hier te Lande (daer het nochtans aen uytstekende Geesten in dese Konste niet heeft ontbroken) in druk zijn uytgegeven.' (Van Noordt's dedication to four burgomasters and rulers of the city of Amsterdam.)

Van Noordt does not mention Speuy's *Psalmen* of 1610, but this does not mean they were unknown to him, for his tablature ranks anyway as the earliest *engraved* Dutch keyboard edition. The peculiar notation which he employs—the English-Dutch keyboard score with six-line staves for the manuals and the German letter notation for the pedals [1]—is symptomatic of his stylistic traits. While maintaining a few of the figural techniques of the Virginalists and of Sweelinck, he has also absorbed the more recent German emphasis on the pedals, on motives with stepwise movement, and on unity of *Affekt*. Van Noordt might be the 'musician of Amsterdam' who, according to an anecdote related by Burney, so much admired Scheidemann. [2] The latter's music would in any case have been well known to him. The very year his tablature appeared, there was published in Amsterdam a eulogy of the Rotterdam organist, Crabbe, by a certain J. Dullaart; he mentions various contemporaries, including Van Noordt, but his highest praise of Crabbe is: 'how flatteringly you follow Jesses' son, through organ pipes, shrill in tone! You even rival Scheidemann!' [3]

The difference between Van Noordt's and Sweelinck's styles is best observed by comparing their fantasies. Van Noordt's, like those of Scheidemann and other later Germans, are shorter, more unified, and without much sectional contrast. The steady, consistent movement is almost never interrupted, and a limited number of rhythmic motives prevails throughout. The lines have been stripped of any fanciful figuration, and a well-balanced, sober network of stepwise motives has replaced the vigorous triadic figures of Sweelinck and the English school. The same stylistic transformation can be seen in Dutch architecture: the cool, balanced classicism of Van Campen replaces the more sectional, lively, and highly

---

[1] This combination may already have been used by Sweelinck, but never to such an extent and probably not for more than one or two pieces.

[2] See Reinken, 49.

[3] 'Hoe vleijend volgt gij Jesses zoon, Door Orgelpijpen, schel van stem! Zoo steekt gij Scheidman na de kroon!' (See *Bouwstenen*, I, p. 63.)

decorated 'strapwork' of Hendrick de Keyser and his school. Certain more retrospective stylistic elements do, nevertheless, preserve an aspect of English influence. One of the most striking (and at this late date surprising) is the preservation of cross relations in the English manner, including even the typically English cadence denounced as 'stale' already in 1597 when Morley described it, attributing its introduction to Taverner. [1] As we have seen, this same cadence may be found in Morley's own keyboard works as well as in those of many of his colleagues. In Van Noordt we see it persisting longer in Holland than anywhere else on the Continent.

Although Van Noordt's restrained, sober lines eschew triadic figuration, they are in a few instances enlivened by the same rhythmic displacements characteristic of much earlier English figuration. The use of three-note motives in a simple duple metre, the most common manifestation of these 'contrametric figurations', had been adopted by Sweelinck— usually with a restriction to a single measure and with less playful effect than in the hands of his English predecessors. Van Noordt is still more sparing of the device: he never exceeds the bounds of a measure and his sequential three-note figure is in each case merely a conjunct ascent. The best example may be found in the opening *bicinium* of Psalm 119.

All the retrospective features of Van Noordt's style seem to be concentrated in his *bicinia*. The second two-part 'Vers' of Psalm 38 includes, in fact, the only instance of larger rhythmic displacement—cf. the middle of m. 7 with the beginning of m. 9—and of a line that approaches triadic and 'zigzag' figuration in the English manner. Its first half (to the middle of m. 18) could easily be mistaken for a *bicinium* of *c.* 1600 or earlier, but in the latter half of the 'Vers' Van Noordt breaks up the rigid *cantus firmus*, introduces simple stepwise motives, and returns to a more up-to-date style.

Van Noordt is a composer of considerable originality. He is not just an imitator of English or German styles, nor is he a

---

[1] See above, p. 112; and cf. especially Van Noordt's third *Fantasia*.

slavish follower of Sweelinck. The lucky preservation of his
collection shows us that serious Dutch keyboard music must
have remained on a high level after Sweelinck's death, continuing to build on an English as well as a native Dutch
heritage, but now turning with more and more admiration
toward Germany as the fount of new developments in keyboard music.

On the much lower level of the keyboard dilettante (to
which we must now return for lack of other sources) the
recent developments in Germany had no effect whatsoever.
In notation, ornamentation, and chordal texture, no essential style change is evidenced either in the G. H. Broekhuijzen
MS. (1668–69) [1] or in the closely contemporary opening
section of the Gresse MS. copied by an unknown hand. [2] The
latter may be a few years later than the Broekhuijzen source
since it has a larger preponderance of French dances. But both
treat French, English or Dutch tunes alike in a style obviously
carried over from earlier English-dominated years. The
following 'Engelsche Panttelont' may serve as an example,
illustrating at the same time the jejune level of these tiny
pieces. The second half is almost identical with part of the
'Brande Champanje', a work which opens the Susanne van
Soldt MS. and therefore dates from probably a century
earlier. One would think that nothing had happened in
dance music during those hundred years.

Anon.,Brande champanje (ca.1570):

Anon.,Engelsche Panttelont(1668-69):

---

[1] Ed. in *Weekblad voor Muziek* (3 and 10 January 1903). The manuscript
was formerly in the possession of J. C. Garms Jr. of Amsterdam but can
no longer be traced.   [2] See *MMN* III, xx.

Even the dilettante's level was seldom so consistently low. Anna Maria van Eyl's book, [1] written at Arnhem in 1671, represents a considerably higher *niveau*, from both technical and aesthetic standpoints. The quality of these pieces, however, also leaves much to be desired. English variation techniques have now degenerated in the hands of mediocre composers to sterile formulas. The result is a stiff, curiously antiquated effect, particularly when these formulas are applied to the latest French tunes. (Cf. Steenwick's *Tricabijlie*, or *La Princesse*, one of his best efforts.) The treatment is more appropriate for *Heiligh, Saligh Bethlehem*, or *More Palatino*; and in the latter Steenwick achieves some modest degree of success in his dilatory attempts to revivify an obsolescent technique. Perhaps a series of variations by Sweelinck on the same tune [2] aided by serving as models. Part of Steenwick's opening (mm. 7–10) with its scalar four-note motive in *stretto* closely resembles the first variation of the anonymous set attributable to Sweelinck. [3] Indeed, all four variations could almost have been written by some younger, and lesser, contemporary of Sweelinck. Only a solitary hint of *style brisé* in one cadence (m. 24) betrays the date of the work.

Elsewhere in the collection, more overt traces of recent French innovations in keyboard style may be found. The presence of a Froberger allemande in the French style is symptomatic, as is the abundance of French tunes, including the popular 'Bell' Iris' from Lully's *Ballet de l'Impatience* (1661). Their incidence increases toward the end of the manuscript— just at the time when French troops were advancing toward Arnhem. [4] But the Lullian invasion anticipated that of Louis XIV. In music, as in other arts, French influence was in its ascendancy during the decade or more immediately prior to the invasion. In fact, French keyboard music had found a

[1] Ed. F. Noske, *MMN*, II.
[2] See J. N. Forkel, *Allgemeine Geschichte der Musik* II (Leipzig, 1801), p. 703.
[3] S. 6 = N. 7.
[4] They occupied the city in 1672, and Miss van Eyl's collection was terminated about this time, or at any rate before 1675.

Dutch champion already much earlier in the personage of Sir Constantine Huygens whom we encountered in Chapter I as a young prodigy playing the English viol in the presence of Sweelinck.[1] By the end of his long and active life, this nonagenarian had seen many musical fashions come and go. Having learned the cittern at five, the viol at six, the lute at eight, and at ten the organ and harpsichord, his early environment was not only markedly musical but was also strongly Anglophile. Later, his musical interests turned more toward Paris. We know from his correspondence[2] that he ardently imported the latest French music for lute and *clavecin* in the 1640s and 1650s and himself composed allemandes, courantes, sarabandes, and especially gigues—but not a note of these instrumental pieces is known to have survived. His allemandes and courantes were always bipartite with twelve bars per section, he tells us; but as for what these dances sounded like—we can only assume they must have resembled the works we know by his friends and correspondents, De la Barre and Du Mont. The latter, in fact, borrowed the opening of an allemande by Huygens for one of his own. Unfortunately, since it had a 24-bar opening and a 17-bar closing section—according to Huygens, who disapproved—it cannot be among the preserved allemandes of Du Mont.

In addition, we know the specific titles of some French pieces Huygens played and perhaps composed himself, quoted in a letter to his beloved English pupil Utricia Ogle (Mrs. William Swann) in March 1654: 'Whensoever you come and find me alife, you are to heare wonderfull new compositions, both upon the Lute (in the new tunes) and the virginals,— lessons, which if they will not please your eares with their harmonie, are to astonish your eyes with their glorious titles, speaking nothing less than Plaintes de Mad. la Duchesse de Lorraine, Plaintes de Mad. la Princesse sa fille, Tombeaux et

[1] See above, p. 33 f.; and Bachrach, *passim*.
[2] Portions concerned with music ed. Jonckbloet and Land (Leiden, 1882). The complete ed. by J. A. Worp in 6 vols. (The Hague, 1911–17) also contains additional musical material subsequently discovered.

funerailles de M. Duarte, and such gallantrie more.'[1] By 'new tunes' Huygens means the recent French triadic tuning (*ton nouveau*) which he had called 'plus harmonieux' in 1653, after using it only for a few weeks. By 1656, however, he had decided that the old quartal tuning was plus 'riche'. Béatrice de Cusance, Duchesse de Lorraine, and her daughter, Princesse de Lillebonne (born 1639), were close friends of Huygens and ardent amateurs of the *clavecin*. In this very winter, 1653–54, the Duchess had engaged one of the finest harpsichord makers in Europe, Jean Denis, to come to Nancy for an extended period and repair her harpsichord.[2] It is probable, then, that the 'Plaintes' were for *clavecin* rather than lute. Caspar Duarte had died the preceding November, and Huygens may have been preparing a published musical *Tombeau* for him. In a letter to Du Mont in 1655 he said of the latter's pavan: 'je l'ay envoyée joindre aux pieces dediées au Tombeau de M. Duarte, où elle a esté fort bien receüe.' Presumably the 'Plaintes' were also intended for this *Tombeau*, although it is not at all clear whether they were composed in France and sent to Huygens by the Duchesse or whether he composed them himself.

Another non-professional musician, of lesser musical talent no doubt, but with great skill as a painter, was Gesina Terburg or Ter-Borch (1633–90), sister of the famous artist. To judge from the titles listed by André Pirro,[3] her keyboard book was full of French music: 'La Gavotte d'Anjou, La Boisvinette, Belle Iris, La Mostarde Nouvelle.' (Pirro gave no source for his information and the manuscript cannot be located.) The repertory would indicate that the book was compiled at some time shortly after 1661[4] and consisted only of simple settings of popular tunes in the manner of those in

---

[1] Quoted by J. A. Worp, 'Nog eens Utricia Ogle en de muzikale correspondentie van Huygens', *TVNM*, V (1897), p. 134.
[2] See the author's forthcoming introduction to a facsimile reprint of Denis' *Traité de l'accord de l'espinette* (Paris, 1653).
[3] *Les Clavecinistes* (Paris, 1927), p. 44; cf. also 'Louis Couperin à Paris', *Revue Musicale*, I (1920–21), p. 148, n. 3.
[4] 'Bell' Iris' comes from Lully's *Ballet de l'Impatience* of that year.

the Broekhuijzen book and its counterpart, the opening of the Gresse MS.

Later Dutch keyboard music [1] tends increasingly toward eclecticism and toward mediocrity. Never again does it approach the heights to which Sweelinck, for a brief but glorious period, had brought it; never again does it equal even Van Noordt in excellence or originality. Certainly this flowering at the beginning of the seventeenth century is not due solely to the genius of a single man; or even to the widespread influence of his teaching. The flowering is not confined to keyboard music alone, but extends to nearly all aspects of artistic creation. It had been a vigorous 'Golden Age'; and precisely in the loss of this vigour did Huizinga see the cause for the eighteenth century's artistic decline, beginning already in the 1670s. [2] There was no loss of wealth, luxury, or artistic cultivation, it is true; but the remarkable energy of the earlier age became softened (if not submerged) upon the arrival of a more courtly elegance and the refined fashions of French taste. The aureate splendour of the *Gouden Eeuw* is gradually eclipsed by the rise of the *Roi Soleil* and his age of grandeur.

Dutch art is seldom, if ever, grand or heroic, and at its best does not strive for elegance. Perhaps for this reason, late seventeenth-century French music had an essentially debilitating influence on Dutch keyboard composers, whereas the rough, pungent vigour of Elizabethan virginal music proved to be highly beneficial. In has been the principal aim of this study to point out the extent of that influence and to elucidate its nature. That we have been so largely concerned with the works of Sweelinck is testimony to his dominating position in Dutch music, and an unavoidable, happy consequence of his genius.

[1] See, for instance, *Niederländische Klaviermusik um 1700* (Berlin, 1931); or the author's edition of three suites by Pierre Bustijn (*c.* 1710) in *Exempla Musica Neerlandica*, I (Amsterdam, 1964).
[2] *Verzamelde Werken*, II, especially pp. 505–7.

APPENDICES

APPENDIX I

C. H. Edskes:

i. *The Organs of the Oude Kerk in Amsterdam at the Time of Sweelinck*

(translated by C. W. Schoneveld)

There is certainly no reason for confining Sweelinck's music to the possibilities of the instruments he used in his professional capacity as organist, or to form decisive judgements from the nature of these particular organs as to which compositions were intended for organ and which for other keyboard instruments. However, since throughout his musical career Sweelinck was associated as organist with only one church, the Oude Kerk in Amsterdam, a study of the organs there is useful for obtaining an insight into the manner in which Sweelinck's keyboard music was meant to be performed.

Although several authors have already devoted considerable attention to the history of these two instruments, [1] there is still room left for further investigation. The extant primary sources are also worth reconsidering, as the transcriptions published have often been lacking in due accuracy. They are given in full as part ii of this appendix.

The history of the large organ in the Oude Kerk begins in the last few months of 1539 when an agreement was made up for its construction. [2] It was entrusted to a combination of organ-builders, probably to provide the maximum of certainty for a succesful completion of the job. Their names are Henrick Niehoff and Hans van Coelen. The former's brother Herman Niehoff was, if necessary, also to be involved. According to M. A. Vente, Hans van Coelen (= Cologne) may have been the same as Hans Suys from Nürnberg and Jan van Zwanenbroek from Cologne. [3] (Both 'Hans' and 'Jan' are shortened forms of Johannes.) Judging

---

[1] See B. Bijtelaar in *Het Orgel*, XLIX (1953), pp. 137–39, 151–53, 165–67; and L (1954), pp. 1–4. M. A. Vente, *Proeve van een repertorium van de archivalia betrekking hebbende op het Nederlandse orgel en zijn makers tot omstreeks 1630* (Brussels, 1956), pp. 9–15.

[2] The contract is undated, but was no doubt concluded shortly before that for the organ-case, dated 29 Dec. 1539.

[3] Vente, *Die Brabanter Orgel* (Amsterdam, 1958), pp. 64–75.

from the evidence available, this is indeed possible, but by no means certain. In a cultural centre like Cologne one or two of the no doubt many organ-builders may well have been called Hans. Jan Zwanenbroek (or Zwanenberg) was established in Cologne and perhaps descended from the village of Schwanenberg between Cologne and Aachen, near Erkelens, whereas Hans Suys clearly stems from Nürnberg. The latter is mentioned as organ-builder in the accounts of the St. Bartolomäus-Stift at Frankfurt a.M. as early as 1498. [1] After 1520 his name does not occur any more, but this does not prove that he was no longer alive in 1539, the year of the contract. In any case, whether Hans Suys and Hans van Coelen are identical or not, the organ-builder involved was advanced in years, for Wagenaar calls him (Jan) Bestevaer, [2] which means grandfather. Elsewhere he is named 'Myster Hans den Ouden' (= Master Hans Senior). [3] He possibly established himself in Amsterdam as a result of the commission to build the Oude Kerk organ, for one 'Jan van Colst, oergelmaeker' became a citizen on 25 September 1542, [4] while at about the same time a 'Mr. Jan, orgelmaker' lived on the east-side of the Oudezijds-burgwal. [5]

The other organ-builder, Henrick Niehoff, was well-known at Amsterdam. He received his training from Jan Kavelens (also called van Cavelen). [6] Niehoff was, according to the contract, resident as an organ-builder at Den Bosch. It is not clear how and when the collaboration with Hans van Coelen was established. Vente supposes that this happened during Henrick Niehoff's trip to Maastricht and Liege in 1537 and 1538, which he undertook to get acquainted with the new stops in the organs there. [7] At any rate, this was not the first project they shared. This appears from the 1539 contract, where it is expressly stipulated that they

---

[1] Theodor Peine, *Der Orgelbau in Frankfurt am Main und Umgebung von den Anfängen bis zur Gegenwart* (Frankfurt a. M., 1956), pp. 38, 40.

[2] Jan Wagenaar, *Amsterdam in zijne opkomst, aanwas, geschiedenissen etc. beschreven*, II (Amsterdam, 1765), p. 100.

[3] Ch. M. Dozy, 'Jan Pietersz. Sweelinck en andere organisten der 16e eeuw', *Oud Holland*, III (Amsterdam, 1885), p. 281. This document can no longer be traced.

[4] Amsterdam, Gemeentearchief, tresoriersrekening 1542, f. 30ᵛ.

[5] *Ibid.*, kohier van de 10de penning.

[6] Vente, *Die Brabanter Orgel*, on p. 49 reproduces the autograph of Jan van Kavelen, but misreads it as 'Jan Franckens'. Unfortunately, the latter has already found its way into the literature.

[7] M. A. Vente, *Bouwstoffen tot de geschiedenis van het Nederlandse orgel in de 16de eeuw* (Amsterdam, 1942), p. 145.

shall not undertake new projects, but will be allowed to finish the organs at Schoonhoven and Naaldwijk. It was not only the art of his teacher Jan Kavelens, but also that of Hans van Coelen which must have greatly influenced Niehoff and helped him to develop into one of the most important organ-builders of his time.

Of his descent nothing certain is known. Vente connects the name with Niehove, [1] one of the villages from which Leeuwarden was constituted. This is not very likely, for the name Niehoff would rather suggest Overijsel or Westphalian origin. Moreover, in the contract for the construction of the small organ he is called Hendrick van Niewenhuis, which again makes a Leeuwarden descent unlikely. On the other hand, his brother Herman Niehoff, the third organ-builder, was established precisely at Leeuwarden, as early as 1532. About him little else is known. Once more we find him in conjunction with Henrick. This was the year before the Amsterdam contract, when he received payments for the organ built in the church at Breukelen, [2] because Henrick was then abroad, as we have seen. His role in the construction of the Oude Kerk organ must have been a very minor one. He did not sign the contract and may not even have been present at the occasion. but probably served only as an extra guarantee.

The agreement for making an organ case was drawn up on 29 December 1539. So the contract for the organ itself, which is undated, must have been concluded before that time. Henrick Niehoff had apparently left Amsterdam in the interval, as the later contract was only signed by Hans van Coelen. The contract bears various signatures. On the left—the less prestigious side— the two organ-builders signed, along with the organists Arent Lambrechtz. of the Oude Kerk and Claes Jansz. of the Nieuwe Kerk. The latter, judging from the handwriting and from what is possibly an abbreviation of 'fecit' behind his signature, also penned the contract. The right-hand side shows the signatures of the churchwardens of the Oude Kerk, and also those of the brothers Quyrijn Arijsz. and Hubrecht Arentz. Verhoech, regents from Delft, who were probably involved as experts. They may also have played a part in the building of the organ at Naaldwijk, as this village lies very near Delft. Over Quyrijn Arijsz.'s signature is an autograph, probably reading C. H., which could be explained as Cornelis Hendricksz., priest of the Oude Kerk. That he was one of the undersigned may also be gathered from the text.

[1] Vente, *Die Brabanter Orgel*, p. 76.
[2] 's Hertogenbosch, Rijksarchief, rechterlijke archieven van de stad Den Bosch, invent. no. R. 1330, f. 18, 30 Oct. 1538.

According to the contract the disposition of the organ was as follows:

Great [1]
a 12 foot 'Doef' of fine tin
an Octave with a Superoctave
a Mixture
a Scharff
These four will constitute the Principal chorus ['Great']

Pedal, 2 basses by themselves
a 6 foot Trumpet
a Nachthorn

Oberwerk, a windchest [2] with seven stops
a 6 foot Rohrflute
a Gemshorn
a Sifflöte
a Zimbel
a full Trumpet [3]
a Zink
a 3 foot Flute

Rückpositiv of 6 foot with 8 stops
a 6 foot Principal of fine tin
a 3 foot 'Coppeldoef' [Principal]
a Scharff
These four will constitute the Principal chorus
a 3 foot Quintadena
a 3 foot Schalmei
a Regal
a Bärpfeife sounding 6 foot

Coupler between the upper and lower keyboard
Tremulant
6 Bellows
Compass of the Great: 4 Octaves
Compass of the Pedalboard: a Twelfth

---

[1] The Dutch term here is 'Principael' (sometimes also called 'Naturael'). It is used for the Great, which originally consisted of one large undivided Mixture. In the Oude Kerk organ it was already divided into rows of pipes that could be used separately.
[2] The Dutch has 'Secreet', which is an old term for windchest, from the Latin 'secretum': to be explained as either 'a secret place where rather mysterious mechanisms, e.g. the spring-chest are stowed away', or, more likely, 'place where "secretion" of wind for the pipes takes place'.
[3] See below p. 189, n. 2.

The churchwardens-archives contain a memorandum about a contract with Henrick Niehoff, undated but earlier than October 1545, for making a number of alterations in the large organ:

1. the Principal chorus will be made stronger as the size of the church demands this.

2. in the Oberwerk a Quintadena, apparently supplied outside the origan specification, will be replaced by a Nasard.

3. in the Rückpositiv the Regal will be renewed, a Krummhorn will be replaced by a Sifflöte, and three of four pipes of the Schalmei will be repaired.

4. overhaul of the entire organ and improvement of the tremulant.

Oddly enough, the first paragraph of the memorandum mentions a new Krummhorn, whereas in the second paragraph it says that this stop will be replaced by a Sifflöte. Probably they changed their mind while the work was already underway. The Krummhorn itself, however, does not appear in the original contract. The work is executed by Henrick Niehoff and Jasper Johanson, also called Jasper Jansz.. In a postscript to the contract of 15 39, dated 28 October 1545, the renewal of the three organ-stops is mentioned as having been finished and the costs, amounting to 16 guilders, as now being paid in the presence of 'Mr. Claes' and 'Mr. Arrent'. These are the organists we already encountered. Jasper Jansz. is a new organ-builder, succeeding Hans van Coelen, who probably died in 1544. According to Vente, he was Van Coelen's son. [1] If this were so, he would have lived for a very long time entirely in his father's shade, for Van Coelen was more than seventy years old by 1544. Moreover, whereas Henrick Niehoff in 1539 designated his brother Herman to replace him in his absence, why did the then already aged Hans van Coelen not designate his (supposed) son Jasper?

As we saw, the organ-case was contracted on 29 December 1539. Its construction is entrusted to Adriaen, otherwise Scalck, from 's-Hertogenbosch. Niehoff collaborated with him several times. [2] One of the witnesses to the contract is Hans van Coelen. Remarkably enough, it was the case, more than the organ itself, which was meant to carry the fame of the organ abroad, as can be read from the contract. That Niehoff did not fail to achieve this, can be inferred from the fact that later on he also received commissions in Hamburg and Lüneburg.

Between 1550 and 1565 the Oude Kerk was thoroughly reconstructed. The organs, too, needed overhauling. For this Pieter

---

[1] Vente, *Die Brabanter Orgel*, p. 65. [2] *Ibid.*, p. 79.

Jansz. from Utrecht was invited. Next to the Niehoff family, this pupil and successor to Cornelis Gerritsz. of Utrecht was one of the most important organ-builders in the Northern Provinces during the second half of the 16th century. [1] Apparently he was preferred to Nicolaes Niehoff and his associate Arend Lampeler van Mill, who together continued Henrick Niehoff's business. [2] The contract, dated 1 September 1567, is an indenture, very gracefully written by Pieter Swijbertsoen of Deventer, Jan Pietersz. Sweelinck's father. It is one of the very few organ indentures of which both halves survive. It describes the organ as follows:

The large windchest of the Great.
The large 'Doef' standing in front: 12 foot
an Octave
a Mixture
a Scharff
These stops constitute the 12 foot Principal chorus ['Great']

Above this Great lie another two windchests, one above the other.
a 6 foot 'Doef'
a 6 foot Rohrflute
a 3 foot open Flute
a Nasard sounding on a fifth
a 1½ foot Gemshorn
a Sifflöte
a Zimbel
a Zink
a Trumpet sounding 6 foot

The Pedal.
a 6 foot Trumpet with a Nachthorn

The Rückpositiv also has two windchests.
a 6 foot 'Doef' of tin, standing in front
a 3 foot Octave
a Mixture
a Scharff
These stops constitute the Principal chorus
a 6 foot Quintadena
a 3 foot Rohrflute
a Sifflöte
a Bärpfeife
a 6 foot Regal: for this he shall make a 6 foot Krummhorn of tin
a 3 foot Schalmei

[1] Vente, *Bouwstoffen*, pp. 80, 81, 82.
[2] Vente, *Die Brabanter Orgel*, p. 94.

In addition to the repairing of defects, six new organ-bellows with their trunks are to be installed, to supply the work with a perfect wind. The tremulant is also to be renewed. By comparison with the disposition of 1539/1545, the following points may be noted: As far as the large Principal-chorus is concerned, which was made stronger in 1544/45, there is no longer any question of an Octave with a Superoctave, but of an Octave only. This alteration had probably also been made in 1544/45. In the Rückpositiv we now find a 6 foot Quintadena instead of the 3 foot one in the 1539 contract. It is, however, possible that '3 foot' indicated its length, which in a stopped register like a Quintadena would still imply, a 6 foot sound. The 3 foot Rohrflute which is now also mentioned may have been added in 1539 above the contract. The Regal, renewed in 1544/45, is now replaced again by a 6 foot Krummhorn. In the Oberwerk we find nine instead of seven registers, which must have necessitated the division into the two chests now mentioned. This concerns a Quintadena and a 6 foot 'Doef' (= Principal). The Doef was probably not actually placed in the front, for unlike the other front registers, this is not indicated as being situated there. The specification 'of tin' is lacking too. Unfortunately, there are no indications about the size of the keyboard and the couplers.

In 1568, Pieter Jansz. de Swart finished the job and received the total amount of money owed him. From the church accounts of the Oude Kerk it appears that from 1582 until his death in 1586 a certain Harman Jansz. took care of maintenance. But in 1588 Pieter Jansz. de Swart again carried out repairs, at the sum of 125 guilders, his assistants receiving another 5 guilders each. On 17 November 1595 a Jan Pietersz. was paid 6 guilders and 15 pence for 'a certain reparation to the organ'. The repairer was in all likelihood Sweelinck. This is the only time he occurs as organ-maker. On 29 July 1613 14 guilders were paid 'for adjusting some pipes of the large organ, they being out of tune'. The name of the organ-builder is not mentioned.

In 1619, shortly before Sweelinck's death, fairly extensive repairs were carried out by Dirck Petersz. de Swart and his associate Jacob Jansz. van Lin. The former was Pieter Jansz. de Swart's son who, after his father's death in 1597, continued his business together with the latter, his nephew. [1] According to the account-book, the organ was renovated and repaired and the bellows covered with new leather. The cost amounted to 450 guilders. Although a contract is mentioned, it has not been found—which

---

[1] Vente, *Bouwstoffen*, p. 78.

is a great pity. It might have informed us about Sweelinck's opinions on the organ which he played for so many years. The amount paid suggests that, in addition, minor changes in disposition were made, but about their nature we remain in the dark.

On 26 June 1646 a Mr. Adam Haesebeen, organ-builder, was paid 10 guilders for small repairs to both the large and the small organ. Particulars are lacking. In 1659 an extensive job was done by the organ-builder Jacobus van Hagerbeer. [1] Again a contract could not be found, but lists of the wages paid do exist. They show the great extent of the work, and when it was started (29 June 1659) and finished (January 1662). They also give the names of Hagerbeer's assistants: Roelof Barentsz. (Duyschot), [2] Gerrit (without patronym) and the junior assistant Jan (perhaps Jan Slegel [3]). Fortunately, in the archives of the Oude Kerk there is a 'remonstrance and reminder' by Jacobus van Hagerbeer, in which he mentions the operations he carried out outside the specifications. They are as follows.

The compass of the Oberwerk was extended from F to G. For the nine stops of this division 139 new pipes were made. The stop-rollers underneath the chests as well as the other stop-rollers of this keyboard were renewed. The roller board was altered, also in connexion with the extension of the keyboard. The front pipes were fixed anew. The broken and decayed 'tuimelaars' (hooks) of the stop-mechanism of the Great were replaced by iron ones. The roller board of the Great got a number of new rollers. The windchest was improved and the stop-knobs corresponding directly with the stop-rollers were fortified with iron. Three 'Sperr-ventile' were placed and the tremulant was again renewed. The keyboards were placed into alignment above each other. The pedalboard and the corresponding roller board were renewed. The stop mechanism of the Rückpositiv was altered and partly renewed. New stops added were: a Trumpet, a Sesquialtera and a Principal-quint. The case of the Rückpositiv was altered. The bellows received new counterweights to obtain a more stable wind. In total 312 new pipes were added.

---

[1] The Hagerbeer family to a great extent determined the modes of organ construction in 17th century Holland. They stemmed from Norden in Oostfriesland. Galtus Germersz. established himself at Amersfoort in the late 16th century. His sons Gerner Galtus and Jacobus continued his business. They died out with Jacobus in 1670.

[2] Roelof Barentsz. Duyschot, from Goor in Overijsel, was Jacobus Hagerbeer's foreman and he carried on the Hagerbeer tradition together with his two sons.

[3] Jan Slegel later was an organ-builder at Kampen.

The next important reconstruction took place between 1682 and 1686. On 7 October 1682 a contract was concluded with the organ-builders Nicolaes van Hagen and Apollonius Bos. The following changes were made:
All keyboards were extended upwards with the tones G-sharp, B-flat, B, and C. Middle keyboard and Rückpositiv were extended downwards from F to C. In the Rückpositiv the Flute 4' was replaced by an 8 foot Rohrflute; in the Oberwerk a new Quintadena and Vox Humana were installed. The disposition of the middle keyboard as mentioned indicates that in addition to the 12 foot Principal, 6 foot Octave, Mixture, and Scharff, an 8 foot Trumpet was also present. Finally, all windchests were renewed. During the work Nicolaes van Hagen died, probably early in 1684.[1] Since it proved possible in the course of construction to add more stops, a further agreement was made with Apollonius Bos. The organ was ready on 29 July 1686. It was formally approved with high praise by the organists Gerbrand van Blankenberg of Gouda, Joan Dusart of Haarlem, Cornelis van Nek of the Nieuwe Kerk at Amsterdam, and Jan Jansz. Backer of the Nieuwe Zijdskapel.
What the organ looked like after this reconstruction cannot be ascertained from the records. A printed document of 1701 containing a 'legend on both sides under the large organ in the Oude Kerk at Amsterdam' has it that after Nicolaes van Hagen's death, Apollonius Bos was assisted by Gerard van Giesen, and that after delivery the organ was extended with five stops. It also states that in 1700 Gerard van Giesen succeeded in adding a totally independant Pedal, consequently enlarging the disposition with another ten stops. According to the 'legend' the organ now had forty stops in all.
It is hardly to be believed that this instrument, still regarded in the agreement of 1682 as one of the best organs in Christendom, should have been replaced so soon as in 1724. Yet this did happen. An entirely new organ was built by the pupil of Schnitger, Christian Vater from Hannover, and the old organ was dismantled by Christian Müller, later famous as the builder of the organ in the St. Bavokerk, Haarlem. Very probably he removed two stops to the small organ. Remains of these, a 3 foot Quint and a 2 foot Octave, are now still to be found in the Oosterkerk organ at Aalten.

[1] Amsterdam, Gemeentearchief, archief van de Kerkmeesteren der Ned. Herv. Gem., Oude Kerk inv. no. K 3–9 (shortly after 1 Febr. 1684). Appollonius Bos, continuing the business, in 1686 built the organ in the Dutch Reformed Church at Vollenhove.

The small organ in the Oude Kerk—situated on the north wall not far from the choir—was also built by Henrick Niehoff and his associate Jasper Johanson. The contract for its construction was concluded on 5 November 1544. Only Jasper was present, undersigning also on behalf of Henrick. The price was very low: 90 carolus guilders. This was because two other instruments in the church were taken over by the builders. According to a postcript the organ was ready and approved of on 28 October 1545. It is described in the agreement as follows:

An entirely new work of 3 foot, sounding 6 foot, with two keyboards.

A windchest with an upper chest with nine stops.
a 'Doef' of fine tin
a 6 foot Rohrflute
a 6 foot Quintadena
a 'Coppeldoef'
a Mixture
a Scharff
a Gemshorn
a Zimbel
a 3 foot Schalmei

The second keyboard shall have a windchest by itself with 3 stops
a 3 foot Rohrflute
a Sifflöte
a good Regal sounding 6 foot

Also a Pedal speaking with a 6 foot Bass Trumpet
Manual coupler
Tremulant
3 Bellows, and if necessary a fourth.

Finally the builders shall undertake to provide a new organ-case, with shutters. They are also to construct the organ balcony.

The second time that the small prgan is described in detail is in the contract of 1567 already mentioned in connexion with the large organ. The agreement with the organ-builder Pieter Jan de Swart, lists:

The stops standing on the chest
a 3 foot Principal
a 6 foot Rohrflute
a Mixture
a Scharff
a 1½ foot Octave
These stops are the Principal chorus

a 6 foot Quintadena
a Zimbel
a Gemshorn
a Sifflöte
a Schalmei

In the Brustwerk, in front:
a Rohrflute
a Regal with
a Krummhorn both sounding 6 foot
a Trumpet in the 6 foot Pedal.

Nothing is said about couplers or compass of the keyboards. The three present bellows are insufficient, according to the builders, and will be replaced by three others taken from the large organ in which, as we have seen, new bellows were installed.

Although after 1567 the small organ occurs more than once in the records, the alterations appear to be so small that changes of disposition can hardly be assumed. Around 1658, however, it was entirely renewed. The resulting instrument has often wrongly been taken to be the organ which Sweelinck played. Originally it was thought to have been constructed by Jacobus van Hagerbeer, on account of his work on the large organ a few years later. But from the records pertaining to that reconstruction it can be concluded that the 1658 instrument was not built by Jacob van Hagerbeer. A careful analysis of surviving pipes tends to show that it was supplied by Hans Wolf Schonat,[1] who also built the large organ in the Nieuwe Kerk at Amsterdam. Several authors have asserted that a relatively large number of pipes of the small Niehoff-organ has been preserved via the 1658-instrument, but a recent article has proved on solid grounds that such cannot be the case.[2]

Analysis of these data and their practical implications, by categories, yields the following results:

The Large Organ

Wind-supply. According to the contract of 1539 the large organ was to be provided with six bellows. Further particulars are not

---

[1] Harpsichord and organ maker from Kitzingen, who settled in Amsterdam and married there in 1662. In Jan. 1659 he bought a house from the Oude Kerk carilloneur Herman, son of Artus Gheerdinck See *Dutch HM*, 50.
[2] J. J. van Os, 'Het kleine orgel in de Oude Kerk te Amsterdam', *Het Orgel*, LXXI (1967), pp. 8–12, 34–37, 62–68, 73, 90–96.

given. But from their number it can be inferred that these already were hinge bellows (single-fold bellows) loaded with weights. The blacksmith's bellows—in Germany called 'Froschmaul' bellows, after their shape—which were used at an earlier stage, would have necessitated a far greater number, because they had to be pumped by the feet of the bellows-blower, and this of course set limits to their size. As there were only six bellows, they must have been fairly big in order to supply a reasonable wind, but apparently not big enough, for they were replaced by six new ones in 1567. These served during Sweelinck's career, until they were recovered with new leather in 1618.

According to the contract, the bellows of the small organ were to be folded 'like those at Delft'. It is not clear which Delft organ is meant—possibly one that the same organ-builder had recently supplied with new bellows. In any case, the reference could indicate that they were hinge bellows with more than one fold—a familiar construction at the time, but later on replaced by single hinge bellows. [1] From the 1567 contract it appears that the bellows of the small organ had also proved too small, but instead of adding the fourth stipulated in the original contract, the builders now replaced them by three of those that had served for the large organ and had a greater capacity. The requirements had apparently become more strict. The wind-supply of the large organ, too, had to be 'good and perfect'. It can, however, hardly have been completely even. It must have given a pleasant, slightly undulating movement and lively quality to the sound, depending on the style of playing and the stops used. At the reconstruction by Jacobus van Hagerbeer the bellows were supplied with counter-weights to render the effect of the blowing less audible.

About the wind-pressure of old organs many unfounded speculations have been made, which alas have often resulted in disastrous organ restorations. Generally speaking the wind-pressure was comparatively high, especially in the days of the simple 'blacksmith's' bellows. When, probably in the late 15th century, hinge bellows came into use, the pressure could be somewhat lowered, but not much, so that the organs in the Oude Kerk must have been played on a fairly high wind-pressure. This is the opposite of Vente's conclusion, arrived at through the general relation between manner of playing and wind-pressure. [2] The relevance of this relationship is less applicable in the present case

---

[1] Michael Praetorius, *Syntagma Musicum*, II: *De Organographia* (Wolffen-büttel, 1619), p. 179.
[2] Vente, *Die Brabanter Orgel*, p. 138.

because the ventils of the Niehoff organs are rather small and very narrow. This indeed points to a high pressure, as does the distribution of the pipes over two chests, the upper getting its wind by way of an air-duct from the lower. All this, together with the physical properties of certain old pipes that almost certainly stem from the large organ in the Oude Kerk (now at Aalten, as stated earlier), points towards a figure of about 90 mm. water-pressure. This was normal for 16th-century organs in large churches, and even in smaller ones it was hardly any lower.[1]

That tremulants were intensively used is once more proven by the frequent repairs which that of the Oude Kerk organ underwent. It was probably situated in the trunks, for when in 1567 the bellows and connecting trunks were renewed, the tremulant had to be replaced as well. When it was again renovated a century later by Hagerbeer, three 'Sperrventile' were fitted as well—whether new or renewed is not clear. In the records about 16th-century organs they do not often occur, except when two divisions had to be operated from one keyboard, in which case they were used to disconnect one of the divisions. But in the Oude Kerk instrument all divisions had their own keyboard, so that there seems to have been no direct need for 'Sperrventile'. They are therefore likely to have been first installed by Hagerbeer for purposes of registration.

Windchests. The only statement we have about the nature of the chests is in the contract of 1567, where it says that the Oberwerk has spring-chests. Later, Jacobus van Hagerbeer reports renovation of the stop-rollers underneath the chest of the Oberwerk, which also strongly points to a spring-chest. He also replaced the 'tuimelaars' of the middle chest by iron ones. Unfortunately, what is meant by 'tuimelaars' is not certain, but probably they are the so-called 'winkelhaken' (hooks) which by means of a bar are connected to the stop-rods. In that case the middle keyboard would also have had a spring-chest, as the function of those stop-rods is to command the pallets of the spring-chest by as many pins as there are keys.

The Rückpositiv often had a slider-chest even if the other divisions had a spring-chest, for a number of reasons. A spring-chest is deeper because of the space taken up by the stop-rods, and as organs were mostly built on unsupported balconies—which obviously could not be made too deep—the Rückpositiv was kept

---

[1] Thus the organ of the Dutch Reformed Church at Oosthuizen (probably built in 1521) has a wind of 87 mm. water-pressure.

as flat as possible. This also entailed keeping the partition of the windchest in the treble as small as possible. An 8 foot Quintadena was therefore mostly preferred to wider 8 foot Flute stops as the scaling of the former differs but little from an 8 foot Principal. In the Reeds, too, almost exclusively those with short resonators were used. Trumpets, requiring a wider space in the treble, were exceptional. Another reason for using a slider-chest is that the Rückpositiv can be kept low by mounting its pallet box not underneath but in front of the chest. The latter can then be put directly on the beams of the balcony, which saves height. With a spring-chest this construction would also be possible, but it would seriously impair the accessibility of the pipe pallets. Even if they were placed in the channels—one of the oldest constructions, which can be seen in the surviving spring-chest of the former organ in the Nicolaikerk at Utrecht—the pallets could only be reached by taking away a bung board. This would become impossible if a pallet box were fitted at the front of the chest.

On account of the constructional conditions of the large organ, however, it does seem possible that a spring-chest was used in which the pipe pallets would have lain in the channels, for it is not likely that in those days the pipe pallets were already mounted in a channel-cover which could be removed, or in a pallet rod which could be pulled out. [1]

Mechanism. The construction of the tracker action no doubt was of the kind still used today in mechanical organs. The rollers of the key and stop mechanism were of wood until 1660, in which year Hagerbeer replaced them by iron ones. The Hagerbeers generally preferred iron in the stop mechanism. This appears also from the changes made in 1660/61. The trackers of the middle keyboard probably connected with their roller board through the keys of the Oberwerk. Both roller board and pallet box were placed at the front in most organs of the period, which ensured a very direct contact with the pallets. The pallet box could easily

---

[1] These constructions probably came into use in the late 16th century. Vente (*Die Brabanter Orgel*, p. 137) mentions a document concerning a project, never executed, for an organ in the 's-Hertogenbosch St. Janskerk, where the rods of the chest to which the pipe pallets were connected were to be fixed with screws. He considers this to be a construction with pallet rods that could be pulled out, like those of the organs at Stade and Lemgo. This seems to me incorrect. What is meant is a pallet rod fixed with screws on the chest, as was still the case with the organ of the Nieuwe Kerk at Amsterdam built in 1655. The construction with a pallet rod that could be pulled out is a still later development.

II. The large organ of the Oude Kerk in Amsterdam. Drawing by Jan Goeree, 1700.

be reached by removing the carving or friezes in the lower cornice. In France this construction continued far into the 18th century. It can only be applied if the case of the main organ protrudes but little or not at all over its pedestal. Pictures of the Oude Kerk organ show that, unlike many other Niehoff organs, the pallet box could have been at the front. The organ-balcony would have caused no difficulty in reaching a pallet box in that position. Very likely the trackers of the Oberwerk would then have been conducted to the chest of the Oberwerk past and behind the chest of the middle keyboard, for which reason the pallet box of the Oberwerk must have been placed at the back.

The manner of playing was probably light, as the chests were carrying relatively few ranks, and the pallets were not very large. The pallet openings, which strongly influence the touch, were also not very wide—in spite of what we have seen to be a fairly high windpressure. Nor would the only coupler of the instrument, that of Rückpositiv to Oberwerk, when in use, necessarily have made the touch much heavier.

The measure of the keys is not known, but existing records and fragments from comparable instruments tend to show that their breadth was very much the same as what is still usual. Only the accidentals were slightly broader than today. This caused no difficulties, and indeed made their playing easier, as no use was made of keys with many sharps or flats. Both the accidentals and the naturals were considerably shorter, however, which is in accordance with the totally different fingering employed, as well as the use of keys with few accidentals. As a result of the spring-chest construction, the stops probably were pushed in to be engaged, and pulled out to be disengaged, being notched into position to prevent their falling back. [1]

The Pedal, according to the 1539 contract, had two independent stops. A close examination of the contracts seems to indicate that they might have been placed on the chest of the Great rather than on an independent windchest. The pedal keys may have been shorter than nowadays, but somewhat broader, and their position slightly inclined, becoming horizontal when pressed down. They were played with the tip of the foot—use of the heels is out of the question—sliding from the accidentals down to the naturals.

---

[1] This is also the case with the spring-chest of the Oberwerk of the former organ of the Nicolaikerk at Utrecht. The slider-chest of the organ at Oosthuizen has a similar construction, and, according to Willem Lootens in his *Beschrijving van het Oude en het Nieuwe Orgel in de Grote of St. Lievensmonsterkerk der stad Zierikzee* (Zierikzee, 1771), this was the case too with the Niehoff organ in the St. Lebuinuskerk at Zierikzee.

Contrary to what is sometimes assumed, organists of the time had an excellent pedal technique—adapted of course, to the prevailing practices—which even included the playing of more than one note at a time.

Organ case. A number of pictures of the organ front are extant, most of them by the artist Emanuel de Witte. He gave free rein to his fantasy, however, so that the results are not always very trustworthy. There is also a drawing by J. Goeree, unfortunately not very detailed (see plate II). Yet, by combining these pictures and the various data from the contracts, a good impression of the organ front may be obtained. The Great had nine pipe-flats and the Rückpositiv seven—that is, if the term 'capellen' used in the contract with Adriaen Scalck means 'flats of pipes', which seems to be the only possible explanation. Right in the middle of the Great was a round tower in which the biggest pipes of the 12 foot stop were placed. On either side of this central tower were pointed towers, each filled with two flats of pipes of nearly equal size. On both sides of these stood again two flats, the one on top of the other, the lower having considerably longer pipes than the upper.

The Rückpositiv also had a round middle tower, containing the biggest pipes of the 6 foot stop, and was flanked by two pointed towers. These contained three flats of pipes each. Both the inner sides probably had two small flats of pipes joined at the feet and the outer sides one larger flat. The Rückpositiv as well as the Great were provided with shutters, lined with linen by Adriaen Scalck and decorated with paintings by Maarten van Heemskerk. They served not only for protection but also to direct the sound. The Great organ was topped with five tower-like crownings, the Rückpositiv with three. Like Niehoff's other organ-cases it must have been of oak and covered with painted decorations. Some of the pipes would have been embossed, probably the bigger ones of the towers of the main case and perhaps also of the Rückpositiv. The organ must have had a highly graceful and well-proportioned appearance, even though rather small in relation to the size of the church.

Pipes. Although hardly any pipes of the large organ have been preserved, an impression of what they were like may be obtained from other pipes by Niehoff. The front pipes would have been made of tin of a high degree of fineness for those days. Probably, like most Dutch tin at the time, it was imported from Cornwall. The lips were undoubtedly pointed and may have been gilt. The inner ranks of the Niehoff organs consisted mainly of pure thick-walled lead, which had been hammered first to improve its physical and sonorous properties. Judging from even the present condition of surviving specimens, they must have been of excellent quality.

The scalings of the various Niehoff organs do not show any marked differences. The Principals are on the whole relatively narrow in the bass. The progression of the scaling towards the treble is slight so that these pipes are relatively wide. The result is a sound quality closely related to vocal principles, with a Principal which is somewhat lighter in the bass, and by comparison rather round in the treble. Notably the many double ranks in the treble caused a fairly strong choral effect, which again underlines the vocal quality. As a result, the entire Principal chorus sounded considerably milder than in modern instruments, without, however, losing in transparency. The Flute stops mostly had a wide to very wide scaling, sounding particularly round as they produced only few overtones. Thus the opposition between Principals and Flutes became very pronounced. The Reed stops generally were of a penetrating nature. In the bass the Trumpets were especially powerful. The shallots of the Reeds had small adges, were beak-shaped and were possibly not covered with leather in the basses. All this was to ensure a strong, penetrating tone. The Flue stops had a high cut-up, especially in the treble. The voicing was effectuated with a large supply of wind through the pipe foot and a wide adjustment of the Flues. Nicking was hardly ever used, if at all.

As a result, this and other Niehoff organs, as has also been pointed out by others, had a sound that was vigorous, intensive and clear, yet agreeable, sonorous and not sharp.

Keyboard compass. This is a much debated point with the Sweelinck organs. Klotz and Vente on the basis of the phrase: 'up to four octaves' in the 1539 contract, believed that the Great ran from contra FF to g″, a″ (without g-sharp″). According to Klotz the upper keyboard, moreover, extended from C, D, E, F, G, A to g″, a″. [1] Hagerbeer's remonstrance, however, clearly states that the upper keyboard will be expanded from F down to C, which proves that in Sweelinck's time it ran from F, G, A to g″, a″, the same as the Rückpositiv, about which there is no doubt.

---

[1] Vente, *Die Brabanter Orgel*, 2nd impression (1963), p. 267. In the 1st impression (p. 73) the compass is given as from F to a′. Hans Klotz, 'Sweelinck spielt Sweelinck', *Beiträge zur Rheinischen Musikgeschichte*, Heft 36 (1960), p. 37.

As far as the Great is concerned, the 1682 contract stipulates that it has to be enlarged from F down to C, and all keyboards up to c''', which proves that they originally ran to g'', a''. Now, if one should still adhere to the theory of an original contra octave, this would imply that after 1682 the total compass would have amounted to five octaves, which is so unusual that it can safely be rejected.

Another method for establishing the keyboard compass is by the division of the front which, especially in such early organs, was quite functional, reflecting faithfully the position of the pipes on the windchests. The number of front pipes in the Niehoff organ in the St. Johannis Kirche at Lüneburg would certainly justify the presence of a contra octave. Judging from the size of the middle tower in the fairly simple Amsterdam front, it would have contained seven pipes, the outer lower flats four each, and the pointed towers nine or possibly eleven. This would make a sum total of 33 or 37 pipes respectively. With a compass of F, G, A to g'', a'' there are 38 keys, so that in either case practically the whole of the 12 foot Principal would have been placed in the front. If there would have been another octave at the upper end, then the front, considering the period of its construction, would hardly have been functional. This, then, is another reason for not assuming the presence of a contra octave. Yet the 1539 contract mentions four octaves, which is more than is taken up by F to g'', a'' but less than what would be required for contra FF to g'', a''. Many other contracts give more precise information, for instance four octaves and a third. [1] However, the contract of Niehoff's St. Janskerk organ at Gouda also gives four octaves, but intends the lowest for the 'Bass Trumpet', which cannot mean anything else than the Pedal Trumpet, implying that the Great started one octave higher, and that with the lowest octave the Pedal Trumpet could be played. [2] Whether this was also the case in Amsterdam is uncertain.

[1] The organ of the cathedral in Trier, dating from 1537. Here a keyboard is mentioned with '5 times the f key and a perfect third', and for the Rückpositiv '4 times the f key and a perfect third'. Cf. Hans Klotz, 'Niederländische Orgelbaumeister am Trierer Dom', *Die Musikforschung*, II (Kassel and Basel, 1949), pp. 36–49. Cf. also the Onze Lieve Vrouwe-kerk at Harderwijk (mid-16th century?), with a keyboard of four octaves and a third, and a keyboard of three octaves and a third (The Hague, Algemeen Rijksarchief, inv. no. 834). In *Bouwstenen voor een geschiedenis der toonkunst in de Nederlanden*, ed. C. C. Vlam and M. A. Vente (Utrecht, 1965), p. 93, the 3 was misread as 'enz.' (= etc.). The expression 'of 4 octaves' does occur more often, e.g. with Münster St. Lambertus, 1590: 'ein lanck Clavier vonn 4 octaven', cf. Vente, *Repertorium*, p. 180.
[2] Vente, *Bouwstoffen*, p. 126.

Another noteworthy remark in Hagerbeer's remonstrance is that he had put all keyboards directly above one another. This would mean that until then the middle keyboard had been placed in a position different from that of the Oberwerk and Rückpositiv. It would also explain the fact that the Oberwerk and the Rückpositiv, being as they were in alignment above one another, were coupled together instead of to the middle keyboard, which would have presented great technical problems.

What the exact position of the middle keyboard had been is unknown, but there are grounds for speculation. Starting from the certainty of 38 tones, a shift to the right is not impossible if, like the Gouda organ, it had a bottom octave for the Bass Trumpet. But, of course, it must have been less than an octave, otherwise the keyboards could hardly have been said to be disparate. The interval might have been a fifth, as this was a favoured distance for transposing. If there was no bottom octave for a Bass Trumpet—which would mean that, like several other items of the 1539 contract, the four octaves had been effected in a different way or not at all— it might have been a fourth to the left, again in view of transposition practices. In either case the F of the middle keyboard would lie directly above or below the C of the other two. The conjecture can be further elaborated on the basis of Sweelinck's music. This often shows motivic repetition with an octave shift downwards. In the Echo Fantasies, in which many echoes are thus employed, the effect may seem strange compared to the natural phenomenon of the echo. It could, however, be explained by assuming an octave difference in pitch between the keyboards, since the middle keyboard is based on the 12 foot, the others on the 6 foot, which is precisely the difference of an octave. If the middle keyboard then shifted a fifth to the right, the difference would have been reduced from an octave to a fourth, so that, for instance, the leap of a twelfth became one of an octave. Obviously this would make leaps from one keyboard to another much easier.

The pedalboard had a compass of a twelfth, according to the 1539 contract, and thus must have extended from F, G, A to c'. This keyboard was connected to the middle keyboard (Great), while it had a Trumpet and a Nachthorn as independent stops.

It has often been stated that a compass of F, G, A to g", a"—the normal vocal range—would make it impossible to perform several of Sweelinck's compositions. In some cases this problem is solved if the basic difference of one octave between the middle and the other keyboards is taken into account. Where a range of C, D,

E, F, G, A to g ", a " is required, harpsichord performance may have been intended. This is supported by a contract of the year 1633 for the reconstruction of the Nieuwe Kerk organ at Delft, which stipulated the extension of the upper keyboard from F down to C, adding the revealing remark: 'just as the harpsichord is now usually made.' The same extension was made in the Amsterdam organ by Jacobus van Hagerbeer as late as in 1660/61. From a technical point of view it is quite natural that only the upper keyboard was affected, as this is the one to which large pipes could be added without calling for any drastic alterations. At the same time the keyboards were, as we saw, placed into alignment above one another. This is in agreement with the changes in the technique of organ playing that took place at the time.

Pitch. On this point the records do not give any clues. They only mention numbers of feet (12 foot, 6 foot, etc.), which was a measure so little standardized that it is impossible to base any conclusion on it. Comparison with other Niehoff organs could point to a pitch just below that current today, but this is by no means certain, since the Oude Kerk organs need not have conformed to Niehoff's others.

Temperament. The only thing known about this is that it was unequal. There is reason to assume that meantone tuning (with eight pure major thirds), as revived today, was not used by Dutch organ-builders of Sweelinck's time. They may have employed some sort of intermediary system between Pythagorean and meantone tuning, sacrificing some of the eleven pure fifths of the Pythagorean tuning in order to get better thirds. Systems of this kind had been published by Arnolt Schlick and Salomon de Caus (see above, pp. 133–147, under 'Chromatic fantasies and meantone tuning').

Specification. The division of the stops of the large organ as it stood in Sweelinck's time—apart from possible subsequent changes of minor importance —was probably as listed in the 1567 contract. At the reconstruction of 1619 changes may have been made. If their nature were known—which unfortunately is not the case— they might have given an insight into Sweelinck's opinions concerned. However, throughout almost his entire career he had made use of the organ in its 1567 state.

Contrary to what Miss Bijtelaar has suggested, [1] the middle

---

[1] B. Bijtelaar, *Het Orgel*, L (1954), p. 23.

keyboard was not provided with an 8 foot Trumpet in 1619. This was first installed by Hagerbeer, for the Trumpet mentioned in his remonstrance could have concerned neither the Oberwerk, which already had one, nor the Rückpositiv, which had a narrow treble scaling and thus too little space. Sweelinck would therefore always have used the Great without a Trumpet. For neither of the Sifflöte stops is the pitch mentioned in the 1567 contract. Vente seems right in assuming that, because the Oberwerk had a Nasard as a quint, the Sifflöte was a 1 foot. [1] The Gouda organ, too, had a 1 foot Sifflöte along with the Nasard. [2] Although for the Pedal Nachthorn the pitch is not given either, this may be expected to have been at 2 foot level. The Bärpfeife on the Oberwerk was an 8 foot, as already appeared from the 1539 contract. The 1 foot Sifflöte on the Oberwerk makes a quint-Sifflöte on the Rückpositiv very plausible.

Most of the Principal stops will have had double pipes in the treble, possibly even triple pipes. The same uncertainty applies to the composition of the Mixtures. They must have had many ranks, owing to the size of the church. According to Willem Lootens, the Niehoff organ at Zierikzee, in a church smaller than the Oude Kerk, had three to eight ranks in the Mixture, four to twelve in the Scharff of the Great, and two to six and four to six respectively in those of the Rückpositiv. [3] In the Oude Kerk they may therefore have had even a few more. Only the Zimbel of the Oberwerk (called 'ruisende cimbel' in the documents) would have had three ranks. The epithet 'ruisend' indicates that it was not composed merely of fifths and octaves, for it takes other overtones to achieve such an effect. Although the term Terzzimbel has been employed in this connexion, it should be used with caution, for hardly any 'ruisende cimbels' have survived, while those few extant show signs of alterations. Moreover, the effect of those stops as preserved is in most cases unsatisfactory. Thus they may originally have been quite different from a Terzzimbel, or any other stop known today.

Of the Reed stops, the Trumpets no doubt had the usual construction. Of the Reeds with short resonators, the Zink of the Oberwerk (always a treble stop) had, to judge from existing fragments of this type, a cylindrical resonator placed on a cone. This is confirmed by a picture in Praetorius' De Organographia. [4] He describes the sound as somewhat hollow, like that of a Flute stop,

---

[1] Vente, *Die Brabanter Orgel*, p. 74.
[2] Vente, *Bouwstoffen*, p. 126.   [3] Lootens, *op. cit.*, p. 14.
[4] Praetorius, *op. cit.*, plate XXXVIII.

but vigorous, through the great supply of wind, while a rattling effect was avoided by using relatively thick tongues. [1] The fragments corroborate this. It had the same compass as the corresponding wind instrument from which it takes its name, starting with c′ (sometimes with the a or f below) and extending to g″, a″, in 8 foot pitch. The scaling too corresponded with that of the instrument, the Zink, the resonator having a constant diameter, possible because of the limited compass of this stop. Only the size of the cone and the length of the cylinder became smaller upwards, causing an interesting, changing sound pattern. Of the Reed stops in the Rückpositiv the 4 foot Schalmei would have had a trumpet-like resonator, possibly with a flaring bell top as in the corresponding wind instruments. The Bärpfeife was undoubtedly also a Reed stop. Praetorius mentions only one general characteristic: the resonators are narrow at the bottom and widen up rather quickly towards the top. [2] He shows 5 different ones, all having short resonators of a rather complicated shape. [3] Which one was used by Niehoff is not known. At any rate, its sound was relatively modest. The Krummhorn had longer resonators than the Bärpfeife, but of what shape is again not clear. According to Praetorius the best sound was produced by one of a constant width along its entire length, the latter being 4 foot on C. [4] This is very similar to the classical Cromorne in French organ building. Whether this type was also used by Niehoff we do not know, as no specimen has been preserved from any of his organs.

Of the Flutes, both stops called 'Holpijp' in the documents should be regarded as Rohrflutes. All stopped pipes will have had caps soldered at the right length, instead of movable ones. The Nasard and the Gemshorn were possibly conical; the shape of the Sifflöte is again unknown.

How the pipes of the Rückpositiv and the Oberwerk were divided between their upper and lower chests can be made out with certainty, both on technical grounds and by comparison with similar instruments, such as the Niehoff organ in the Petrikirche at Hamburg, in which these divisions are known. [5] The disposition, then, is as follows: [6]

---

[1] *Ibid.*, p. 146.   [2] *Ibid.*, p. 147.   [3] *Ibid.*, plate XXXVIII.
[4] *Ibid.*, p. 145.   [5] Vente, *Bouwstoffen*, p. 183.
[6] Foot measures have been modified according to the present-day standard, for the sake of convenience (although it is in fact unrealistic). The order in which the stops are listed is that of their presumed position on the chest starting from the front.

Great
Principal   16'
Octave   8'
Mixture
Scharff

Rückpositiv

Lower chest	*Upper chest*	
Principal 8'	Quintadena	8'
Octave 4'	Rohrflute	4'
Mixture	Sifflöte	$1^1/_3$'
Scharff	Schalmei	4'
	Bärpfeife	8'
	Krummhorn	8'

Oberwerk

Lower chest	*Upper chest*	
Principal 8'	Rohrflute	8'
Sifflöte 1'	Open Flute	4'
Gemshorn 2'	Zimbel	3 rank
Nasard $2^2/_3$'	Trumpet	8'
	Zink	8' treble

Pedal
Trumpet   8'
Nachthorn 2'

Coupler between Rückpositiv and Oberwerk
Tremulant, probably functioning for the whole organ
6 Bellows
Manual compass F, G, A, to g″ a″: 38 notes
Pedal compass F, G, A to c′: 18 notes; linked to the Great

The Small Organ

Matters are less complicated with the small organ. The wind-supply has already been treated above. As to keyboard range, pipes, pitch, and temperament, what has been said about the large organ applies here in similar fashion.

Windchests. Owing to scarcity of space, the Brustwerk must have had a slider-chest. Representations of the instrument show that it was much narrower than the present one with its breadth of 2.13

m. It cannot have been more than about 1.65 m. wide, which is not enough for a spring-chest. As a consequence, the Great must have had a slider-chest, too. In fact, all pipes may therefore be assumed to have been mounted on slider-chests.

Mechanism. This was very simple. The pallet box can only have been on the wall side, because the main case protrudes rather much over the pedestal, and also because there was a Brustwerk. This Brustwerk would not have extended much beyond the width of the keyboard. Most of the pallets were then connected directly with the corresponding keys. Only in the lowest octave a number of channels might have been fitted in at the right hand side of the chest, entailing the use of rollers. Thus the arrangement of the pipes on the chest was chromatic. From a constructional point of view the only logical place for all stop levers was at the right hand side of the keyboards.

Organ case. The small organ was pictured—apparently rather faithfully—on a number of paintings by Emanuel de Witte (for the most accurate of all, see Plate III). The ground-plan of the front was segmental. This mostly occurred with Rückpositivs. The case was rather high for a 3 foot organ. A number of front pipes may therefore have been mute—a not uncommon feature at the time. Such was, for instance, the case with the front pipes of the Rückpositiv in the St. Janskerk organ at Gouda. [1]

This circumstance makes it difficult to establish the exact number of front pipes. The front probably consisted of a round middle tower with 7 pipes; a pointed tower on either side, standing somewhat back owing to the segmental ground-plan, and next to each of these a presumably undivided field of a slightly rounded shape. The pointed towers may have had two flats of pipes joined at the feet on the inside and bigger pipes on the outside. The case was crowned with three decorative towers. The pedestal with the keyboards receded rather strongly in comparison to the upper case, so as to keep the balcony as shallow as possible for reasons of balance. The Pedal Trumpet was possibly mounted in a separate case on the balcony, rather than in the main case.

Disposition. In Sweelinck's time, this was still as described in the 1567 contract. Owing to the large number of stops, the Great must have been fitted on two chests. Again nothing is known about the ranks and composition of the Mixtures. Here too the Zimbel

[1] Vente, *Bouwstoffen*, p. 183.

('ruisende cimbel') probably had three ranks. The Sifflöte may
have been a quint. [1] Undoubtedly the Pedal was connected to
the Great. The order in which the stops occur in the 1567 contract seems rather arbitrary, yet it might still reflect their actual
order on the chest. A number of pipes of the Quintadena may
have stood in the front, as this was not ususual. What shape the
resonators of the Reeds in the Brustwerk had is unknown. Unlike
that of the large organ, the Krummhorn possibly had short reson-
nators in view of the limited height available. The Regal must
have had relatively narrow resonators because of the narrowness
of the chest division.

The disposition given below is in the order of the stops on the
chests, starting from the front with the Great, and in reverse
order with the Brustwerk. The foot measures are modern:

Great

Lower chest		Upper chest	
Principal 4'		Quintadena	8'
Rohrflute 8'	Principal	Zimbel	3 rank
Mixture	chorus	Gemshorn	2'
Scharff		Sifflöte	$1^1/_3'$ (?) or 1'
Octave 2'		Schalmei	4'

Brustwerk

Rohrflute   4'
Krummhorn 8'
Regal   8'

Pedal

Trumpet   8'

Tremulant, probably functioning for the whole organ
Manual coupler
Manual compass: F, G, A to g", a"
Pedal compas: F, G, A, to c'
3 Bellows

To attempt to derive registration possibilities for Sweelinck's
music from the various facts presented here would lead us beyond
our present scope. However, some remarks of a technical nature
may be made in conclusion. The number of registrations possible

---

[1] It is remarkable that the 1544 contract mentions a Sifflöte in the Brustwerk. In view of the rest of the stops it must have been a quint, in which
case that of the manual must have been a 1 foot.

can be quickly surveyed if the maximum wind-supply needed for them is taken into account. This at once eliminates the simultaneous use of all stops on both chests of the Rückpositiv or Oberwerk. The Reeds, standing as they do on the upper chest, could hardly be used in conjunction with the full Principal chorus, owing to the danger of losing their pitch. They would therefore seem to fall outside the Principal chorus, unless they were tuned to this purpose, but then they would become unfit for use in other combinations. So, if the whole of the lower chest is used, a maximum of two stops from the upper chest could be added, not counting the Reeds since they take too much wind. But the latter could be combined with other voices of the upper chest, the Zimbel in particular which because of its position on the upper chest did not belong to the full Principal chorus either.

In connexion with the small organ, it may be pointed out that an 8 foot Principal not being present, an 8 foot Flute (the Rohrflute) could be joined to the Principal chorus. This is true of 4 foot organs, including of course most Rückpositivs.

Further information on possibilities of registration can be found in the relevant literature, especially Vente's *Die Brabanter Orgel*. One should, however, realize that some registrations derive from organ builders who, wanting to show the versatility of their instruments, included many combinations of only theoretical value. Yet, if one is able to review and thoroughly comprehend the registration possibilities available on Sweelinck's Oude Kerk organs, the difficulties in adapting his works for modern performance should be less than is often assumed.

ii. *Original texts of the documents concerning the Oude Kerk organs*

1. *Contract for the large organ (undated, possibly December* 1539)

In manieren hiernae ghescreven hebben Pieter Smit van Jabec, Claes Meeusz., Pieter Wilmz. Canter, Burchman Woutersz. als kercmeesteren in Aemstelredam in Sinte Niclaes-prochie in der tijt wesende, besteet een orghel te maken dese meesters bij namen

---

[1] The transcription follows the *Regels voor het uitgeven van historische bescheiden, in opdracht van het bestuur van het Historisch Genootschap* (Utrecht, 1954). Most of the texts were published, fully or partly, earlier by Bijtelaar and Vente, except Hagerbeer's Remonstrance which is given here for the first time. The 1682 contract appeared in *TVNM*, X (1915), pp. 69–70. Only major differences from previous readings will be given in foornotes.

meester Henrick, wonende ten Bosch, ende meester Hans ende meester Harman, denselfden meester Henricks broeder, soe vard alst [1] hem in sijn absentie ghelieven sal.

Te weten dese meesters sullen maken een werck van XII vuet. In den eersten soe sal dat principael wesen suuaer ende sterc van gheluijt nae den eijsch van den kercken. Ende datselfde principael sal hebben vier registeren, te weten

voert eerst een doef van tuualef vuet van fijne tin

tueede een octaef met een superoctaef

tderde een mixtuer

tvierde een scarp ende deze vier sullen maken een principael.

Item daerboven sal dit voerscreven werck hebben een pedael tot een duodecim, twelc sal hebben tuuee bassen op hemselfs, te weten een trompet van ses voet ende het ander een nachthoern, diewelcke men sal moghen ghebruijcken tot die XII voet of elx bijsonder soe dat den organist ghelieven sal.

Item dit voerscreven werck sal hebben een clavier op hemself tot vier octaven toe.

Item boven int werck sal zijn een secreet met sijn toebehoren ende met seven registeren:

In den eersten een holpijp van ses voet, item een gemtsenhoern, item een cijvelet, item een cimbel, item een trompet gaende [2], item een cingke, item een floijte 3 vuet.

Ende dit secreet sal hebben een clavier op hemzelf.

Item noch sullen dese meesters voerscreven maken een positijf achter den rug van ses voete met acht registeren, te weten

voer eerste een prestant van ses vuet van fijnen tin

een coppeldoef van drie vuet

een mixtuer

een scarp

dese vier sullen maken een principael.

Item noch sullen sij maken een quintadena van drie vuet

item een scalmeij van drie vuet

een regael

een barpijp ludende op ses vuet.

Item dit positijf sal hebben een clavier op hemzelfs.

Item daerboven soe sal men dat bovenste clavier met dat onderste tesamen moghen spelen als men wil.

Item noch soe sal hierin wesen een trambulant.

Item dit werck sal hebben ses guede balghen daertoe dienende.

---

[1] 'Soe vard alst' = in so far as.

[2] 'Gaende' = going on (all over the keyboard): in opposition to the Zink which is a discant stop only.

Item die kercmeesters moghen die structuer ter sien maken of breken soet haer ghelieft, oec die hoechte ende breete.

Item die kercmeesters sullen betalen alle materialia, tcoperdraert uutgheseijt. [1] Voer welcken arbeijt dese meesters voerscreven sullen hebben vierdalf hondert gulden current, te weten een hondert gulden alst werck begonnen wert ende ten ende des leverings [2] sullen sij ontfanghen die reste.

Item noch sijnt voerwaerden dat dese meesters en sullen anders gheen werck maken voer dit dan twerck tot Scoenhoven ende tot Naeldwijck ende daernae gheen werck maken noch beghinnen dan dit.

Item tot sekerheijt dattet aldus ghesciet is in presentie van mijnheer die pastoer, heer Cornelis Henrickz., pastoer tot Sinte Niclaeskercke binnen Aemstelredam, Quijrijn Arijsz. met Hubrecht Arijsz., ghebroederen van Delft, heer Claes Janz, organist van de Nieuwe Kerck ende meester Arent Lambrechz., organist van de Oude Kerc, hebben haer namen ende hancteijken hieronder gheset tot sekerheijt.

	C[ornelis] H[endrickz.] [4]
	Quirijn Arijsz.
Hansken van Coelen	Peter Smetsz. van Jabeck
Arent Lambrectz. orghe[nist] [3]	Pieter Kantert Willemzoen
Henrick Niehoff Claes Janz. fecit	Claes Mijensz.
	Burrichman Wouterz.
	Hubrecht Arentz. Verhoech.

Utrecht, Rijksarchief, familiearchief Huydecoper, inv. no. 2136.

2. *Contract for the organ case* (29 *December* 1539)

A° 1539 den 29ste decembris ten huijse van Goessen Jansz. int vuijsgen so hebben wij kerckmeesteren van Sinte Nicolaes-prochie binnen Amsterdam Pieter Smit, Pieter Kanttert Willemsz., Burchman Woutersz. ende Claes Mijensz. bestaet den eersamen Aerdriaen alias Scalck, meester kistwercker binnen tSiarttoghenbosse woenaftich een gheheel houtwerck van een orghel te weten in

---

[1] 'Uutgheseijt' = excepted. Bijtelaar incorrectly reads 'ghescijr', and so does Vente in *Die Brabanter Orgel* (in German: 'Geschirr'). In the *Repertorium* he gives the correct reading.
[2] Vente and Bijtelaar both read 'kuering'.
[3] Vente in *Die Brabanter Orgel* reads 'Jonghe' (= junior).
[4] Possibly the autograph of the pastor of the Oude Kerk, mentioned in the text.

deser manieren: In den eersten so sal Adriaen voirsz. binnen tsiairs maken dit voirsch. ghehele werck ende leveren met alle sijnen toebehoren op sijn paesdaecghs, [1] wuijtghesondert ijserwerck, kanijfas [2] om den dueren mede te becleeden ende den balcken mitten solder daert 'tghele werck op staen ende rusten sal. Boven dit voirsch. ghespecificeert sal Adriaen voirn. ghehouden wesen ons binnen dattum voirsch. te leveren ende setten op sijnen kosten een gheheel houtwerc[k] van sijn selfs hout ende dat gheeff [3] sonder spijnt ofte vierichheit also ghoet ende duerachtich ende proeper ghevrocht.

Den kas boven met neghen cappellen ende dat positijve met seven cappellen met sijne toerns, loeveren ende allen anderen sneewerck, so cossel, proeper ende welghedaen dat dit werck van diversse nacien ghepresen ende gheiudiciert wart proeper, goet ende wel cossel ghemaeckt te wesen.

Ende want arbeit loen weerdich is, so sal Adriaen hiervoer hebben eens die somme van hondertendevierentneghentich karolus guldens 20 stuvers voir die gulden gherekent.

Mond [4] of die betalinghe op daghen navolghenden, te weten 44 guldens corrent ghereet ende noch vijftich guldens sodra als Adrian den stoel, posijtijff ende borst ghelevert ende gheset sal hebben, welcke hij sculdich is te setten voir petrij ad vincula toecomende, [5] 14 daghen onbegrepen, ende den trest sodra als hij den kas, dueren mit allen andere accidentten toebehoerende ghelevert ende gheset sal hebben op sijn paesdaecghs, so dat een goet meester van eeren toebehoert. Ende want wij kerckmeesteren voirsch. ons niet seer ende verstaen van den houtwerck voirsch., so verbijnt [6] hem den voirsch. Adriaen ons op sijnen costen te leveren ende setten dit voirsch. houtwerck met alle sijnen toebehoeren, so ient, [7] so excellent dat hij Adriaen sijn levedaghen daer eeren of hebben sal omme anderen wercken daeruuijt te sprutten tot sijn profijt ende dat daeromme, want hier veel diversse vreemde nacien verkeren.

Ende bij ghebreke van den duechdelijke leverancie, so sal men Adriaen cortten van sijn penninghen bij meesters secgghen hem daerof verstaende. Hierbij an tot verijficacie van deze hier twee cedullen.

---

[1] 'Op sijn paesdaecghs': litt. '[dressed] as on Easter Day', so: in the most perfect way.
[2] 'Kanijfas' = linen. [3] 'Gheef' (gaaf) = sound, whole.
[4] Improved reading from the margin, ignored by Bijtelaar and Vente.
[5] St. Peter ad vincula: 1 August (1540).
[6] Vente in *Repertorium* incorrectly reads 'wynt'.
[7] 'Ient' = handsome, fine.

Item over geweest Jacob Lucas, item meester Cornelis Jansz. int hart ende meester Hans orghelmaker als soenlijden. [1]

[In the margin:] Maen Petersz. *[with mark].*
[On the back]: Item op 't selffen tijt heeft Adriaen hierop ontfanghen ghereet ghelt vierenveertich guldens corrent per Pieter Willemsz. Kanttert, Claes Mijensz. ende Pieter Smit.

Utrecht, Rijksarchief, familiearchief Huydecoper, inv. no. 2136.

3. *Contract for the small organ* (7 *November* 1544)
In den name ons Heeren, amen. Op den VII den dach van november anno XV[C] vierendeveertich hebben Sijmon Marten Dircxzoonsz., Burchman Wouter Dobbenzoonsz. ende Cornelis Jacobsz. kerckmeesters van Sinter Niclaes-prochiekercke binnen der stede van Aemstelredamme in absencie van Claes Meeusz. bestaet ende mr. Jasper Jansz. van den Bosse, orgelmaicker voir hemzelven ende gem[achtichte] van mr. Henrick van Nijeuwenhuijs oick orgelmaicker ten Bosse ende voir hem beloovende ende vaststaende heeft anghenomen een gans nijeuw werck van drie voet, zes voet luijende, mit twee clavijeren wairvan dat eerste zal hebben een secreet mit een operlae mit neghen registers wairvan dat eerste wesen zal een doeff van fijne thinne, [2] dat andere een holpijpe van zes voet, dat derde een quintodeen van zes voet, dat vierde een coppeldoeff, [3] dat vijfde een mixtuer, dat zeste een scarp, dat zevende een gheemshoern, dat achste een ruijssende cijmbael, dat negende een scalmaij van drie voet. Item dat tweede clavier zal hebben een secreet op hemselven mit drie registers, the weeten een holpijpe van drie voet, dat andere een sijvelet, dat derde een goedt regael van zes voet luijende. Noch een pedael sprekende mit een bas-trompet van zes voet.

Item dese twee clavijeren zal men mogen spelen tesamen ofte elcx bijsonder zoe dat den organist believen zal. Item noch zal in dat voorsz. werck zijn een goede trambulandt. Ende tot dit voorsz. werck zullen sijn drie goede balgen van hout, gevouden [4]

---

[1] This last sentence is lacking in Vente and defective in Bijtelaar. 'Meester Hans' (not 'mr. Hanrick' as Bijtelaar has it) is Hans van Coelen. This is the only time that he is mentioned independently. 'Soenlijden' = arbiters.
[2] Bijtelaar thinks that this is an 8 foot Principal. This is not true, as the 1567 contract shows.
[3] Not a 4 foot, as Bijtelaar assumed, but a 2 foot octave.
[4] Vente incorrectly reads 'gevonden'.

III. The small organ of the Oude Kerk in Amsterdam. Painting on copper by Emanuel de Witte, before 1658.

gelijck die tot Delft zijn geweest ende wairt saicke dat mr. Cornelis Scaegen, onse organist, mit een ander goedt meester zeijden dat die wint van de drie balgen tot dat voorsz. werck nijet sterck genouch en wair, dat alsdan die voorsz. meesters gehouden sullen zijn die vierde ballech dair bij te maecken op haeren costen ende voert zullen die voorsz. meesters leveren een nijeuwe borst mit een nijeuwe casse ofte vidimus mit zijn tabernaculen, net ende wel gewrocht mit die doeren daertoe ende voort alle materialen ende al dat daertoe behoort tot dat voorsz. werck, wairvoir die voorsz. kerckmeesters die voorsz. meesters weder leveren zullen die oude leeghe casse van twaelf voet mit zijn stoel staende in de voorsz. kerck bij dat Hamburger choer ende noch dat geheele Edammer werck mit zijn gheblaes ende dat sonder stoel ende dairenboven noch an ghelde wanneer dat werck opghelevert zal sijn tnegentich karolus guldenen van XL grooten vlaems tstuck. Welverstaende dat de voorsz. meesters gehouden zullen zijn die kerckmeesters te leveren een fraije welgemaicte patroen voir kersmisse toecomende in alle manieren zij dat werck zouden willen leveren ende soe zullen oick die voorsz. kerckmeesters gehouden zijn voir jaersdach eerstcomende te zeggen off zij dat werck gemaict willen hebben ende ist dat zijluijden tevreden zijn, dat dit voorsz. werck aldus gemaict sal wordden alst voorsz. is, zoe sal meester Jasper gehouden zijn dit voorsz. werck te helpen ofte te accorderen ist saick dat dairnae dat werck gelevert zal sijn eenich gebreck in quaem ende hij in levende lijve waer hier omtrent. Ende oick zullen die voorsz. kerckmeesters gehouden zijn die leghe cas van twaelf voet beneden op die vloer van de kerck te leveren op kercx costen ende die meesters voorsz. zullen die ouwe wercken wel mogen vercoopen, mair die kerckmeesters zullen nijet gehouden zijn eenige leverancie die voorsz. meesters te doen voirdat die meesters die kerck eerst gelevert zullen hebben.

Sonder arch ende list in kennisse der waitheijt zoe sijn hiervan gemaict twee cedullen alleensluijdende ende per A B C D uuijt malcanderen gesneden ende oick bij den voorsz. partijen ondergeteijckent.

bij unss beijden mester Hijndrijch Sijmon Marten Dijrickzzoen ende Jasper Johanson orgelmachkers

[mark]

Postscript (28 *October* 1545)

Item dijt voerscreven werrick is tho vollen optghelievert actum den 28 in october, verstaende dat mijster Jasper hem varbonden heft dijt voerscreven werck soe lanck als hij leeft tho onderhouden

ende tho accorderen ende heft dijt beloeft in presencije van mr.
Claes ende mr. Arrent ende Hanrick Fransen ende meer ander die
daerbij ghevest sijn. — a° 45 —
Sonder dair eet of tho nemen. ¹

*Amsterdam, Gemeentearchief, archief Kerkmeesteren der Ned. Herv. Ge-
meente, Oude Kerk, file* 294.
In Rijksarchief, Utrecht, familiearchief Huydecoper inv. no. 2136, *a dupli-
cate with minor variant readings.*

4. *Postscript to the* 1539 *contract, page* 1 (28 *October* 1545)

Item ² dijt groete werrick is bij mister Hanrick ende bij mister
Jasper varbetert en drie ander gheluden inghebrocht als die seel
daerof sijnde breeder varmelt ende hebben se betaelt bij bijweesen
van mister Claes ende Mr. Arrent ende ghaven haer XVI gulden
corent.
Actum den 28 in october anno 45 ende bij seeghen van hemluden.³

Utrecht, Rijksarchief, familiearchief Huydecoper, inv. no. 2136.

5. *Memorandum about the reconstruction of the large organ* (*undated*,
1544 *or* 1545)

Item dit zijn die ghebreecken die hierna ghescreven staan, 'tgheen
dat die kercmeesters van die Oude Kerck begheeren volmaickt
ende gherenoveert te hebben int groet werck staende in die Oude
Kerck.
Item een nyen regael met een nyen cromhoren.
Item men zal drie ofte 4 schalmeyen vermaicken ofte vertonghen
om hair perfect gheluyt te hebben.
Item men zal dat 't ghehele werck boven ende beneden doirsien
ende helpen dat 't selfde gebreck datter in is met die tramblant
etc.

Item alsoverde ⁴ alst die kercmeesteren gelieven zal ende met Mr.
Henrick tesamen kuenen accorderen, so zal men die quintedeen
boven wechnemen ende brengen in dieselfde plaets een regyster
ghenoemt die naezaet.

---

¹ Last line defective in Vente. 'Eet' (eed) = oath, not 'iet' as Vente has it.
² Vente wrongly reads 'int'.
³ These words omitted by Bijtelaar and Vente.
⁴ 'Alsoverde' (voor zover) = in so far. Not 'also verder' as given by Vente.

Item achter int posetyf zal men uuijtnemen dat cromhoiren ende
brenghen een suflet in die plaets.

[*other hand*]

Item dat princepael sal men maecken stercker nae den eijshe van
dije kerck.

Amsterdam, Gemeentearchief, archief Oude Kerk, file 294, no. 2.

6. *Indenture, text of the lower half* (1 September 1567.)

Item op den yersten dach septembrys anno sovensestych synt dye
ersaeme kerckmeysters van dye Oude Kerck bynnen Amsterdam,
te weten Jan Ryser, Cornelys Janson, Mr. Derryck Florys, Claes
Bueck overeengecoemen unde geaccordyer[t] met Mr. Peter
orgelmaeker resydyrende bynnen der stede van Uutrycht um
beyde dye orgelen te renovyren unde te vermaeken van dye voerschreven kerck yn dyer ffuege unde manyere hyerna volgende:
Item yn den yersten sal hy vorsyen dat groete sekreet van dat
groete pryncypael dat het guet unde perffeckt wesen sall.
Yn den yrsten spreckt up dat sekreet dat groete doeff dat voer
staet van 12 voet, noch den octaeff, ynt myxtuer met noch een
scharp. Desse voerschreven regysters maeken dat groete pryncipael
van 12 voet unde dat voerschreven pypewerck sal dye meyster
versyen, wat gebroeken ys sal hy moeten vernyen.
Item boeven dyt pryncypaell lyggen noch twye secreten dye een
boeven dey anderen, daerup sprekende negen spryngende regysters, hyerna volgende:
Yn den yrsten een doeff van 6 voet, noch een holpyep van 6
voet, noch een oepen ffloeyt van 3 voet, noch een [n]asaet,
ludende up een quynt, noch een gemsenhoern van 1½ voet,[1] noch
een sufflet, noch een rusent symbell, noch een synck, noch een
trumpet, ludende 6 voet. Dese voerschreven regysteren met dye
twe voerschreven secreten sal hy maeken guet ende perfeckt, als
boeven voerschreven ys. Item dat pedaell een trompet van 6 voet
met een nachthoern. Item den stoel achter den rugge synt ock
twye secreten, daerup sprekende dese nabeschreven geluden: Iyn
den yrsten een doeff van 6 voet van tyn dat voer staet, noch een
octaeff van 3 voet, noch een myxtuer, noch een scharp. Dese voerschreven regysteren maeken dat pryncypaell. Noch een quyntedeen van 6 voet, noch een holpyep van 3 voet, noch een sufflet,
noch een baerpyep, noch een regaell van 6 voet, daer sal hy voer

---

[1] Vente reads '2 voet', which is incorrect.

maeken een kromhoern van 6 voet van tyn, noch een schalmey van 3 voet. Item tot dyt voerschreven werck sal hy maeken 6 guede nye leren blaesbalken met syen bussen[1] als dat tho behoert dat dat voerschreven werck gueden ende perffeckten wynt hebben sall. Noch sal meyster Peter maeken een ny trambulant off bevende stem. Iten van[2] dye regysters van kleyn orgell dye boeven up dye lae staen, te weten dat prestant van 3 voet, holpyep 6 voet, myxtuer ende scharp, noch een octaeff van 1½ voet.[3] Dese voerschreven regysters ys dat pryncypael. Item noch een quyntedeen van 6 voet, noch een symbel, noch een gemsenhoern met een sufflet, noch een schalmey van 3 voet. Item noch voer yn dye borst een holpyep van 3 voet, noch een regaell met een kromhoern, beyde ludende 6 voet, noch een trompet yn dat pedaell 6 voet.

Item noch sal dye meyster maeken van dye 3 blaesbalken dye an dat groete werck hebben gelegen sal hy leggen an dat kleyne werck. Ende dyt alles sal hy gehouden wesen te maeken voer dye summe van vyerhondertvyerentwyntich[4] carolus guldens van twyntych sts b. dat stuck, hondert geryet unde dye rest als dye voergeschreven meyster Peter beyde dye wercken hefft upge-levert by organysten dye dye kerckmeysters belyeven sal, dyt alles sonde[r] arch off lyst yn kennys der waerheyt. Synt van desen gemaekt twe sedulen alleens sprekend unde geteykent met dye letteren a. b. c. d., dye een uut den anderen gesneden, waeraff dye voerschreven karckmeyster[s] dye een off hebben ende Mr. Peter dye ander.

Dyt aldus gedaen unde gesloeten, so hebben wy onse gewonte-lycke hant hant daerunder geset.

bij mijn Peter Jansz.　　　Jan Rijser Janszoen
orgelmaker　　　　　　　Cornelis Jansz. int
　　　　　　　　　　　　Root Cruijs.[5]

Dese voergeschreven werken sollen
ryede wesen te mey naestkoemende.

Utrecht, Rijksarchief, familiearchief Huydecoper, inv. no. 2136.

7. *Hagerbeer's remonstrance* (*undated, probably* 1661)

Remonstrantie ende memorie van 'tgeene Jacobus Galtus van Hagerbeer, orgelmaacker, buijten besteck ofte contract (dogh op

---

[1] 'Bussen' (buizen) = windchannels.
[2] Not 'noch' as Vente has it.
[3] According to Vente again '2 voet'.
[4] Vente and Bijtelaar both read 425 instead of 424.
[5] Names omitted by Vente.

't hooghste noodigh) heeft gemaackt aen 't groot orgel in de Oude
Kerck deser stadt Amsterdam, als naementlijck:

Eerstlijck in 't bovenste werck in't voorsz. orgel beijde de seekreten
op de acht voet gemaackt van F tot C.

2. Hondertnegenendertigh pijpen gemaackt op de negen registers staande op de secreten.

3. Onder de voorschreven secreten de roeden nieuw gemaackt.

4. D' roede van de voorsz. sekreten, gaande naer de benede
   registers, einsgelijcx nieuw gemaackt ende aen de ende met
   iser beslagen.

5. Het bovenste welbort mede vermaackt ende de wint in 'tselve
   op een beter maeniere als voordesen.

6. De prestandtpijpen met nieuwe houvasten gemaackt en in de
   velde verbetert anders als voordesen.

7. In 't prinsepaal sekreet nieuwe tuijmmelaars gemaackt van
   iser, welcke voordesen van hout waeren ende teenemaal ge-
   broocken ende vergaan.

8. Het welbort van 't selve sekreet versien met eenige nieuwe
   tuijmmelaars, item de wintlade op een ander ende beter
   maenier als voordesen vermaackt ende de roeden aen de
   registers met iser beslagen.

9. Drie affsluijtinge gemaackt, als naementlijck een tot het
   bovenwerck, een tot het priszepaal ende een tot het postieff.
   Ende buijtendien noch een trammelant gemaackt.

10. Alle de drie clavieren in 't voorsz. orgel reght oover malckan-
    der gemaackt, die voordese schieff ende ingevallen waeren.

11. Een nieuw clavier van 't pedaal gemaackt met een welbort
    daeraan.

12. De registers van 't postieff vermaackt ende de roeden van de
    registers vernieuwt.

13. Drie registers pijpen gemaackt, als naementlijck de tromp[e]t,
    sexqualtera ende de quint-prestandt. Item de stoel nieuw ge-
    maackt in 't postieff.

14. In 't blaashuijs aen ses blaasbalcken tegenwight gemaackt
    merckelijck tot verbeteringhe van 'tselve.
    De pijpen die ick hebbe gemaackt in 'tgeene vooren verhaalt
    beloopen 't samen driehondertende twaalff.

15. Hebbe voortz. tot noodige ende verdere verbeteringe van
    't meergemelte orgel, niettegenstaende hetselve buijten 't

voorsz. besteck gelijck het voorstaende is, gewerckt geruijm den tijdt van ses maanden ende dienvolgende noch wel een merckelijcke zomme van penningen daeraan verdient, doch niet begrotende hoeveel, stelle hetselve ter discretie van Haer Edele

Amsterdam, Gemeentearchief, archief Kerkmeesteren der Ned. Herv. Gemeente, Oude Kerk, inv. no. K 3–9.

8. Contract for reconstruction of the large organ (7 October 1682)

Accoord tusschen kerkmeesteren van de Oude Kerk ter eenre ende Nicolaes van Hagen ende Apolonius Bosch, orgelmakers, ter andere sijde.

Door speciale authorisatie vand Ed.grootachtbaren heeren burgemeesteren en regeerders deser stadt Amsterdam sijn kerckmeesteren van d'Oude Kerck alhier ter eenre ende Nicolaes van Hagen ende Apollonius Bosch, orgelmaeckers, ter andere sijde geaccordeert ende verdragen gelijck sij accorderen en verdragen bij desen, dat de voorsz. orgelmaekers het groot orgel in de gemelde kerck, 'twelck nu alrede voort geene datter in is, een van de beste orgels van ['t] Christenrijck mach werden geroemt, verder te suppleren, te volmaecken ende daerinne te brengen het navolgende:
Voor eerst het rugwerck
Al de registers verlanght tot bovenuijt met 4 pijpen gis, b, h, c, daertoe een nieuw sekreet met alle wat daeraen dependeert, oock 4 stecken int clavier met sijn toebehooren, oock in plaets van de fluijt 4 voet moet een holpijp van 8 voet gemaeckt worden.
Ten tweeden het bovenwerck.
Al de registers verlanght tot bovenuijt met 4 pijpen gis, b, h, c, een nieuw sekreet met sijn toebehooren, een nieuwe vox humana[1] met een nieuwe quintadeen, daertoe een nieuw secreet, int clavier 4 nieuwe stecken gemaeckt worden.
Ten derden het middelclavier.
De navolgende registers onderuijt verlenght te worden van F nederwaerts tot C, dat is de prestant van 12 voet tot 16 voet, trompet van 6 voet tot 8 voet, octaeff van 6 voet tot 8 voet.
Oock het mixtuur en het scharp tot onderuijt, oock alle de registers tot bovenuijt gis, b, h, c, hiertoe een nieuw sekreet met al

---

[1] This shows that there already was a Vox Humana on the Oberwerk, which probably had replaced the Zink, as often happened.

sijn toebehooren, oock het heele orgel schoongemaakt en geaccordeert met goet accoord.

Ende eijndelijck het onderste clavier van F tot C voluijt door al de registers heen met alle 'tgene daertoe behoort. [1]

Voor alle 'twelcke de voorsz. orgelmaekers sal werden betaelt de somme van achtienhondert guldens.

Ende dat na het voorsz. werck ten vollen wel ende behoorlijck sal sijn gemaeckt ende goetgekent bij diegene, dewelcke de welgemelte heeren burgemeesteren daertoe gelieven sullen te committeren.

Mits en onder expresse conditie, dat het oude werck van het voorsz. orgel in geenderlije manieren en sal mogen werden verergert, maer in alle manieren soo goet gehouden moeten werden als het tegenwoordigh is.

Ende oock dat het nieuwe werck immers soo goet ende deugtsaem sal moeten wesen als het oude.

Ende dienvolgende alles ten vollen moeten accorderen.

Onder expresse conditie, dat bij sooverre eenigh gebreck bevonden wierde, dat in sulcken gevalle sij niet en sullen vermogen van de voorsz. achtienhondert guldens ijets te pretenderen, maer integendeel het oude werck wederomme herstellen ende soo goet maecken als 't is geweest tot hunne costen.

Waerbij sooverre volgens de hoop en het vertrouwen van de voorsz. aenneemers hun werck soodanigh comt te succederen en uijt te vallen, dat het geheele orgel bevonden wert onverbeterlijck te sijn ende de reputatie te hebben gelijck als nu het oude heeft.

Dat alsdan in sulcken gevalle de voorsz. aenneemers sullen genieten en aen haer betaelt werden in plaetse van de achtienhondert guldens als boven tweeduijsent guldens.

Voor al hetwelck de aenneemers tesaemen en ijeder in 't besonder sijn verbindende haer personen ende goederen present ende toecomende, ten bedwangh van alle rechten ende rechteren, renuncierende van de benefitie, ordre, excussie ende devisie in effecte verstaende, ter goeder trouwe ende in oirconde van dien. Dit aldus gedaen ende gepasseert voor mij Nicolaes Brouwer, openbaer notaris tot Amsterdam, ende de getuijgen naergenoemt, dese sevende october 1682 in 't bijsijn van Sijbrand van Noort, orgelist van de voorsz. kercken, ter presentie van Gerrit Stoffelsz. van Haer ende Bernardus Coop van Groen als getuijgen.

N. Listingh als kerckmr.   Nicolaus van Hagen
Joan Pels   Aplonius Bos

---

[1] It is remarkable that a pedal-chest is not mentioned. This could indicate that the pedal stops stood on the chest of the Great.

S. v. Noord   Gerrit Stoffselen van Haer
                                     B. Coop van Groen

                                     N. Brouwer nots.

Amsterdam, Gemeentearchief, Notariële archieven no. 3945, *f.* 321 *IV.*

9. *Printed legend about the large organ* (1701)

By-schrift ten weedersyden onder het groot-orgel
in de Oude Kerk tot Amsterdam.

A°. 1540 is dit orgel eerst aan dry meesters besteet. A°. 1567 heel
vernieut door mr. Pieter van Utregt en met syn positief vermeert,
van sulk een heerlijk geluyt, dat geen mr. ooit dorste bestaan
't soo goet daarby te leveren. [1] Tot A°. 1685 Apollon. Bosch en
Ger. van Giesen, in plaats van syn gestorven mr. Nicolaas van
Hagen, dat nog wel met vyf registers, van die eygen aart, hebben
vergroot.

Maar heeft hy Gerard van Giesen, de konstigste mr. A°. 1700 onder
de regeeringe van de hier mette wapens aangeweesen Eed.Groot-
agtbare Burgemeesteren en Thesorieren, daarenboven ook een vry
pedaal en verder tot thien registers meer (nu t'samen veertig)
van deselve deugt, nog seer subtiel, in die kleyne kas weten te
brengen en soo dit beroemde werk, tot syn groote lof, dus eyndelyk
te volmaken.

t' Amsterdam, door ordre van de kerkmeesteren gedrukt,
by d'erfg. van Paulus Matthysz., in 't muzyk-boek, 1701.

Utrecht, Rijksarchief, familiearchief Huydecoper, inv. no. 2136.

[1] This is not correct (Pieter Jansz. de Swart only repaired the organ),
but it does give proof of the excellent quality of its sound.

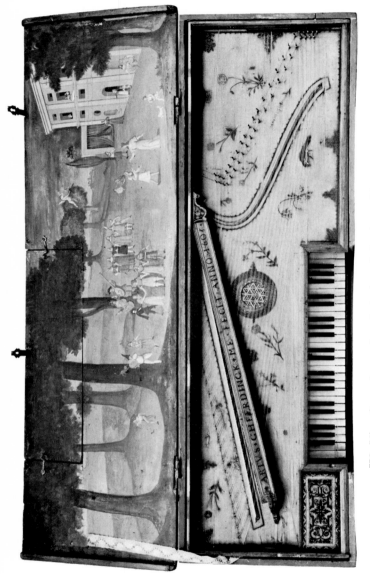

IV. View from above of a virginal made by Artus Gheerdinck, 1605.

APPENDIX II

Domestic keyboard instruments Sweelinck might have played

Even if Baudartius had not told us of a visit to Sweelinck's house where he heard him play 'op zijn Clavecymbel', we might well have assumed the presence of keyboard instruments of various types and sizes in Sweelinck's house in the Koestraat. Nothing whatever is known about them, however. The only 'reconstruction' left to us is negative: the harpsichords would not have had a 16-foot register and would most likely have been single manual; if they were two manual, the second would probably have been for purposes of transposition only (thus he would not likely have composed echo fantasies for the harpsichord); the range would probably not have exceeded C (with short octave)-c''' (his preserved keyboard music calls for a compass of only C-a''); if there were clavichords, they would most likely have been simple practice instruments.

Within these limitations, the enormous variety of keyboard instruments available at the time is difficult to imagine today. Most familiar to us now are the four basic shapes in which Ruckers instruments were made: the harpsichord (*staartstuk* or *clavecimbel*), normally with an 8-foot and 4-foot but occasionally with two 8-foot registers only; the virginal with keyboard on the left, giving an evenly-voiced compass, with the bass strings plucked near the bridge (*virginaal* or *spinet*); the somewhat more common virginal with keyboard on the right, giving a bright treble and 'booming' bass, plucked near the center of the string (called *virginaal* or *muselar*[1]); and the polygonal virginal (called *spinetta* in Italy, built only rarely in the Netherlands). It should be stressed that these were only four basic designs, however; and we may form some idea of the variety available if we consider an excerpt from an inventory made up for a lottery at Utrecht in 1622, sponsored by the harpsichord maker, Cornelis Hartung.[2] Among the items were: 1. a positive organ with five and a half registers of pipes, a

---

[1] According to Claas Douwes, *Grondig Ondersoek van de Toonen der Musijk* (Franeker, 1699), p. 104.
[2] *Dutch HM*, 51.

harpsichord above, of the length of six feet; 2. a positive organ with three and a half registers of pipes, a harpsichord above of the length of five and a half feet; 3. a harpsichord with two manuals, one above the other, with harp and lute (two types of buff stop?); 4. a large double harpsichord of two registers, a lute, and in the chest (*i.e.* built into the bent side) an octave (4-foot virginal) which can be played separately; 5. a beautiful English harpsichord with two registers, made of walnut with a cypress soundboard; 6. a double virginal, 'mother-and-child' [1]; etc.

Sweelinck would probably have owned some instruments by local Amsterdam makers. His colleague, Artus Gheerdinck (1564–1624), who became *carilloneur* of the Oude Kerk in 1594, was a prominent harpsichord maker whose four-octave virginal (C-c''', short octave, keyboard left), dated 1605 and surviving today in the Neupert collection, Nürnberg, might well have been played by Sweelinck (see Plate IV). Another instrument, in the Smithsonian Institution, is signed by him (1603) but only the nameboard seems to be original. Artus Gheerdinck was succeeded by his son, Herman, and by a nephew, Lucas van Hoven, [2] who was making harpsichords already in 1616. Some other harpsichord makers active in Amsterdam in Sweelinck's day were Jan Aertz., Marten van der Biest (whose beautiful double virginal made in 1580 for Alessandro Farnese and preserved in the Germanisches National-Museum, Nürnberg, was made in Antwerp shortly before he fled to Amsterdam), Hendrik Mensen, Daniel van der Oort, and the composer Willem Swart (see pp. 92 and 100 f.), who worked 13 years on the invention of a 'porcelain' harpsichord in order to find 'the correct amount of resonance for the requirements'. [3]

When the Burgomasters of Amsterdam decided to present a harpsichord to the visiting Secretary of the King of Denmark in 1597, they naturally asked Sweelinck for advice. The commission was given to Daniel van der Oort, who was paid 75 guilders. The excellence of his work can be imagined when we realize that he was in competition with Marten van der Biest, whose splendid double-virginal still survives. However, in 1604 the city of Amsterdam sent Sweelinck to Antwerp to buy a 'Stadts clavecimbel', which was to be transported to various places and used at the behest of the Burgomasters. For the protection of the instrument they authorized Sweelinck to buy a flannel covering. The cost of this harpsichord was considerable—200 guilders, including

---

[1] For a discussion of 'mother-and-child' instruments, see J. H. van der Meer, ' ''Per Ogni Sorte di Stromenti da Tasti'' ', *TVNM*, XIX–1,2 (1960–61), p. 71 f.   [2] *Dutch HM*, 52.   [3] *Dutch HM*, 61.

transport—but they were evidently so pleased with it that they spent another 300 guilders in 1606 to have it decorated by Pieter Isaecksz., a fashionable painter of the period. [1]

We may presume that in Antwerp, after visiting his friends—the composer Verdonck, the writer Sweertius, and his publisher Phalèse—Sweelinck would have gone to the Ruckers workshop and selected one of their instruments. There were many other makers to choose from, of course. But we know that when Alewijn, son of Sweelinck's pupil Pieter de Vois, went to Antwerp in 1631 to buy a city harpsichord for Utrecht, he returned with one by 'I. Ruckers': he was probably following an example set by his father's teacher. Dordrecht may also have been following this pattern when, in the same year 1604, they purchased a city harpsichord. We are not told where it came from, however—only that it was purchased from a certain 'Jaques Narrot' for 153 pounds. It was kept, 'to the honour of the city', by the organist, Henderick Speuy. [2] A decade later, on 13 August 1614, Speuy was paid 36 stuivers for having transported the harpsichord several times to the inn 'Inde Paeuw' ('At the sign of The Peacock') where Sweelinck, invited by the churchwardens as an organ expert, was royally entertained.

[1] He had been a pupil of Cornelis Ketel, around the time when Ketel was Sweelinck's neighbour on the Oude Kerksplein and had married a girl from Antwerp in 1593. In 1607 he left for Denmark. Perhaps he had also decorated the harpsichord sent to Denmark in 1597.
[2] *Speuy*, 144 f.

APPENDIX III

English and Dutch ornament symbols

In spite of the lack of autographs of Sweelinck's keyboard music, we may assume that he used the notation of the English school. His pupil, Samuel Scheidt, in a prefatory note to *Tabulatura Nova* (1624) speaks of 'sechs Linien auff Engel- und Niederländische Manier adornieret', and he would hardly class the two as identical if his famous teacher had not used the English system. It thus seems more than likely that Sweelinck would also have used the curious ornament symbols peculiar to the English Virginalists: ♯ or, more rarely, ♩ . Such signs are found already in the earliest Netherlands keyboard source,[1] though used sparingly and only in two works (nos. I and XVII) from the earlier section of the manuscript. Although lacking in Speuy's rather retrospective *Psalmen*—where they would, in any case, have been inappropriate to either the austerely unadorned *cantus firmus* or the already florid counterpoint to it—they are found, in one form or another, in all remaining Dutch keyboard (and some other instrumental) sources even into the eighteenth century. They are fairly frequent in the *Tabulatuur-Boeck* (1659) of Anthoni van Noordt, which conservatively carries on some of the Amsterdam traditions of a half century earlier. Most telling of all is their presence in *Ly* A 1.[2] Being the most authentic source, its abundance of ornament signs (far more numerous than in all other sources combined) argues strongly for the necessity of adding them to other works if we are to restore Sweelinck's intention.

Although *Ly* A 1 begins with a fairly plentiful supply of ornaments—see Sweelinck's toccatas S. 30 = L. 19, S. 25 = L. 22, S. 24 = L. 21, S. 28 = L. 18, etc.—their number diminishes as the scribe proceeds, and by page 166 ('Mein junges Leben hat ein

[1] The so-called Susanne van Soldt MS. written perhaps mainly in Antwerp *c.* 1570 (see Chapter II and *MMN*, III). The ornament symbols may well have been added in England at a later date, around 1599.
[2] The description by vdSM, 162 of a note by the scribe (to the effect that ornaments and fingering were added later) is erroneous fabrication according to Lydia Schierning (*op. cit.*) who, unlike Van den Sigtenhorst, examined the manuscript at first hand.

Endt') the supply is reduced to one, by page 195 ('Est-ce Mars') to nil. On page 150, we find a fantasia (S. 18 = L. 14) which ceertainly needs ornaments, but which opens unadorned except for a few written-out trills at cadences. Towards the end, however, when the passage-work becomes more difficult, the scribe has added fingering and, at the same time, profuse ornament symbols. Clearly this suggests that ornaments should normally be heard but not seen. They are implied and must be realized, but need not be notated. They are added only by the scrupulous scribe, and in places where their employment would not be obvious. By comparing part of this section with a similar passage (m. 217f) in another fantasia (S. 17 = L. 13) preserved only in German tablatures, we can suggest a manner by which ornaments can be added to most of Sweelinck's works.

Fantasia S.18 L.14 in Ly A 1 :   Fantasia S. 17 L.13 :

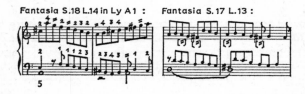

It will be noticed that the double strokes in the quoted excerpt from *Ly* A 1 are beside the note rather than through the stem. Both placements are found in this source, which thus represents a transitional stage (mid-seventeenth century) in the usage of the double-stroke symbol. It seems to have been placed *beside* the note first in Germany, perhaps through the influence of the tablatures —although the placement beside stemless semibreves or breves would also provide a precedent in English notation. The symbol was used in a variety of ways during the middle of the century and its meaning is often unclear. Sometimes it was employed in conjunction with the abbreviation 'tr' and may possibly, in such cases, signify a mordent rather than a trill. In some manuscripts (cf. KN 147) it is difficult to distinguish it from the sign later used regularly to indicate a trill. In fact, a study of such sources suggests a new hypothesis: that the double stroke, liberated from the stem and slanted down rather than up \\, developed into the common sign for the *Triller* W. Such a transformation is easily explainable graphologically. Whether its musical meaning remained the same is uncertain. In any case the double-stroke symbol seems to have been preserved unchanged in the Netherlands longer than in any other country. After about 1675 it began to be placed beside the note, in which form it continued to be preferred to any other symbol well into the following century. In an Amsterdam edition from the second decade of the eighteenth century, Pierre Bustijn's *IX Suittes pour le Clavessin*,[1] both double and single strokes (slanting down) are placed beside the note, and seem to indicate a trill and a mordent respectively.

To extend such a solution backwards in time to cover the Elizabethan period is tempting, but dangerous, for it oversimplifies a complicated issue. The most elaborate, and most accurate discussion of the Virginalists' symbols written thus far is by Robert Donington.[2] The simplified scheme recommended by Thurston Dart[3] has nevertheless found wide acceptance recently due to its inclusion in current editions of early English keyboard music. Dart's interpretation of the single stroke as a slide (*Schleifer*) is open to criticism. The table of ornaments attributed to Edw[ard] Be[vin] in British Museum MS Add. 31,403 is the source for his view. This manuscript dates, however, from the period of Purcell or later. Moreover, of the four ornaments given, three are never found employed in the music of any period, not even in the Bevin works copied in the same manuscript. The remaining ornament in the table, the single stroke, is given in the following peculiar solution, quite unlike any slide or *Schleifer* to be encountered elsewhere:

To use this peculiar slide as an interpretation of the virginalists' single stroke would, in many cases, result in stylistic absurdities. In the passage cited below, a solution according to Bevin (or Dart) would result in sharp dissonances patently out of keeping with the style of the period. A solution as a mordent would be better from the point of view of both stylistic consistency and musical sense.

Bull, Fantasia #12 :

---

[1] Three of which were edited by the author in *Exempla Musica Neerlandica*, I (1964).
[2] Grove, 'Ornaments'.
[3] Cf. the relevant volumes of *MB* and the Stainer & Bell series of *English Keyboard Music*.

As pointed out by Donington, both the double and the single stroke must have different meanings according to their context and should, accordingly, be freely interpreted. The modern performer need not be hopelessly baffled by such extensive freedom. First of all, that some definite distinction between the single and the double stroke was indeed intended is clear from consistent passages such as the following.

Bull ,"Fantastick" Pavan :

Secondly, while neither sign was restricted to a single meaning, the number of possible appropriate interpretations was by no means unlimited—both symbols would have been used with certain preferences in mind.

To begin with the more common ornament, the trill, we should note that the English preferred trills starting with the upper auxiliary, contrary to contemporary Italian usage. Earlier in the sixteenth century, upper-note trills were common in Italian keyboard music, too. They were, however, nearly always prepared, as in the following exceptionally dissonant example.

M.A.Cavazzoni (1523) :

Less frequent was the type of main-note trill illustrated below, but its incidence increased toward the end of the century. By the time of Frescobaldi and the late works of Merulo it had become usual, and the upper-note trill (still always prepared through suspension or tone repetition) was most exceptional.

Cavazzoni :   Frescobaldi, [Typical]: [rare exception]:

In England, however, the preference for upper-note trills may be clearly seen not only by their frequent occurrence in the works of all Virginalists but also by the dissonant character they often assume. Unlike the Italians, the English felt no necessity to prepare the dissonant upper-note trill, and the line may leap to the most surprisingly strong dissonance, as in the following excerpt from a typical 'Praeludium' (anonymous in the *Fitzwilliam Virginal Book* but printed as William Byrd's in *Parthenia*).

Byrd, Preludium :

Main-note trills, on the other hand, are notably absent from the English sources. The only exceptions are occasional appearances in works connected with the Continent: for instance, the anonymous setting of 'Susanne un jour' in British Museum. Ms. Add. 30,485, [1] or the later works of Peter Philips. The preference for dissonant, accented, upper-note trills as consistently written out is so strong that it seems safe to infer that other shorter or simpler kinds of trills, to be supplied when an ornament symbol appears, should also begin from the upper note. [2]

Why then were trills written out at all? Perhaps in order to indicate a longer trill with afterbeat (*Nachschlag*). Among the hundreds of written-out trills in English sources, not one simple trill (i.e. without afterbeat or some other ending) may be found. It is inconceivable that this most basic of ornaments, present throughout the history of the literature for harpsichord and related

---

[1] See *MMN* III, xxviii.

[2] Johannes Wolf, *Handbuch der Notationskunde*, II, p. 281, equates the two symbols in Reinken's *Hortus Musicus* (1687) with those of the virginalists, and prints solutions showing the double stroke as a main-note trill. However, this interpretation stems from Wolf rather than from Reinken, whose Latin description merely speaks of a trill 'qui superne tonum contingit'. Moreover, the signs Reinken prints are an x and two parallel, perfectly vertical, lines—and the latter sign never occurs in the music. Although these might have been adaptations of the Virginalists' symbols especially designed for ease of printing, there is no real evidence of such a connexion. Reinken would certainly have preferred the upper-note trill; witness the written-out ornaments of his toccata in *G*, ed. R. Buchmayer, *Aus historischen Klavierkonzerten*, III (Leipzig, 1927), pp. 29 ff.

instruments, should not have been used by the Virginalists. On the
contrary, this must have been a principal interpretation for the
common double-stroke ornament symbol. Trills were written out
only when they could not be represented by such a sign. Occasionally one finds the double stroke symbol followed by a written-out
afterbeat. To return to Bevin, his symbol for a trill with afterbeat
was never adopted. Its form suggests that the curved line above
the double stroke was meant to indicate an afterbeat.

Thus the double stroke alone would have meant a simple upper-
note trill of short but indeterminate duration.

Some writers have noted that a written-out trill may occur in
one manuscript precisely where another source for the same piece
gives a double-stroke symbol. From this is drawn the faulty conclusion that the one represents the solution or proper interpretation of the other. Concurrence of this sort happens only spora-
dically, however, never consistently, and such comparison could,
moreover, be made to argue as well for the absurd conclusion that
every ornament must be equated with every existing written-out
ornament. Comparison of different manuscripts yields this conclusion: that compilers of manuscripts were sometimes arbitrary
and always extremely free in their notation of ornaments; and
that some few chose apt ornaments fairly consistently, while others
did not at all.

In all trills, whether written-out or indicated by a symbol,
there remains the perplexing question of speed and flexibility.
Donington cites Diruta and Frescobaldi as supporting the free
(unmeasured) interpretation of written-out trills, adding that

in the English keyboard music of the late sixteenth and early seventeenth
centuries, written-out figures of this kind must almost invariably be
regarded as ordinary trills. The same is true of Sweelinck and others
on whom the influence of the great English school was so considerable. [1]

We must remember, however, that the rhythmic freedom characteristic of the early Baroque in Italy should not be unreservedly
applied to all aspects of the Northern school, i.e. to Sweelinck or
the Virginalists. Such ornaments as the *ribattuta* or the *trillo* (goat
trill), characterized by extreme rhythmic freedom, were experi-

[1] *Op. cit.*, pp. 403-4.

mentally introduced into England at a later date, but they were never truly incorporated into Northern styles and remained essentially Italian. Moreover, the stylized, measured trill is sometimes treated sequentially in Sweelinck's works, serving as a figure, as in the excerpts below. It should probably be played more or less as written, in order to underline its function.

Sweelinck, Allein zu dir, Var.2 :

There are, nevertheless, certain instances in Sweelinck's music where a written-out trill cannot possibly have been intended to be played exactly as notated. In fact, an example occurs in the same variation as quoted above. Not only is the beginning of the measure too stiff as notated, but the thirty-second notes at the end are almost unplayable at a tempo suitable for the rest of the piece.

Ibid. :

It also happens, in several cases, that different sources give varying speeds for the same trill, or, as below, vary the length. Something in between the two extremes (perhaps fourteen 'sixteenth'-notes) could have been intended but would not have been notated, since custom dictated that one could only double or halve a trill in duple meter.

Sweelinck, Ps.140 *(Fitz.V.B)*: *(Lübb. B1)*:

In general, however, written-out ornaments appear consistently and aptly in the principal sources for Sweelinck's works. It seems likely that they should in most cases be played as notated, though with some slight degree of rhythmic flexibility.

Finally, one special problem is presented by 'double' trills, found already in the *Dublin Virginal Book* and especially frequent in *Parthenia*, both in thirds and (as in the exceptionally difficult example below) in sixths.

Byrd,Mrs.Brownlo's Galliard:

In the Elizabethan age, double trills were apparently cultivated by keyboard players from their very first lessons,[1] however, and would consequently not have seemed so clumsy or hazardous as today. Only a century after Sweelinck and the Virginalists, François Couperin strongly approved of double trills in thirds, saying 'sy l'on pouvoit gagner cette pratique, cela donneroit un grand ornement au jeu', but warning that one must begin practising early. Only one of his pupils—a young lady—was able to do them well, and the difficulty it caused others 'ne m'a point encouragé à me donner la torture pour ariver à les faire comme je souhaiterois qu'ils fussent faits'.[2]

[1] See the simple preludes opening the London Royal College of Music MS. 2093.
[2] *L'Art de toucher le Clavecin* (Paris, 1711), ed. Anna Linde (Wiesbaden, 1933), p. 20.

V. Jan Pietersz. Sweelinck. Engraving by Jan Muller, 1624, with the epitaph by Joost van den Vondel.

VI. Portrait of Jan Pietersz. Sweelinck(?). Part of an altarpiece, attributed to Gerrit Pietersz. Sweelinck, representing St. John the Baptist.

APPENDIX IV

Portraits of Sweelinck

Only two identified portraits of Sweelinck are known: an engraving made three years after his death, and the fine painting, done when he was 44, which forms the frontispiece of this book. Although generally attributed to his brother Gerrit Pietersz. (1566–after 1610), the painting is not signed. The abbreviated Latin inscription around the inner edge of the oval reads: 'M. Io. Pet. Swll Ams. Or.' As pointed out by Van den Sigtenhorst Meyer, [1] the implied spelling of 'Swellinck' with a double LL is curious, since members of the family seem never to have used that variant. Moreover, if we compare the two paintings signed by Gerrit Pietersz. in 1606— *John the Baptist preaching in the Wilderness* (exhibited by Douwes of Amsterdam at the Delft Antique Fair, 1967) and *Christ on the Cold Stone* (coll. H. J. van Gelder, Bamlach/Baden)—it is very difficult to believe the same hand could have painted the 1606 portrait. It is infinitely more accomplished, refined, and subtle in both draftmanship and colour. Also, it seems later in style—the work of a confident, daring master who extends his subject's hands outside the illusionistic stone frame in a conceit rarely found so early as 1606.

It is dangerous, however, to compare paintings of such different genres. We should rather look to the group portrait Gerrit Pietersz. painted for the St. Sebastian Guild in 1604 (Amsterdam, Rijksmuseum, but presently in storage): *Het korporaalschap van Kapitein Jan Jansz. Carel en Luitenant Thys Pietersz. Schrijver.* This large work is in a style not too distant from that of the 1606 portrait, contains several faces of similar mien, but certainly ranks lower in quality. It is not signed; but Carel van Mander, whose *Schilder-Boeck* (Haarlem, 1604, expanded in later editions) is the source for most of our information about Gerrit Pietersz., in an Appendix written at the time of its execution praises it highly but says that the hardworking Gerrit was dissatisfied. Van Mander also tells us that Gerrit was the pupil of Cornelis Cornelisz. van Haarlem and, in turn, the teacher of Pieter Lastman, Rembrandt's teacher.

[1] vdSM, 270.

Relying largely on van Mander, P. J. J. van Thiel [1] has recently reconstructed Gerrit's career, which is of special interest for its parallel relationships to his brother's: study in Haarlem, a trip to Italy (which Jan may or may not have made), connexions with Antwerp, and a return to Amsterdam where he did all his mature work and remained until his death.

Visiting Italy at the same time as Gerrit was Jan Muller, [2] also a member of the Haarlem School, who made the posthumous engraving of the famous organist. There are several versions of this portrait, the most common of which bears a Latin verse by Plemp. The rare copy reproduced in Plate V has instead the epitaph by Vondel, copied in ink. The engraving was probably based on a drawing or painting made during Sweelinck's last years. The author of this original is not likely to have been Gerrit, who is never mentioned after 1610 and who probably died even earlier than his elder brother.

It has recently been suggested [3] that a 'St. John the Baptist', part of an altarpiece at Utrecht attributed to Gerrit Pietersz., might be a portrait of 'John' P. Sweelinck. The focus on facial expression certainly suggests a portrait, and there is some resemblance to the identified representations of Sweelinck. This hypothesis would become more attractive if the matching panel, a 'St. Nicholas', could be identified with some other prominent resident of Amsterdam connected with Gerrit Pietersz., and named 'Nicholas'.

[1] 'Een vroeg schilderij van Gerrit Pietersz. Sweelinck', *Oud-Holland*, LXXVIII (1963), pp. 67–74. Cf. also K. Bauch, 'Gerrit Pietersz. Swellinck, der Lehrer Lastmans', *Oud-Holland*, LV (1938), pp. 254–65.
[2] For information on Muller as a draftsman, see E. K. J. Reznicek, 'Jan Harmensz. Muller als tekenaar', *Nederlands Kunsthistorisch Jaarboek*, VII (1956).
[3] By Mr. Pieter Fischer of Amsterdam in a private communication.

APPENDIX V

Lyck-Klacht

Over de doot des
Voortreffelycken ende wijt-beroemden *Meesters*

IAN PIETERSZ:
SVVEELING
ORGANISTA
Binnen der Stadt
AMSTELREDAM,

Ende overleden den 16. October 1621.

T'AMSTELREDAM,

Voor Ian Benningh, Boeck-verkooper / wonende op de
Dam-Sluys inden vergulden Bybel. Anno 1621.

Lyck=Klacht.

W AT oorsaeck hebstu? spreeck, o ! *Niobe* te
klagen
Over dyn *Amphion*, u vande dood ontdra-
gen:
Thebanen waerom sucht ghy over *Iovis*
Soon,
En m' t veel tranen vlocht een droeve
Myrten Croon?
Beweent ghy zyn vernuft hem van geen God geschon cken,
Of zyn brood-droncken keel die u plach te ontfoncken?
Die door een bloot gehoor u dartel heeft gemaeckt,
En u bereyt gemoet met ydelheyd ontschaeckt,
Ontschaeckt en so verleyd, ia u verstant verduysterd,
Dat ghy meer naer zyn stem,als Gods-dienst hebt geluysterd,
Gelastert aen den Al, verweten aen den throon,
Dat *Iupiter* niet meer con teelen sulcken Soon.
O ! smaetheyd al te groot, o ! lasterlijcke tongen,
Om dat u *Amphion* eens kunstigh heeft gesongen,
Maer laes ! zyn nieuwe konst niet verder heeft gegaen,
Als u gehoor en hart op eenmael kon verstaen,
Wat doet u boos gemoet uytbarsten sulcke woorden,
Waer mee ghy op het hooghst het Hemel-rijck verstoorde,
Na dien de mogentheyd der Goden alles mach,
Noch maeckt haer niet gemeen met menschelyck ontsach,
Noch sterffelyck begrip, noch ydele voorslagen
Voor haer volmaeckte stoel niet hebben af te vragen,
Na dien *Saturni* Soon *Europa* heeft bevrucht,
Dat al de breede maar van *Amphion* vervlucht.
Europa heeft gebaert met lieffelycke smerte
Een Soon een grooten Soon, een Sone naer haer herte,

A 2

Deelach-

LYCK-KLACHT.

Deelachtich van het breyn, en Vaderlyck verstant,
Begaeft met een geheym, en Goddelycke handt,
Bevocht met soete dauw, en lieffelycken regen,
Alwaer wy ons begrip meest hebben af gekregen,
Een Sanger van het lof, en 't Goddelycke beeld,
Die door zijn brave kunst den Hemel heeft verveeld,
Dat *Iupiter* most selfs af-komen om beneden
Hem by de halve God des Amstels te besteden;
Daer al de schoone rey der Nymphen niet om sunst
Noch stoffen te vergeefs op *Sweelings* hoge kunst,
Waer in zy geene lust tot ydelheyd omgorden,
Maer Gods-dienst ende vreughd te saem geoeffent worden:
De Gods-dienst door het woord, waer op zyn konste drijft,
De vreughde die de galm en thoon is ingelijft:
Maer ach! hoe komt de doodt hoe komt de bleecke rover,
En wint al voor de vuyst des levens schansen over,
Hy lost zyn taije booch ô! *Sweeling* op u hert,
Dat ghy door zyne flits nu over-rompelt werdt:
Dat wy ons hert en ziel gaen droeffelycken leyen,
Beklagen uwe doot, en laetste uyr beschreijen.
O licht dat heden zyt met glory uyt gegaen,
Nochtans u konste blyft ons tot een bake staen;
Waer ons verlegen boot komt met een graecht na perssen,
Om u beminde maets en sangers te ververssen,
Die singen daer bedroeft u naergelaten stof,
Wt boecken inde rouw, het Goddelycke lof:
Dat een vermaerd *Propheet* heeft op zyn Harp geslagen,
Met thoonen veelderley den Hemel toe gedragen,
Dat een Heyligh Poët, en Coningh heeft gespeelt,
Door dijn geswinde geest so treflyck is verdeelt,
Dat ghy zijt in gelijft met eenen strael beneven
Die *Hecäergos* u van verde heeft gegeven,
Waer mee ghy waert verlicht, verlichte uwen geest,
Dat al u kunstich werck uytmuntend is geweest:

Verdeelt,

LYCK-KLACHT.

Verdeelt, ia so gemaeckt, dat alle herten ryfen,
En door het zoet geklanck u groote eer bewyfen.
  Hoe vloeyden uwe thoon, hoe dreef u juyfte maet?
  Als elck gegoten pijp zyn toetfingh had gevaet:
O ! wonder van het land, ô ! Phœnix van het fpelen,
O ! dichter vande fangh, en meefter van het quelen,
  Als wy u hoorden aen, fo werden wy beroert,
  En datelyck ons hert en finnen wech gevoert
Op rotzen hoogh en fteyl, en hoogh gelegen wijcken,
Van waer wy uwen lof niet konden over kijcken:
  Want al u neerfticheyd, en yver overwon
  't Gefleepen criftalyn, 't welck fo verd niet en kon
(In een gefette tyd en voorgeftelde jaren)
Ons 't eynde van u kunft, en waerde openbaren:
  Hoe meenigh vreemdelingh fwurf om u lichaem heen?
  Alleer ghy op den trap des Orgels waerd getreen.
En hoorden u verftand van uwe kunft en handen,
En tot u eer vertaeld in Vaderlycke Landen,
  En waffer dan een *Arts* of Meefter in haer oort,
  Die quam u met zyn wenfch en groetenis aen boort:
Dat u geruchten tot haer verde plaetfen vloden,
En fchier de heele werldt tot uwe maeltijd noden:
  Daer elck van uwen difch quam nuttigen de fpijs,
  Beminders van u kunft, en kunftigh onderwijs.
De fpyfe was 't begrip van 't ongehoorde fpeelen,
Die ghy met miltheyd ginght de hongerige deelen:
  Den dranck, de foete vocht, die onfe ziel verheughd,
  Was uwe lieflijckheyd ; een vroe-Vrou vande vreughd
Een rechte Voefteres, die ons gemoet gingh prangen
Tot geenen ydelheyd, maer Goddelycke fangen,
  Die hebben hert en ziel door haer beweechlyckheyd,
  En ons in eenen hof vol zoete reuck geleyt.
Een hof op wiens verdeck, en groene gaelderijen
De *Mufa* met haer fpel vrypoftigh quamen vlijen,

Apollo

LYCK-KLACHT.

*A*pollo fat by u, en heeft u breyn geraeckt,
En hebt zyn groote geeft van 't *hooge Huys* gefmaeckt.
De bloemen loocken op, dyn zoete kruyden groeyden,
De ftammen van u kunft feer loffelycken bloeyden,
   Verdorden nimmermeer, maer bleven altijdt ftaen,
   Verwelckten door geen coud', verlooren geene blaen.
De bloemen die de fchoot van 't aerderijck befpreyen,
Verlaten haer cieraet, verdorren ende fcheyen
   Wt een vercierde rock, en duycken met veel leedt,
   Gekarckert by de mol, weer in het fwarte cleedt:
Maer uwen blyven groen, noch paffen op geen blafen,
Of *Boreas* fchoon komt te knorren en te rafen,
   Dyn luft-hof is voorwaer gefegent in dat kas,
   Gelijck de gulde Eeuw' daer geenen winter was.
He! wat een kettery de Heydenen bedreven,
Om haren *Amphion* den grooten loft te geven,
   Die met zyn *Niobe* feer ydelijck geleeft,
   Noch trooft, noch goeden naem, haer na gelaten heeft.
Waerom zyn wy bedruckt? 't is beft wy ons bedwingen,
Vermids dat *Sweeling* fteeds in Goddelycke dingen
   Zijn tyd gekoefterd heeft : zyn bloemen by ons ftaen
   Veel langer als wy doen; en blyven als wy gaen.
Den loffelycken naem, die naer hem is gebleven,
Sijn eygen vyant felfs voldoeninge fal geven.
   Wat fegh ick vyant? neen, wie foud een vyant zyn?
   Na dien hy yder fchonck dien lieffelycken Wijn
Van vreughd en vrolyckheyd, wie foud zyn vyant wefen?
Als 't eenigh onverftant, die men niet hoeft te vrefen?
   Wiens vyantlyck gewelt, en kogels fonder macht
   Meeft fonder anghft en vrees, hier werden in gewacht.
„ De treffelyckfte krans die ons vernuft mach halen,
„ Wanneer het om zijn winft loopt inde wereld dwalen,
   „ Wanneer de vruntfchap van het aengenaem geniet,
   „ Ons op den hooghften graet haer foete vruchten biet,

                             „ Is;

LYCK-CLACHT.

„Is; dat wy inden gront van oneer niet verſmooren,
„Maer neygen ons gemoet, en neygen onſe ooren,
„ Waer toe de gulde mont van recht en billijckheyd,
„(Dat is een goeden naem) met wyſe woorden leyd.
Een naem een goeden naem heeft *Sweeling* na gelaten,
En werd daerom te meer geroemt op onſe ſtraten,
Maer of het onverſtant haer vyantlyck bethoond,
„ *Den naergelaten naem haer Meeſter wel verſchoond.*
Nu zit hy inden Throon, betreet de hooge ſalen,
Drinckt necktarlycke dranck uyt koſtelycke ſchalen;
De hoocheyd van de plaets zijn waerdicheyd getuyghd,
Dat *Ganimedes* ſtuypt en ſedich voor hem buyghd;
Hy was de werelt loof, en woud de werelt laten,
Haer onſtantvaſticheyd, en groote ſonden haten,
De *Parcæ* hebben hem ſo haeſt niet afgekort,
Of ſtracx zijn eygen ziel in een nieuw leven word
Veranderd en geleyd, getrocken inde wolcken
By al den Edeldom, en 's Hemels heylige volcken,
Van waer hy ſach zijn Lijck vaſt dragen na de aerd,
Dat baerd zijn Moeder weer die hem eerſt had gebaerd.
Hy ſach ons uyt zijn kunſt, hy ſach ons uyt zijn boecken,
Hy ſach ons uyt zijn werck, de oeffeninge ſoecken,
Zijn ziele keeck om laech, en merckelijck kon ſien
Hoe zijn warande bloeyt, en al 't gewas beſpien:
Hy ſach ons altemael vaſt dringen en crioelen,
Om uyt ſijn rijcke Born een aderken te voelen
Beſprengen ons vernuft, dat nimmermeer en ruſt,
Ten zy het heeft geboet in *Sweelings* kunſt haer luſt.
Ha! kon myn pen het ſtof der loffelijcker dingen,
Na haer waerdy en lof, eenſamentlijck uyt bringen,
Niet lievers wou mijn hert, niet anders wenſcht mijn geeſt,
„ *Maer ſchoeyt voorwaer te kleyn, op ſulcken grooten leeſt.*
Dus aengename trooſt wy vinden naer zijn ſterven
Zijn na-zaet; die de Croon zijns *Vaders* ſoeckt te erven,
A 4 Wy

LYCK-KLACHT.

Wy hopen op zijn kunft,verlangen meer en meer,
Dat ons nu is vergunt den tweeden *Sweeling* weer.
't Is trooftelyck dat wy met zijn vermaerde wercken,
Ons klaechelyck gemoet oprechten en verftercken,
Oprechten een pylaer van ftof die hy ons laet,
Van kunft die eeuwigh blyft, en nimmermeer vergaet.
Daerom lief-hebbers al, beminders van zijn konfte,
Bewijft met my u ernft, en onbevleckte ionfte,
Laet ons de droefheyd nu veranderen in vreughd;
Om dat wy fien zyn werck, en na gelaten deughd:
Zijn moeyte werd bekroont, zyn neerftichcyd en wenfchen
Is aengenaem gemaeckt voor God en alle menfchen,
Voor menfchen, om dat hy de menfchen vreughde iont,
Voor God, om dat hy looft de Godheyd met zijn mond;
Niet met den mond alleen, maer toe-bereyden herte,
Bepalingh inde vreughd, en trooft in alle fmerte.
Dus laet geen droefheyd meer verwinnen u gemoet,
Maer in zijn heyligh werck een nieuwen yver doet:
Verblyt u : want hy is ten Hemel op ontboden,
En fpeelt op 't hooge Choor ter eeren vande Goden.

N. VOOCHT.

Vitam vitiofam vita.

EYNDE.

APPENDIX VI

Chart for comparison of the 1943 and 1968 editions of Sweelinck's Werken, I

1943, ed. M. Seiffert	1968, Fascicle I, ed. G. Leonhardt

Fantasias:

1 (Chromatic Fantasy)	1
2	2
3	3
4	8
5	4
6 (Hexachord Fantasy)	5
7	—
8	6
9	9
10	7
11	32*
12 (John Bull's 'God Save the King')	33*
13	—
14	11

Echo Fantasias:

15	34* & 34a*
16	12
17	13
18	14
19	—

Toccatas:

20	15
21	16
22	17
23 (H. L. Hassler?)	31*
24	21
25	22
26 (Jacob Hassler?)	30*
27	23
28	18
29	24 & 24a
30	19 & 19a
31	20
32	25

1943, ed. M. Seiffert	1968, Fascicle I, ed. G. Leonhardt	
Praeludium:		
33	27	
— Fantasia	10	(Leningrad MS.)
— Toccata	26	(Leningrad MS.)
— Ricercar 'Johann Peterle'	35*	(Tor G 7)
— Fantasia, Annegarn supplement No. 1	36*	
— Fantasia, Annegarn supplement No. 2	37*	
— Fantasia, Annegarn supplement No. 3	38*	
— Fantasia, Annegarn supplement No. 4	39*	
— Fantasia, Annegarn supplement No. 5	40*	

1943, ed. M. Seiffert	1968, Fascicle II, ed. A. Annegarn	
Chorale variations:		
34 Ach Gott vom Himmel sieh darein	—	
35 (Var. 1–4) Allein Gott in der Höh sei Ehr	1	
36 Allein zu dir, Herr Jesu Christ	—	
37 Christe qui lux es et dies	3	
38 Da pacem, Domine, in diebus nostris	4	
39 Dies sind die heilgen zehn Gebot	—	
40 Durch Adams Fall ist ganz verderbt	—	
41 Erbarm dich mein, o Herre Gott	5	
42 Est ist das Heil uns kommen her	—	
43 Es spricht der Unweisen Mund wohl	—	
44 Herr Christ der einig Gottes Sohn	—	
45 Herzlich lieb hab ich dich, o Herr	14*	
46 Ich ruf zu dir, Herr Jesu Christ	6	
47 Nun freut euch, lieben Christen gemein	—	
48 Nun freut euch, lieben Christen gemein	7	
49 Nun komm der Heiden Heiland	—	
50 O lux beata trinitas	—	
51 Psalm 116	11	
52 Psalm 140	12	
53 Puer nobis nascitur	8	(Ons is gheboren een kindekijn)
54 (Var. 1,3,4) Vater Unser im Himmelreich	15*	(Onse Vader in hemelrijck)
54 (Var. 2)	9	(Var. 1)
55 Wie nach einem Wasserquelle	—	
56 Wir glauben all an einem Gott	13	
57 Wo Gott der Herr nicht bein uns hält	—	
— Allein zu dir, Herr Jesu Christ	2	(*Ze* 1)
— Psalm 36	10	(Tor G 5)
— (Var. 2,3) Onse Vader in hemelrijck	9	(*Ze* 2)
— Psalm 60	16*	(*Ly* B 2)

1943, ed. M. Seiffert

1968, Fascicle III, ed.
F. Noske

Secular variations:

58 Est-ce Mars........................ 3
59 Ich fuhr mich vber Rheine.......... 4 (Ick voer al over Rhijn)
60 Mein junges Leben hat ein End..... 6
61 More Palatino 7
62 Soll es sein .... 12 (Poolsche dans)
63 Unter der Linden grüne .... 8 (Onder een linde groen)
64 Von der Fortuna werd ich getrieben 2 (Engelsche Fortuyn)
    (Attrib. to H. L. Hassler
    in Tor F 8)
65 Balletto del granduca .... 1 (Ballo del granduca)
66 Paduana Lachrimae .... 10 (Pavana Lachrimae)
67 Passamezzo .... 13* (Passamezzo moderno)
68 Pavana Hispanica 9
69 Pavana Philippi 11
— Malle Sijmen .... 5 (Leningrad MS.)

Anhang:

70 Capriccio .... L. 29* (Fascicle I)
71 (John Bull's 'Fantazia op de Fuga van
    J. P. Sweelinck').................. —
72 Toccata (incomplete) .... L. 28* (Fascicle I)
73 Praeludium (different version of S. 33) L. 27a (Fascicle I)

SELECT BIBLIOGRAPHY

i. Editions

An Anthology of English Lute Music, ed. D. Lumsden (London, [1954]).
Archives des Maîtres de l'Orgue, ed. A. Guilmant, X (Mainz, 1914).
John Bull, Keyboard Music: I, ed. J. Steele and F. Cameron, *MB*, XIV (London, 1960).
John Bull, Keyboard Music: II, ed. T. Dart, *MB*, XIX (London, 1963).
Collected Works of William Byrd, ed. E. H. Fellowes, XVIII–XX (London, 1950).
Choralbearbeitungen und freie Orgelstücke der deutschen Sweelinck-Schule, ed. H. J. Moser and T. Fedtke, I–II (Kassel, 1954–55).
Choralbearbeitungen aus der Tabulatur Lynar A 1, ed. H. J. Moser and T. Fedtke (Kassel, 1956).
The Dublin Virginal Book, ed. J. Ward (Wellesley, Mass., 1954; 2nd ed. 1964).
Dutch Keyboard Music of the 16th and 17th Centuries, ed. A. Curtis, *MMN*, III (Amsterdam, 1961).
Van Eyl. Het Klaviaboek van Anna Maria van Eyl, ed. F. Noske, *MMN*, II (Amsterdam, 1959).
Fitzwilliam Virginal Book, ed. J. A. Fuller Maitland and W. Barclay Squire, 2 vols. (Leipzig, 1894–99).
Lueneburg. The Free Organ Compositions from the Lueneburg Tablatures, ed. J. R. Shannon, I–II (St. Louis, 1958).
Thomas Morley, Keyboard Works, ed. T. Dart (London, 1959).
The Mulliner Book, ed. D. Stevens, *MB*, I (London, 1952).
My Ladye Nevells Booke, ed. H. Andrews (London, 1926).
Anthoni van Noordt, Tabulatuur-Boeck van Psalmen en Fantasyen (1659), ed. M. Seiffert (Leipzig, 1896).
Parthenia, ed. T. Dart (London, [1961])
Heinrich Scheidemann, Choral-bearbeitungen, ed. G. Fock (Kassel, 1967).
Werke von Samuel Scheidt, ed. C. Mahrenholz, V–VII (Hamburg, 1934–53).
Henderick Speuy, Psalm Preludes, ed. F. Noske (Amsterdam, 1962).
46 Choräle für Orgel von J. P. Sweelinck und seinen deutschen Schülern, ed. G. Gerdes, *Musikalische Denkmäler*, III (Mainz, 1957).
Jan Pieterszn. Sweelinck, Werken voor Orgel en Clavecimbel, ed. M. Seiffert, I (Amsterdam, 1894, 1943; repr. 1957, 1962).
Werken van Jan Pietersz. Sweelinck, Supplement, ed. A. Annegarn, VNM, XLVII (Amsterdam, 1958).
Jan Pzn. Sweelinck, Werken voor Orgel of Clavecimbel uit het 'Celler Klavierbuch 1662', ed. J. H. Schmidt, Exempla Musica Neerlandica, II (Amsterdam, 1965.)
Thomas Tallis, Complete Keyboard Works, ed. D. Stevens (London, 1953).

ii. Books and Articles

Bachrach, A. G. H., *Sir Constantine Huygens and Britain: 1596–1687*, I, 1596–1619 (Leiden/London, 1962).

Balfoort, D. J. (ed.) *Nederlandsch Muziekleven, 1600–1800* (The Hague, 1936).

Baudartius, G., *Memoryen ofte Cort verhael der gedenck-weerdichste so kerckelicke als wereltlicke gheschiedenissen van Nederland den iaere 1603 tot in het iaer 1624*, 2nd ed. (Arnhem, 1624–25).

Bijtelaar, B., 'De orgels van Sweelinck', *Het Orgel*, XLIX (1953), pp. 137–39, 151–53, 165–67; and L (1954), pp. 1–4, 21–24.

Bol, J. H. D., 'Sweelinckiana', *TVNM*, XVII–2 (1949), pp. 158–60.

van den Borren, C., *Geschiedenis van de Muziek in de Nederlanden*, I–II (Antwerp, 1949–51).

van den Borren, C., *Les origines de la musique de clavier dans les Pays-Bas (Nord et Sud) jusque vers 1630* (Brussels, 1914).

van den Borren, C., *Les origines de la musique de clavier en Angleterre* (Brussels, 1912).

van den Borren, C., *The Sources of Keyboard Music in England* (London, 1913)

Boyd, M. C., *Elizabethan Music and Musical Criticism*, 2nd ed. (Philadelphia, 1962).

Breig, W., 'Der Umfang des choralgebundenen Orgelwerkes von Jan Pieterszon [*sic*] Sweelinck', *Archiv für Musikwissenschaft*, XVII (1960), pp. 258–76.

Breig, W., *Die Orgelwerke von Heinrich Scheidemann, Beihefte zum Archiv für Musikwissenschaft* (Wiesbaden, 1967).

Breig, W., 'Jan Pieterszoon Sweelinck en de koraalbewerkingskunst van zijn Duitse leerlingen', *Jubileumnummer ter gelegenheid van het 70-jarig bestaan van de Nederlandse Organisten-Vereniging* [1960], pp. 63–71.

Bukofzer, M., *Musik in the Baroque Era* (New York, 1947).

Cohn, A., *Shakespeare in Germany* (London, 1865).

Cole, E., 'Seven Problems of the Fitzwilliam Virginal Book', *Proceedings of the Royal Musical Association*, LXXIX (1953), pp. 51–64.

Curtis, A., 'Dutch Harpsichord Makers', *TVNM*, XIX–1, 2 (1961), pp. 44–66.

Curtis, A., 'Henderick Speuy and the Earliest Printed Dutch Keyboard Music', *TVNM*, XIX–3, 4 (1962–63), pp. 143–62.

Curtis, A., 'Jan Reinken and a Dutch Source for Sweelinck's Keyboard Works', *TVNM*, XX–1, 2 (1964–65), pp. 45–56.

Dart, T., 'Elisabeth Eysbock's Keyboard Book', *Svensk Tidskrift för Musikforskning*, XL (1962), pp. 5–12.

Dart, T., 'English Music and Musicians in 17th-Century Holland', *Kongress-Bericht, Internationale Gesellschaft für Musikwissenschaft, Utrecht 1952* (Amsterdam, 1953), pp. 139–45.

Dart, T., 'Sweelinck's "Fantasia on a theme used by John Bull"', *TVNM*, XVIII–4 (1959), pp. 167–69.

Dietrich, F., *Geschichte des deutschen Orgelchorals im 17. Jahrhundert* (Kassel, 1932).

Dozy, C. M., 'Jan Pietersz. Sweelinck en andere organisten der 16e eeuw', *Oud-Holland*, III (1885), pp. 277–302.

Fedtke, T., 'Der niederländische Orgelbau im 16. Jahrhundert und seine Bedeutung für Sweelincks Instrumentalmusik', *Musik und Kirche*, XXVI (1956), pp. 60–67.

Fock, G., 'Onuitgegeven orgelwerken van de Nederlands-Noordduitse school', *Het Orgel*, LVI (1960), pp. 172–82.

Gerdes, G., *Die Choralvariationen J. P. Sweelincks und seiner Schüler*, typewritten dissertation (Freiburg im Breisgau, 1956).

Glyn, M. H., *About Elizabethan Virginal Music and its Composers* (London, 1934).

Gombosi, O., 'Ein neuer Sweelinck-Fund', *TVNM*, XIV (1932), pp. 1–13.

Hellmann, D., 'Betrachtungen zur Darstellung der Sweelinckschen Werke für Tasteninstrumenten', *Musik und Kirche*, XXV (1955), pp. 287–92.

Heye, J. P., 'Jan Pietersz. Sweelinck', *Bouwsteenen*, I (1872), pp. 36–47.

Houck, M. E., 'Jan Pietersz. Sweelinck en Claude Bernhardt', *TVNM*, VI–2 (1900), pp. 144–50.

Kastner, M. S., 'Parallels and discrepancies between English and Spanish keyboard music of the 16th and 17th century', *Anuario Musical*, VII (1952), p. 77–115.

Kerman, J., *The Elizabethan Madrigal, A Comparative Study* (New York, 1962).

de Klerk, J., 'Sweelincks leraar ontdekt na een duik in de archieven', *Gregoriusblad*, LXXXII (1961), pp. 135–43.

Klotz, H., 'Sweelinck spielt Sweelinck', *Musik im niederländischen-niederdeutschen Raum*, ed. K. G. Fellerer (Cologne, 1960), pp. 37–49.

Land, J. P. N., 'Het luitboek van Thysius beschreven en toegelicht', *TVNM* I–III, [1884–1888] (and pub. as a book, Amsterdam, 1889).

Lindenburg, C., 'De slotvariatie van Sweelinck's Pavana hispanica', *TVNM*, XV–2 (1937), pp. 47–51.

Lowinsky, E. E., 'English Organ Music of the Renaissance', *The Musical Quarterly*, XXXIX (1933), pp. 373–95, 528–53.

Mahrenholz, C., *Samuel Scheidt, sein Leben und sein Werk* (Leipzig, 1924).

Mattheson, J., *Grundlage einer Ehren-Pforte* (Hamburg, 1740).

van der Meer, J. H., 'The Keyboard Works in the Vienna Bull-manuscript', *TVNM*, XVIII–2 (1957), pp. 72–105.

van der Meer, J. H., 'Per ogni sorte di stromenti da tasti', *TVNM*, XIX–1, 2 (1960–61), pp. 67–79.

Mellers, W., 'John Bull and English Keyboard Music', *The Musical Quarterly*, XL (1954), pp. 364–83, 548–71.

Mischiati, O., 'L'Intavolatura d'Organo tedesca della Biblioteca Nazionale di Torino', *L'Organo*, IV (1963), pp. 1–154.

Morley, T., *A Plaine and Easie Introduction to Practicall Musicke* (*1597*), mod. ed. by R. Alec Harman (London, 1952).

Moser, H. J. and F. Piersig, 'Neue Schüler des Jan Pietersz. Sweelinck', *TVNM*, XV–1 (1936), pp. 47–51.

Mueller, P. L., *The Influences and Activities of English Musicians on the Continent* (typewritten Ph. D. thesis, Indiana University, 1954).

Noske, F., 'Een apocrief en een dubieus werk van Sweelinck', *Mededelingenblad VNM*, XX (Sept. 1966), pp. 27–30.

Noske, F., 'Luitkomposities van Jan Pieterszoon Sweelinck', *Orgaan der K.N.T.V.*, XII (1957), pp. 46–48.

Noske, F., 'Nederlandse Klaviermusik uit de 16de en 17de Eeuw', *Mens en Melodie*, XVII (1962), pp. 3–7.

Noske, F., 'Remarques sur les luthistes des Pays-Bas', *Le Luth et sa musique*, ed. J. Jacquot (Paris, 1958), pp. 179–92.

Noske, F., 'Rondom het Orgeltractaat van Constantyn Huygens', *TVNM*, XVII–4 (1955), pp. 278–309.

Noske, F., 'Sweelinck na vier eeuwen', *TVNM*, XIX–3, 4 (1962–63), pp. 125–30.

Plemp, C. G., *Poëmata* (Antwerp, 1631).

Reese, G., *Music in the Renaissance*, 2nd ed. (New York, 1959).

Reimann, M., 'Die Autoren der Fuge Nr. 23 in Lüneburg, KN 208', und der Fantasia Ut sol fa mi in Lübbenau, Ms. Lynar A 1', *Die Musikforschung*, XVI (1963), pp. 166–67.

Riedel, F. W., *Das Musikarchiv im Minoritenkonvent zu Wien (Katalog des älteren Bestandes vor 1784)* (Kassel, 1963).

Riedel, F. W., *Quellenkundliche Beiträge zur Geschichte der Musik für Tasteninstrumente in der zweiten Hälfte des 17. Jahrhunderts* (Kassel, 1960).

van Riemsdijk, J. C. M., 'Sweelinckiana', *TVNM*, II–3 (1887), pp. 200–204.

Riewald, J. C., 'New Light on the English Actors in the Netherlands, *c.* 1590–*c.* 1660', *English Studies*, XLI (1960), pp. 65–92.

Ritter, A. G., *Zur Geschichte des Orgelspiels, vornehmlich des deutschen, im 14. bis zum Anfänge des 18. Jahrhunderts* (Leipzig, 1884).

Scheurleer, D. F., *Het Muziekleven van Amsterdam in de 17e Eeuw* (The Hague, 1904).

Scheurleer, D. F., 'Sweelinckiana', *TVNM*, IX–4 (1914), pp. 224–29.

Schierning, L., *Die Überlieferung der deutschen Orgel- und Klaviermusik aus der 1. Hälfte des 17. Jahrhunderts, Eine quellenkündliche Studie. Schriften des Landesinstituts für Musikforschung Kiel*, XII (Kassel, 1961).

Schmidt, J. H., 'Eine unbekannte Quelle zur Klaviermusik des 17. Jahrhunderts, das Celler Klavierbuch 1662', *Archiv für Musikwissenschaft*, XXII (1965), pp. 1–11.

Seiffert, M., *Geschichte der Klaviermusik I: Die ältere Geschichte bis um 1750*, (Leipzig, 1899).

Seiffert, M., 'Neue Sweelinck-Schüler', *TVNM*, XI–3 (1924), p. 127.

Seiffert, M., 'Sweelinckiana [1]', *TVNM*, V–1 (1895), pp. 40–45.

Seiffert, M., 'Sweelinckiana 2–3', *TVNM*, VI–3 (1899), pp. 173–74.

Seiffert, M., 'Sweelinckiana 4', *TVNM*, VI–4 (1900), pp. 250–52.

Seiffert, M., 'Sweelinckiana 5', *TVNM*, X–1 (1915), pp. 30–32.

Seiffert, M., 'Sweelinckiana 6', *TVNM*, XII–2 (1927), pp. 102–103.

Seiffert, M., 'Ueber Sweelinck und seinen deutschen Schüler', *TVNM*, IV–1 (1892), pp. 1–16.

Seiffert, M., *Ueber Sweelinck und seine direkten deutschen Schüler* (Leipzig, 1891; also in *Vierteljahrschrift für Musikwissenschaft*, VII (1891), pp. 145–240).

Seiffert, M., 'Zu Band I der Werke Jan Pieterszn. Sweelincks', *TVNM*, V–1 (1895), pp. 7–12.

Shannon, J. R., *The Free Organ Compositions from the Lueneburg Tablatures*, (typewritten Master's thesis, University of North Carolina, 1956).

van den Sigtenhorst Meyer, B., 'Hondert Jaar schalmeispelen te Haarlem, 1532–1635', *TVNM*, XIV–1 (1932), pp. 14–27.

van den Sigtenhorst Meyer, B., *De vocale Muziek van Jan P. Sweelinck*, (The Hague, 1948).

van den Sigtenhorst Meyer, B., *Jan P. Sweelinck en zijn Instrumentale Muziek*, 2nd ed. (The Hague, 1946).

van den Sigtenhorst Meyer, B., and C. Lindenburg, 'Sweelinck's Pavana hispanica', *TVNM*, XV (1936), pp. 53–55.

de Smidt, J. P., 'Sweelinckiana', *TVNM*, XVII (1955), p. 310 ff.

Thijsse, W. H., *Zeven eeuwen Nederlandse Muziek* (Rijswijk, 1950).

Tiedeman, F. H. L., 'Jan Pieterszoon Sweelinck, een bio-bibliographische schets, tweede geheel bij- en omgewerkte uitgave', *Jan Pieters Sweelinck, Acht zes-stemmige psalmen*, VNM, VI (Amsterdam, 1876).

Tiedeman, F. H. L., 'Jan Pieterszoon Sweelinck, een biographische schets [met] bibliographie', *Jan Pieters Sweelinck, Regina Coeli*, VNM, VI, (Amsterdam, 1876).

Tusler, R. L., *The Organ Music of Jan Pieterszoon Sweelinck* (Bilthoven, 1958).

Vente, M. A., *Die Brabanter Orgel* (Amsterdam, 1958).

Vente, M. A., 'Nogmaals: de orgels van Sweelinck', *Het Orgel*, L (1954), pp. 73–76, 85–87.

Vente, M. A., 'Sweelinckiana', *TVNM*, XIX–3, 4 (1962–63), pp. 186–91.

Vlam, C. C., 'Sweelinckiana', *TVNM*, XVIII–1 (1956), pp. 37–42.

Voigts, A., *Die Toccaten Jan Pieterszoon Sweelincks, ein Beitrag zur frühen Instrumentalmusik* (typewritten dissertation, University of Münster, 1955).

Wolf, J., 'Sweelinckiana 1', *TVNM*, VI–3 (1899), pp. 170–72.

INDEX